3750

e/ ɔ

MOTIVATION AND EXPLANATION

AN ESSAY ON FREUD'S PHILOSOPHY OF SCIENCE

PSYCHOLOGICAL ISSUES

HERBERT J. SCHLESINGER, *Editor*

MOTIVATION AND EXPLANATION

AN ESSAY ON FREUD'S PHILOSOPHY OF SCIENCE

NIGEL MACKAY

Psychological Issues
Monograph 56

INTERNATIONAL UNIVERSITIES PRESS, INC.
Madison, Connecticut

Library of Congress Cataloging-in-Publication Data

Mackay, Nigel.
  Motivation and explanation : an essay on Freud's philosophy of science / Nigel Mackay.
      p. cm. — (Psychological issues : monograph 56)
  Includes bibliographies and index.
  ISBN 0-8236-3474-4
  1. Psychoanalysis—Philosophy. 2. Freud, Sigmund, 1856-1939.
3. Motivation (Psychology) I. Title. II. Series.
  [DNLM: 1. Motivation. 2. Psychoanalytic Theory. W1 PS572
monograph 56 / WM 460.5M6 M478m]
BF175.M2625 1989   88-645
150.19′52—dc 19   CIP

Manufactured in the United States of America

For Hannah

CONTENTS

PART III. FURTHER ISSUES

ACKNOWLEDGMENTS

Acknowledgment is made to the following sources for kind permission to reprint extracts:

From various volumes of the *Standard Edition of the Complete Psychological Works of Sigmund Freud* translated and edited by J. Strachey. Reprinted by permission of Sigmund Freud Copyrights Ltd., the Hogarth Press, The Institute of Psycho-Analysis and the Hogarth Press, and Allen and Unwin.

From *The Life and Work of Sigmund Freud* by E. Jones. Reprinted by permission of the author's estate and the Hogarth Press.

From "The Medical Origins and Cultural Use of Freud's Instinctual Drive Theory" by J. C. Burnham. Reprinted by permission of the author and the *Psychoanalytic Quarterly*.

From "A Review of Some of Freud's Biological Assumptions and Their Influence on His Theories" by R. R. Holt; from "Freud's Project: An Open Biologically Based Model for Psychoanalysis" by K. Pribram. Reprinted by permission of the University of Wisconsin Press.

From *The Logic of Explanation in Psychoanalysis* by M. Sherwood. Reprinted by permission of the Academic Press.

From *A New Language for Psychoanalysis* by R. Schafer. Reprinted by permission of Yale University Press.

From *Freud's Project Reassessed* by K. Pribram and M. M. Gill. Reprinted by permission of Century Hutchinson Publishers.

From *Psychoanalytic Theory: An Exploration of Essentials* by G. Klein. Reprinted by permission of International Universities Press.

From "Knowing One's Motives" by N. Mackay. Reprinted by permission of the *Journal for the Theory of Social Behaviour*.

From *Freud's Neurological Education and Its Influence on Psychoanalytic Theory* by P. Amacher; from "Drive or Wish? A Reconsideration of the Psychoanalytic Theory of Motivation" by R. R. Holt; from "Metapsychology Is Not Psychology" by M. M. Gill. Reprinted by permission of *Psychological Issues* and International Universities Press.

From *Psychiatry* by T. Meynert, translated by B. Sachs. Reprinted by permission of Macmillan Publishing Company.

PREFACE

In the middle of the 1975–1976 academic year, I had finished some research on the influence of positivist philosophy of science on psychology, and had moved to Oxford to do my doctorate. I was trying to decide on what aspects of psychoanalysis and philosophy I was going to focus when a talk to the Oxford University Psychoanalytic Society (a university interest body) by Roy Schafer, then Visiting Professor at the University of London, concentrated my mind wonderfully. I was convinced his thesis was wrong! The theme of his talk was one to be found in a number of works by psychoanalysts, philosophers of various schools, and even social theorists, that is, that there is in the writings of Freud a cleavage between the insights into psychological, specifically clinical, matters and the metapsychology, which is the theoretical account and model of mind that Freud gives to explain the clinical phenomena. Schafer argued that Freud's metapsychology, which employs the language and causal concepts of natural science, is philosophically mistaken. Schafer's case was that Freud's insights—and indeed any understanding of the person, who must live in a world of meaning—can only be expressed in a language tailored to the articulation of meaning, purpose, responsibility, and related notions. Schafer pressed for a reconstructed language for psychoanalysis, the "action language" outlined in his book, which had then just appeared in print.

This monograph is based on my doctoral work, which followed Schafer's presentation. It sets out arguments for a realist construal of Freud's philosophy of science as well as a critique of the philosophical assumptions of Schafer, George Klein, and others who had argued along similar lines. The debate over the metapsychology and the status of the explanatory concepts of

1

psychoanalysis expanded in the mid-1970s and into the 1980s, becoming perhaps *the* theoretical debate of psychoanalysis. In this debate the "anti-metapsychology" position, often identified with the hermeneutic position, seems to have become almost an orthodoxy (although Adolf Grünbaum's work, *The Foundations of Psychoanalysis* [1984], critical of the hermeneutic thesis and widely noted, has in recent years presented a serious challenge to the anti-metapsychology position).

I believe, however, that the anti-metapsychologists in this debate have nourished themselves on limited accounts of the way explanations of human action work. They have variously depended on hermeneutic and phenomenological accounts, and even arguments from "ordinary language" philosophy that distinguish sharply between explanation by reason, deemed appropriate for human action, and explanation by cause, deemed appropriate only for natural phenomena. In contrast, I attempt to set out a more appropriate philosophy of psychological explanation to underpin Freud's theory, one which shows that a causal theory of mind like Freud's is philosophically viable. There is, fortunately, a substantial philosophical literature providing alternative and better models for the treatment of mental accounts than those on which the anti-metapsychologists have depended. My task has been to argue that a scientific realism (basically a materialism) is appropriate in psychological explanation and that it makes sense of Freud's metapsychology. I have set out Freud's theory as a psychology of motivation, and argued that the causal model of mind he presents is compatible with the language of meaning and purpose that Freud, and everyday psychology, also uses in accounts of human action. Freud is indeed concerned with meaning but, I argue, what is missed in the anti-metapsychological literature is that Freud is concerned with how meaning relates to man's biological nature.

It has become a virtual orthodoxy that, however good a psychologist Freud was, he was also a muddled philosopher, a victim of a naive nineteenth-century scientism. In contrast, in my textual work on Freud I have been surprised at the degree to which he was aware of his philosophy of explanation and how he provided sophisticated arguments for a qualified scientific realism. Gathering and setting out Freud's treatment of various philosophy of science issues became a substantial part of my work.

In doing the work for this book I was particularly fortunate in getting advice and criticism from two philosophers, Brian Farrell of Corpus Christi College, Oxford, and later David Armstrong of Sydney University. I also benefited from contact with John Maze of Sydney University. (None of them of course must be held responsible for my views.) Brian Farrell provided an example of careful, analytic study of philosophical issues in psychoanalysis that is rare and valuable in the field, an example from which Michael Sherwood's book *The Logic of Explanation in Psychoanalysis* (1969) had benefited earlier. David Armstrong has for some time been an important figure among philosophers arguing for a sophisticated materialism and a causal theory of mind. His work, like those of others arguing for a similar or related philosophy of psychology, is not apparently much considered by the critics of Freud's metapsychology, despite its status in modern philosophy of mind. My work draws on the literature supporting this sort of account of mind, arguing against any radical distinction between reasons and causes, and between the sorts of explanations we may offer for human phenomena and for natural phenomena. John Maze provided me with a certain amount of useful opposition as well as an example of a thoroughgoing materialist treatment of Freud's psychology.

To situate the present work more clearly within the current debates in psychoanalysis, it is worthwhile to compare it briefly with Adolph Grünbaum's work, not because it is a work of that scale but because Grünbaum's has become a landmark in the area. There are roughly three general areas of debate in the philosophy of psychoanalysis: (1) what sort of discipline or science psychoanalysis is, and by what standards it should be judged; (2) if it meets the standards of evidence demanded by a genuine science, whether it is true or false; (3) whether it is at all the sort of theory that could be scientific because it may not be possible to show it as true or false, in principle. Grünbaum's work enters all three areas, arguing, first, against the hermeneutic approach, that psychoanalysis must be judged by the canons of scientific evidence (including Freud's own);

second, that it does not, however, meet those standards; and third, that psychoanalysis is, in principle, falsifiable.

My work falls largely within the first of these areas, that is, what sort of enterprise psychoanalysis is. On the positive side I set out a construal of psychoanalytic explanation. I argue that the theoretical concepts of psychoanalysis need to be under-stood in the same way as those of other sciences, as hypothesized causal processes of mind, and that they gain their meaning and their justification in quite complex ways, as do the theoretical concepts of the other sciences. Like Grünbaum, I present a critique of the hermeneutic view of psychoanalysis, or rather against the anti-metapsychologists who endorse that view, though my arguments are presented in a different way, using different target authors. Unlike Grünbaum, I say little directly about whether psychoanalysis meets the standards of scientific evidence. I would not, however, bother writing about psycho-analysis if I did not think that it contains a great deal of truth. Furthermore, and without retreating to the hermeneutic dis-paragement of proof in the social sciences, I think the worth of a scientific theory like Freud's consists in its capacity to fulfill several functions. I spell out something of this idea here. Only one function of a good theory has to do with "correspondence with the facts," although many philosophers concerned with problems of confirmation in psychoanalysis become preoccu-pied with it. They argue as though the whole worth of a theory may be established straightforwardly by showing the corre-spondence of its propositions with facts, whereas other theo-retical functions are also important. Also, unlike Grünbaum, I present no argument against Popper's view that psychoanal-ysis is unfalsifiable. That argument seems to me to be obviated if the concepts of psychoanalysis gain their meaning and make explanations in essentially the same way as is done in other sciences.

At every turn in the discussion of psychoanalysis and its con-ceptual problems one touches on matters that relate to debates in other disciplines, particularly philosophy and the philosophy of science. And for each of these debates there is a large body of literature, sometimes highly technical. In some places, usually to acknowledge sources, I have linked a point I am making with a few examples of the literature in related debates. For the most part, however, I have tried to keep the text uncluttered. Similarly, I have tried to keep my writing plain, analytic and direct, though both Freudian exegesis and conceptual analysis must of course deal with complex matters. Work in psychoanalysis and philosophy is unfortunately often marred by unclear and even pretentious writing. In keeping the writing plain, the scope of the essay modest, and not attempting a tour de force, perhaps the limitations as much as the strengths of my arguments will be visible. In the end, however, and regardless of these strengths and weaknesses, my essay is part of a wider enterprise. I hope it contributes to the debate, and helps to clarify psychoanalytic explanation, its place in psychology, and its place in science.

Nigel Mackay
August 1987

INTRODUCTION

THE THESIS OF THE BOOK

In this essay I put forward an analysis of the psychoanalytic concept of motivation, setting out its place in psychoanalytic explanation. This introduction summarizes the arguments of the book and states where the work hopes to make its contributions. The essay itself is in three parts.

Part One

The first part sets out Freud's psychoanalytic theory. It traces this theory from its prepsychoanalytic roots to its final form. The psychoanalytic concept of motivation is a central part of this theory. Indeed, psychoanalytic theory is above all a theory of motivation.

The content of the theory changes over time: new hypotheses are added to the theory, old ones are removed or changed. For example, Freud comes to change the theory of instincts, and to emphasize aggression in mental life. He drops the early trauma theory of neurosis, changes the theory of anxiety, and much more. Freud also becomes more clearly psychological in his approach, abandoning the attempt to analyze mind in directly neurophysiological terms. Yet behind all these changes in content are a number of major principles that remain stable. These determine the form of psychoanalytic theory, and establish its motivational structure. This form persists throughout the development of Freud's thought. His model of mind, in its successive versions, is always given in terms of forces acting on and through structures. It always assumes that psychic structures evolved because of their functional relation to the environment. It always involves a theory of learning by association, treats mental actions as complex, modified reflexes, retains a theory of primary and secondary processes, and so on.

This account of the background and development of Freud's theory makes clear what sort of theory it is. First, it shows that psychoanalysis is the very type of a theory of motivation. A full motivational explanation of any given behavior or experience is multicausal. It consists in the specification of the internal processes that energize, precipitate, and direct behavior. Psychoanalytic theory is based on just such a principle of multiple causation, and consists of hypotheses about the energizing, precipitating, and directing factors that cause behavior. Second, it points out the interrelationships of Freud's various motivational notions, such as wish, purpose, drive, impulse, memory, cathexis, and others. These derive their meanings from the general theory within which they are set. Third, the account provides material on Freud's philosophy of science. For example, it shows the sources of his physicalism and the persistent influence this physicalism had on his theory. It shows how Freud's views on the mind-brain relation originated and changed. And it shows up his causal conception of psychological explanation.

Part Two

These points are used in the second part of the essay to undertake an analysis of the psychoanalytic concept of motivation. I argue that the concept of motivation that psychoanalytic theory embodies is best construed as a theoretical construct, in a realist sense of "theoretical construct." The theoretical construct approach has a number of implications for the analysis of the psychoanalytic concept of motivation. It tells us about (1) the way it explains behavior; (2) the epistemological status of motives, especially unconscious motives; (3) the relation of motives to behavior; and (4) the ontological status of the concept.

EXPLANATORY STATUS

The ascriptions of unconscious motives to individuals are used in the same way, basically, as the postulations of theoretical constructs in science.

1. They set out in general terms the conditions under which a type of behavior occurs.
2. They provide a link, or some conceptual continuity, between the manifest causal conditions for a behavior or symptom, and the behavior itself. They thus dispel the conceptual discomfort that arises when we consider action at a temporal or spatial distance. The unconscious motive is, for psychoanalysis, something that is part of a mental structure changed by external events at some point in time, and that continues to exist in some form until, under suitable conditions, it results in behavior.
3. Such ascriptions condense and organize data in that a large number of observations of behavior become embodied in relatively simple ascriptions. Ascribing a particular motive is, in part, a shorthand for making a large number of statements about past, present, and future overt behaviors or observable symptoms.
4. Thus, a large number of behaviors, which superficially appear unrelated, are assimilated into one hypothesis about an underlying motive. This is heuristically valuable. The theory links motives to other motives, to mental structures, to probable environmental causes, and to behaviors perhaps as yet uninvestigated. In this way, ascribing an unconscious motive leads from the examination of the original phenomenon to new areas of interest.

EPISTEMOLOGICAL STATUS

Ascriptions of motives explain in the same way as do postulations of the existence and operation of theoretical constructs. It then follows that we get to know motives—in particular, but not only, the unconscious motives of which psychoanalysis speaks—in the same way we get to know the theoretical processes of science. That is, the knowledge we have of motives is indirectly gained and is based on evidence. Further, knowledge claims even about one's own motives are corrigible and can be justified only indirectly. This approach is in accord with Freud's. Psychoanalytic theory implicitly contains a theory of knowledge of minds, a characterization of how we know our own mental states. In some ways psychoanalysis is all about how we know, and yet often refuse to admit, what our motives are. In this it deals with two features that any adequate theory of motivation must deal with (1) the apparent certainty with which people can get to know their mental state; and (2) the fact that individuals may be unconscious of their motives.

THE RELATION OF MOTIVES TO BEHAVIOR

Motives are the postulated causes of behavior. On the general assumption that whatever happens is caused, causes for behavior are sought. Clearly there are environmental events that are causally relevant to behavior. However, as with most complex organisms, a person's behavior does not seem lawfully related to environmental events in any simple manner. Internal factors are then postulated as intermediate causes. The psychoanalytic theory of motivation is about the internal structure of the human organism that causally mediates between the environment and behavior. As such, motives are contingently related to the behavior they cause, even though the psychoanalytic concept of motive was postulated on the basis of the observation of that behavior.

THE ONTOLOGY OF THE MOTIVE CONSTRUCT

This is a realist approach to theoretical constructs. It follows from this view, of motives as causes, that psychoanalytic motives are to be taken as real, existent processes. Of course, they are only real and existent inasmuch as psychoanalytic theory, and its concept of motive, correctly characterizes the processes underlying behavior. Now, a critic might say that Freud has incorrectly characterized the motivational process. Indeed, there is much about Freud's theory that is empirically doubtful, or simply wrong. It is important to distinguish this view, that Freud is empirically wrong, from a second type of criticism. This second type holds that the motivation concept is a mere fiction, no matter how well the concept accounts for behavior. This distinction is like that between saying Dalton's atomic theory was an early and inaccurate conception of atoms, and saying that the concept of an atom is a mere theoretical fiction.

As processes causally responsible for behavior, psychoanalytic motives are not irreducibly purposive; they do not belong to any special, human type of explanation achieved by giving the reasons and purposes behind an action and taken as fundamentally and conceptually distinct from causal explanations. Psychoanalytic motive explanations are purposive, but not in any way that means they are not causal. Ascribing an unconscious motive to a person is, among other things, ascribing a mental property to that person. Treating psychological predicates as mental is a "mentalist" approach, but mentalism here is fully compatible with materialism. Indeed, it seems inconceivable that the processes that are postulated in the mental model of psychoanalysis, and which are held to cause behavior, could be anything but material processes. On the other hand, "unconscious motive" does not directly name any material processes. The identification of material conditions for motives would be achieved by discovering physiological processes that are functionally equivalent to motives—processes that perform the same functions as motives, arousing and directing behavior. The psychoanalytic theory that characterizes motives would then be an abstract description of these underlying physiological processes. But, for the present, it does not matter to the theory of motivation (nor the mental model it implies) whether the mechanisms inside the individual's body are made of neurons, metal, or blue cheese.

The comments Freud makes on the explanatory, epistemological, and ontological status of psychoanalytic concepts show essential points of similarity to my approach. Freud's philosophy of science is a realism, and his approach to psychology is a materialist one. But it is qualified by an understanding that the processes of which science, including mental science, speaks can be known only indirectly.

Part Three

There is a recent critical literature on psychoanalytic theory that takes a position quite opposite to mine. In Part III I deal with the issues raised by this literature. There is a large number of authors, philosophers, psychoanalysts, psychologists, and others who argue for this position. I take as representatives, and targets for my criticism, the psychoanalytic theorists Roy Schafer, George Klein, Merton Gill, and Robert Holt. They in particular have been the vanguard, in the mainstream psychoanalytic domain, of a movement critical of the metapsychology and the philosophy of explanation it embodies.

These critics argue that true psychoanalytic explanation deals solely with "meanings." That is, psychoanalytic explanation is the articulation of individuals' understanding and misunderstanding of themselves, their relationships, and their experience. They argue that this articulation can be achieved only in a language that eschews the causal vocabulary employed by the Freudian metapsychology and model of mind. These critics are "anti-metapsychologists." The motivational concepts of this language, they argue, must be kept free of mechanistic and biological connotations, and have nothing to do with ideas of force and structure. They attempt to disengage the clinical principles and data from the metapsychology, and to rewrite Freud's motivational theory in a purposive, noncausal language.

The anti-metapsychologists are arguing for a "separate domain" view of explanation; they hold that explanations of human behavior belong, on conceptual grounds, to a domain of explanation that is separate from explanations of nonhuman phenomena. In this they oppose the idea that mental (psychoanalytic) concepts can be analyzed as theoretical constructs, and in the terms of a scientific realism.

The anti-metapsychologists make three central arguments.

THE BIOLOGY ARGUMENT

The first argument says that Freud's metapsychology is disguised biology, and as such it is inappropriate for the explanation of psychological phenomena. It mistakes the sense in which Freud's metapsychology is related to biology and the way theoretical constructs work in explanation. According to the analyses given in Parts I and II of this essay, psychoanalytic constructs are putative characterizations of the processes that cause behavior. As such, they are characterizations of neurological processes only in a high-level, abstract, and indirect sense. This is true of all mental concepts, and does not exclude them from being used in explanations of behavior. As long as concepts carry out basic explanatory functions (systematizing, heuristic, and conceptual), they may feature in explanations of behavior. A materialist view of Freud's motivational concepts does not commit one to the type of biological reductionism of which the critics wrongly accuse the metapsychology. It does not commit one to saying that mental terms can be "translated" into biological language, nor does the metapsychology try to effect such a translation-reduction.

THE INDEPENDENCE ARGUMENT

The second of the anti-metapsychologists' assertions is that the clinical insights of Freud (in which, they hold, lies the true value of psychoanalysis) are independent of the metapsychology. Against this, the clinical principles are, as a matter of fact, dependent on the metapsychology in several senses. First, in a general sense: the metapsychology informs the clinical aspects of psychoanalytic theory in that the metapsychology largely predates and conditions the clinical principles. Second, in a more specific sense: an examination of case-study material shows how the model of the mind aids Freud in making clinical interpretations, linking disparate data, and giving the account theoretical coherence. Third, the motivational concept "wish"—which itself bridges the mechanistic language of the metapsychology and the purposiveness of the clinical descriptions—unites these two into a single motivational explanation.

The clinical principles and data may, however, be logically independent of the metapsychological propositions. But then, no theory offered in explanation of a set of data is strictly necessary for the derivation of that set of data.

ON METAPSYCHOLOGY AND MEANING

The third of the anti-metapsychologists' central ideas is that the metapsychology, with its concepts of force and structure, and its causal view of motivation cannot deal with the essential aspect of human behavior, its meaningfulness. They argue that one states the motives behind a behavior by stating the purpose or goal of that behavior, which is its meaning. And they argue that this is not to give its cause.

This argument depends on the supposed distinctions between motives and causes. There is, however, nothing irreducibly purposive, and nothing irreducibly noncausal, about motive ascriptions. Ascriptions of motives function similarly to hypotheses about theoretical processes. Motives may be specified independently of that for which they are motives. They are contingently related to the behavioral data they are postulated to explain, and they satisfy the conditions for being causes of behavior.

Freud's theory offers a plausible type of account for the way in which the goal-directed quality of a motive is derived from a process that is itself not intentional. Initially there are only various somatic requirements, which in turn are evolutionary survival mechanisms. In this process there is direction, in that there is a limited class of objects which, for the same evolutionary reasons, can effect a fulfillment of the somatic requirements. But this is completely independent of any purpose or intention on the part of the individual to attain those objects. It is only after these objects are attained that they, and the actions associated with their attainment, take on the quality of goal-objects. And it is only through a complex learning process and the development of consciousness that the individual has motives in the sense of consciously (or unconsciously) considered goals.

The empirical correctness of Freud's theory is not the important point here. Rather, it is that there is nothing philosophically wrong about treating motives as learned derivatives of nonpurposive processes.

Overall, the anti-metapsychologists fail to make an adequate case for their psychoanalytic version of the separate-domain thesis. Their case stands on inadequate philosophical doctrines. A realist, "theoretical construct" analysis offers better answers to the problems of psychoanalytic explanation.

ABOUT THE ESSAY

The foregoing makes it clear that the essay enters the domains of several disciplines and subdisciplines: psychology, philosophy, psychoanalysis, philosophy of mind, psychology of motivation, and others. Furthermore, it involves, to varying degrees, several types of tasks: philosophical analysis, history of psychology, exegesis of Freudian texts, and a review and critique of a branch of psychoanalytic literature. It is in order, then, to say where among these several areas it hopes to make its contributions.

Psychoanalysis and Philosophy

Freud's attitude toward philosophy was ambivalent. On the one hand, he denied that he was any sort of philosopher; on the other, his work was carried out under the direction of a distinct philosophy of explanation, and his theory, as he acknowledged (1913b), makes inroads into the domain of philosophy. Psychoanalysis since Freud has retained this ambivalence. Psychoanalysts are first of all practitioners. However, they and psychoanalytic psychologists are often forced to be concerned with the troublesome conceptual foundations of the practice. Some examples of this concern with the foundations of psychoanalytic practice, excluding those concerned only with the confirmation of Freudian theory, may be found in the works of Atwood and Stolorow (1984), Bettelheim (1982), Edelson (1984), Gill (1976, 1983), Hartmann (1959), Hartmann, Kris, and Loewenstein (1964), Holzman (1986), Klein (1976), Kubie (1959), Meltzer (1978), Pollock (1980), Reiser (1984), Rubinstein (1967, 1976), Rycroft (1966), Schafer (1976, 1980), Spence (1982, 1983), and Wilson (1973). Furthermore, those psychoanalytic theorists who expand, clarify, or reflect upon Freud's theory are engaged in a philosophical exercise that is not always explicit. For their part, philosophers have always shown interest in psychoanalysis. They have been concerned with its scientific credibility and testability (for example, Cioffi, 1970; Farrell, 1981; Flax, 1981; Grünbaum, 1984; Jones, 1975; Nagel, 1959; Popper, 1983), and with its standing in relation to the natural, social, and behavioral sciences (for example, Farrell, 1981; Grünbaum, 1984; Habermas, 1972; Ricoeur, 1970, 1981; Von Eckardt, 1982; and the collections of Cioffi, 1973; Hanly and Lazerowitz, 1970; Hook, 1959; Wollheim, 1974; Wollheim and Hopkins, 1982). They have also been concerned with the conceptual legitimacy of Freud's theory of mind (for example, Alexander, 1962, 1974; Alston, 1967b; Cioffi, 1974; Dilman, 1972, 1984; Farrell, 1981; Flew, 1956; MacIntyre, 1958; Peters, 1958; Shalom, 1985; Smythe, 1972; Solomon, 1974b). An important part of this literature follows Wittgenstein (1942–1946). And philosophers have been concerned with the political and social ramifications of psychoanalysis and its place in modern thought (for example, Cioffi, 1973; Habermas, 1972; Nelson, 1957; Ricoeur, 1970, 1981; Wollheim 1971), and other topics.

The debate over the metapsychology mentioned above is conducted by psychoanalysts (for example, Gill, 1976; Holt, 1976; Schafer, 1976) as much as by anyone else. However, it is largely philosophical. It is about issues that fall into two related areas of philosophical writing: those concerned with what sort of theory psychoanalysis is—in particular, where it stands in relation to the natural, social, and behavioral sciences; and those about the conceptual legitimacy of Freud's theory of mind. The anti-metapsychologists admit their debt to philosophical literature, citing the analytic tradition of Wittgenstein and Ryle, as well as Ricoeur's hermeneutics, and the views of Sartre and others. And they argue, following the themes in this varied philosophical literature, that the concepts of Freud's theory of motivation are inappropriate for the explanation of human action, and that psychoanalysis needs to be rewritten in a form that disengages completely from natural science. They make it clear that they criticize the philosophy of science that underlies Freud's metapsychology, not his clinical ideas. However, the philosophy these critics draw on is limited. They ignore the literature arguing for realist and causal theories of mind (see, for example, Armstrong, 1968, 1973a; Armstrong in Armstrong and Malcolm, 1984; Borst, 1970; Brandt and Kim, 1963; Davis, 1983; Dennett, 1969; Fodor, 1968a, 1978; Goldman, 1970; Maze, 1983; Solomon, 1973–1974, 1974a). I contend that the philosophical doctrines on which the anti-metapsychologists draw do not give a satisfactory account of mental concepts, and that a realist account can overcome many of the problems faced by analyses of mental concepts: their explanatory, epistemological, and ontological status, the relation of reasons to causes, and so on. With some exceptions (for example, Mackay, 1986; Maze, 1983; Smythe, 1972; Solomon, 1974b), this realist philosophy of psychology has not been applied to psychoanalysis. Indeed, it is not common to see it applied to the concepts of actual psychological theories, Fodor (1968a) being a notable exception. A feature of this essay, which I hope makes a contribution, is that *it sets out Freud's theory of motivation, and it offers a systematic application of a realist philosophy of psychology to psychoanalytic (motivational) concepts.*

Further, there is a need for a clear discussion of Freud's views on such matters as explanation, the mind-brain relation, theoretical knowledge, reduction, and so on. For, even on such a relevant issue as the mind-brain relation, Freud is variously described by different commentators as a parallelist, an epiphenomenalist, a physicalist, and a dualist. Therefore, in the process of providing an analysis of the motivation concept, *the essay clarifies and states Freud's realist views on basic issues in the philosophy of psychology.*

Until a few years ago the anti-metapsychologists had only been criticized in part. This had been done piecemeal by other psychoanalysts, for example, by Anscombe (1981), Barratt (1978), Frank (1979), Friedman (1976), and Meissner (1979). Although the hermeneutic view of social science on which the anti-metapsychologists draw has now been criticized systematically on philosophical grounds (Grünbaum, 1984, for example), there is still much room for a systematic critique of the anti-metapsychology position. Thus, there is another respect in which this essay attempts to make a contribution: *It makes explicit the central arguments of the anti-metapsychologists, dissects them, and gives a critique of their philosophical presuppositions.*

THE STRUCTURE OF FREUD'S THEORY OF MOTIVATION

It has been convincingly argued in a number of works (for example, Amacher, 1965, 1974; Jones, 1953; Sulloway, 1979) that much of Freud's theory derives from his neurological background, and the influence of biology on the metapsychology in particular is taken up by Gill (1976), Holt (1965, 1976), Klein (1976), and Schafer (1976). In this sense Freud never abandons his neurological ideas. It is also sometimes explicitly recognized, though not always in the same places, that the metapsychology is a theory of motivation. Here I draw these two ideas together: *The essay makes explicit the sense in which the metapsychology has the form of a motivation theory. It further argues that this form is determined by the principles derived from Freud's prepsychoanalytic ideas, and shows how they determine the motivational structure of the successive versions of Freud's theory.*

Wider Implications

Finally, the issues I deal with have relevance to more than just psychoanalysis. Many of these issues, such as the status of mental concepts, the mind-brain relation, the nature of motivational concepts, realism, and purposive and causal explanation in psychology are of importance to the psychology of motivation, and to all of psychology. Psychoanalysis is a major psychological theory with application to the study of motivation, psychopathology, and developmental, personality, and social psychology. It is as wide in its range of application as any other theory. The problems it confronts—problems of verification, method, data collection, theory construction, and most of all of what types of concepts are appropriate for explaining human action—are the problems of all psychology. In these respects, psychoanalysis is psychology in microcosm.

PART I

FREUD'S THEORY OF MOTIVATION: ITS ORIGINS, DEVELOPMENT, AND CONCEPTUAL STRUCTURE

1

PRELIMINARIES

THE THEORY AND THE CONCEPT OF MOTIVATION IN PSYCHOANALYSIS

My concern in this essay is not only with Freud's *theory* of motivation, with how Freud considered behavior to be motivated, but also with Freud's *concept* of motivation, with the explanatory, epistemological, and ontological status of the motive constructs that he postulates. However, it is clear that the way to get some understanding of the concept of motivation is to look at the theory within which it is set, and to examine those processes and entities that Freud took to motivate behavior. In this setting both the theoretical and conceptual interrelations of the theory's constructs may be discerned, and the nature of the concept of motivation can be made explicit.

There are, unfortunately, factors that make it impossible to go to psychoanalytic theory and simply extract the desired information about its concepts. Neither the theory itself nor the conceptual and theoretical relations among its notions are so transparent as to allow this. There is no single, coherent statement of the theory. Indeed, there is not really any such unitary thing as "the" psychoanalytic theory. What often passes for the theory is something that has been extracted from some fifty years of Freud's writings. These writings cover a number of theoretical and conceptual shifts. They also represent interests ranging over individual and group psychology, personality theory, abnormal psychology, and so on.

There is also a lack of consistency in Freud's theoretical presentations. The theory is never fully stated in any one place. Most of his theoretical presentation is piecemeal, and is often condensed or elliptically stated, leaving it to interpreters and expositors to put the theory together into a whole. Freud's equivocation on theoretical points, his carelessness in presentation, and the changes he made to the theory all give rise to inconsistencies therein. Freud dealt with such a wide range of abnormal and normal phenomena that consistency in the theory is an impossible demand. Furthermore, the exigencies of psychotherapy required him to produce *ad hoc* explanations: schemes that fitted the patient at hand at the expense of overall theoretical coherence.

The difficulties of extracting the theory from these different sources and welding them into a whole are compounded by another factor. As is well known, there are two sorts of Freudian writings: in one, Freud strives to present the theory in purely mechanistic, causal, and nonpurposive terms; in the other, most usually found in Freud's clinical discussions, the reader is met with a mixture of mechanistic, anthropomorphic, purposive, and experiential concepts.

Thus, there is no concise and unambiguous theory within which to examine the Freudian concept of motivation. Even more important, the psychoanalytic concept of motivation is itself split, for motivation is central to all psychoanalytic explanation and to all psychoanalytic theory, clinical and metapsychological. So it is the motivation concept itself that appears at one moment as a mechanistic, forcelike notion, associated with drives, energies, and mental structures, and at another moment as a purposive, experiential notion. For example, wish is the central motivational concept in psychoanalysis. Sometimes it is treated as equivalent to impulse, the psychological side of an instinctual drive. At other times it is treated as intentional and as implying a goal.

These difficulties set a largely textual task for Part I: to discover and set out which principles, if any, remain constant through the changes and inconsistencies in Freud's theory; and to show in what sense these principles make psychoanalysis a motivation theory. It has been fairly common in psychoanalytic studies, for example, in Gill (1976), Holt (1965, 1976), and Sulloway (1979), to argue that much of Freud's mental model was adapted from the science of his time, and persisted in sometimes disguised form throughout his works. My task, however, is rather more than this. I want to set down the underlying and largely inherited principles of psychoanalysis in a manner that lights the way for my second task, to show them to be part of a reasoned and viable philosophy of explanation, specifically a materialism. This I believe can be done by showing their motivational structure.

There are some comments to be made on terminology. Thus far, no sharp distinction has been drawn between the psychoanalytic theory of motivation and psychoanalytic theory itself. The reason for this is simple enough: there is no sharp distinction to be drawn. Psychoanalytic theory is motivational by nature, and whatever explanations it generates of normal, clinical, or social behavior are essentially motivational in character.

The idea of a theory of motivation as it exists in the discipline of psychology has three elements. A theory of motivation is one that attempts to account for behavior by referring to those factors that energize, precipitate, and direct behavior. Theories of motivation do this by making hypotheses about "internal" or not immediately observable factors in the determination of behavior. Under this definition, psychoanalysis is quite clearly a motivation theory. The inclusion of Freud's theory in texts on motivation is almost universal. Psychoanalysis has had a prominent place in the development of the psychology of motivation as a subdiscipline of psychology.

There are narrower uses of the term "motivation" which restrict it to the energizing or to the directing aspects only of a psychological theory. In the case of psychoanalysis, the motivation theory would then only cover those hypotheses about instinctual drives and their derivatives, or about unconsciously entertained goals. But for the most part, psychologists have recognized the essential unity of the energizing, precipitating, and directing aspects of human action. This recognition is reflected in motivation textbooks, for example, in Arkes and Garske (1982), Atkinson (1964), Cofer and Appley (1964),

Geen, Beatty, and Arkin (1984), Young (1961), and is well articulated in Alston (1967a).

It is clear, even from Freud's early writings, that psychoanalytic explanations give a statement of the precipitating, energizing, and directing factors in human behavior. Freud's accounts provide hypotheses about the internal drive processes that place the individual in a state of readiness for action, about the external and internal signals that precipitate action, and about the ways in which action is directed toward particular ends. Such a motivational approach contrasts with those approaches that treat humans as somehow motivated by their very nature, and that all the psychologist has to do is to account for the directions of behavior. These latter psychologies may try to specify the cognitive, environmental, social, or phenomenal factors which they consider guide behavior, but leave out any attempts to find the engines that drive it.

The Motivation Theory, the Metapsychology, and the Model of Mind

The term "metapsychology" will recur in this discussion of the motivation concept in psychoanalysis. Freud (1915c) defines a metapsychological explanation as one which accounts for psychological phenomena in terms of force, structure, and energy. In their well-known clarificatory paper, Rapaport and Gill (1959) argued that there were two further aspects implied by the sort of explanation Freud termed metapsychological. Such explanations give an account of the adaptive role of the psychological phenomena being explained, and describe the genesis of the particular phenomena by tracing their development in the life of the individual. Both of these aspects—the genetic and the adaptive points of view—reflect the evolutionary basis of Freud's ideas. Freud regarded the metapsychology as the set of assumptions that are most basic to psychoanalytic theory. Fully stated, the metapsychology would comprise a set of axioms upon which psychoanalytic theory stands—the basic psychoanalytic propositions.

However, Freud and others have used the term in a looser fashion. The metapsychology is seen as the general theory of classical psychoanalysis, in contradistinction to clinical data and to rules for data interpretation. According to Freud, the metapsychology explains the clinical data and principles. It covers all those hypotheses about mental events and processes (forces, structures, and energies) that Freud takes to be causally responsible for symptoms, experiences, and behaviors. In this looser sense the metapsychology is identical to Freud's model of mind. This is the sense in which these terms will be used in this essay. Further justification for equating the metapsychology, the model of mind, psychoanalytic theory, and psychoanalytic theory of motivation will be given in the chapters that follow.

2

THE PREPSYCHOANALYTIC MODEL

THE BEGINNINGS OF PSYCHOANALYSIS

The formative influences on psychoanalysis have been well researched. They cover the various theoretical influences from Freud's neurological, anatomical, and medical work (for example, Amacher, 1965, 1974; Bernfeld, 1944, 1951; Burnham, 1974; Holt, 1965; Jones, 1953, 1955, 1957; Pribram and Gill, 1976; Ritvo, 1972, 1974; Rosen, 1972; Sulloway, 1979). They cover the clinical and psychiatric influences (for example, Bernfeld, 1944, 1951; Burnham, 1974; Jones, 1953, 1955, 1957; Serota, 1974; Stewart, 1969; Sulloway, 1979) and extra-scientific influences (for example, Barclay, 1964; Ellenberger, 1970; Erikson, 1955; Jones, 1953, 1955, 1957; Merlan, 1945; Rapaport, 1960a; Sterba, 1974; Sulloway, 1979; Ticho and Ticho, 1972; Whyte, 1960). There is also a rather more exotic recent literature exemplified by Masson (1984), which uses psychodynamic combined with historical forms of investigation to analyze the roots of Freud's ideas. The verdict of these researchers on the genealogy of Freud's ideas is not unanimous. However, it has been possible to give the most plausible of the scientific sources of the main derivative hypotheses in psychoanalysis, and to show how Freud drew upon these sources. Among these derived aspects are hypotheses that are fundamental to all the later formulations of Freud's theory. These are hypotheses about what approach to take to explain behavior, about the mechanisms that underlie human behavior, about the neural

26

basis of activity, about learning, and about the functions of behavior. Together these hypotheses add up to the skeleton of a model I shall call the "prepsychoanalytic" model, though strictly they do not constitute a full and coherent model of mind. This prepsychoanalytic model forms a baseline for the comparison of later versions of the psychoanalytic theory. In particular it is a philosophy of explanation that carries over from the prepsychoanalytic model to psychoanalysis proper. The conceptual puzzles in Freud's psychology of motivation—the referents of motivational terms, the causal nature of psychoanalytic concepts, knowledge of unconscious motives, the role of intention ascriptions in psychoanalytic explanations—are illuminated by an examination of the origins of that psychology.

Freud took over a general physicalism from important nineteenth-century thinkers such as Johann Herbart, whose psychology was probably studied by Freud (Jones, 1953, p. 410); the psychologist Gustav Fechner, a student of Herbart whose influence Freud acknowledges (1920, pp. 8–9); the influential physiologist Hermann Helmholtz; and Charles Darwin. This general physicalism was also transmitted by the life scientists Freud met during his education: Ernst Brücke, who Freud said "carried more weight with me than anyone else in my whole life" (1927, p. 253) and who was a pupil of Helmholtz; Theodor Meynert, in whose psychiatric clinic Freud worked for a while; and Sigmund Exner, successor to Brücke's chair of physiology. From these same sources Freud also inherited a more specific set of views on human functioning, conditioned by the general physicalism. A rough outline of Freud's theoretical inheritance follows:

Freud's general physicalism, or "materialism" to use a more modern term, asserts that the human organism is an integral part of the physical universe, wholly natural and determined in its behavior. Mind is not anything over and above the physical aspects of the organism and, following Herbart's dictum, "the conformity to law in the human mind resembles exactly that in the firmament" (Herbart, 1816, p. 15). The neural structures and mechanisms of this organism are functional in the Darwinian sense in that they developed as survival mechanisms in the evolving organism. The operations or behaviors of the organism are determined by the interplay of forces on and through these structures. Further, since the material that underlies the behavioral capacities of the organism is nervous tissue, any hypotheses made about the operations of the organism are constrained by knowledge about neural functioning. Freud, like Brücke (1874; Bernfeld, 1944), under whom he studied, and like others of the time, accepts that the forces at play within this nervous system are electrochemical; that they have direction and quantity; that they obey the laws of conservation of energy. He also holds that the principal function of the working unit of the system, called a "neuron" or "element," is the discharge of excitation.

Some more specific views on human functioning follow from this more general physicalism. Freud holds that the properties of the neuron determine those of the whole nervous system and, like Brücke (1874; Bernfeld, 1944), that the primary mode of operation of the nervous system is reflexive. It operates to discharge any energy that accumulates within it due to stimulation. It thus transfers excitation from the sensory periphery through the nervous centers of the organism, and out through efferent motor pathways. However, the system is more complex than this or it would not meet the exigencies of life. They are what Freud calls "secondary processes"—modifications to the reflexive process.

Freud did not inherit the theory of primary and secondary processes as such, but he did take over and adapt a number of ideas about nervous functioning that in effect hypothesize secondary modifications to the nervous system—for example, Meynert's ideas on ego (1884). These modifications give it a capacity to retain some energy within it, enabling it to act (rather than just react) in an organized way. It acts (by flight) to remove itself from exogenous sources of stimulation, and it acts to alter endogenous stimulation from somatic sources—for example, by taking in nourishment. Overall, in the prepsychoanalytic model, the system acts to maintain an optimum level of excitation within it as a reservoir of energy for actions. The modifications depend on the properties of the unit of nervous tissue, the neuron. The neuron itself has the capacity to retain an energy charge. This happens where the normal discharge paths, the boundaries with other neurons, are blocked. A path becomes unblocked, depending on the amount of excitation to be discharged, the inborn strength of this "discharge gate," its previous use for discharge, and other factors that facilitate the discharge temporarily.

The principles so far mentioned are given in neurological terms. However, they are intended to account for the psychological capacities of the organism. Physicalism holds that psychological properties are a function of physical, largely neural, processes.

Psychological Processes

The primary process of the organism, the energy-discharging function, has its psychological equivalent in the pleasure principle. High levels of excitation within the system are the neural concomitant to pain (unpleasure). Thus the discharge tendency represents, in psychological terms, the tendency of the organism to seek relief from unpleasure. It is, like the psychology of Fechner (1873), essentially hedonic and echoes Meynert's view that "In all the actions of man, be they ever so complicated, problematic or incomprehensible, the avoidance of greater pain is the determining motive" (1884, p. 176). Unpleasure comes from external sources in the form of excessive stimulation, or from internal stimulation. The unpleasure from internal sources is the basis of drive, or instinct, and is related to somatic requirements of the organism—to breathe, eat, drink, have sex, and so on.

The organism has the capacity to learn. This is a consequence of evolutionary development in the higher cortical centers of the nervous system. All learning is essentially learning what objects, and what actions upon them, lead to the lowering of excitation within the system to tolerable levels. For Freud, the mechanism of this learning is association, a long-accepted assumption about the nature of learning. The capacity of the organism to form associations is a consequence both of the properties of the neuron and of the way the neurons are arranged in the central nervous system, a view found, for example, in the works of both Meynert (1884) and Exner (1894; see Amacher, 1965).

For Freud, and for some of his predecessors and contemporaries in neurology, notably Exner (1894; see Amacher, 1965), neurons have the characteristic that where excitation is present in two adjacent neurons the conduction barriers between them is lowered. As a consequence of this lowering of resistance, energy flows from the higher to the lower potential points. Not only does this effect transferal of energy across the nervous system, it also leads, in at least parts of the brain, to the permanent lowering of resistance. This creates a pathway associating the two neurons. Since the concomitant of neurons in a state of excitation is an idea, this process associates ideas. A particularly important type of associative learning is that where external objects become associated with the release of unpleasure from drive sources. The simultaneous presence of stimulation in neurons linked to the sensory apparatus and in those excited by drive sources facilitates links between them. If effective discharge takes place—for example, by food intake—the object that gave rise to the sensory input is linked with that drive and with the motor actions that gave effective discharge. Pathways have been "grooved" into the nervous system.

This method of tension reduction represents an equilibratory mechanism at work, similar to that put forward by Fechner (1873), in turn following Herbart (1816). For Freud, the nervous system of the organism, through associative pathways, produces learned behavior that results in a decrease of drive tension level. But the decrease is only achieved when the somatic source of the drive tension is affected. The taking in of nourishment, however, provides the body with future sources of energy that can later become increased tension in the nervous system.

The formation of the cortical pathways that lead, in this roundabout fashion, to the discharge of tension is the development of the ego. The complex behaviors that serve the discharge function are all learned. They include most higher-order behaviors: thought, purposive activity, language, consciousness, and so on. All these are ego functions and make up the personality or individuality of the person. Where they break down, there appear forms of neurosis and mental disturbance. It is in this area of the model that Freud is strongly influenced by nonneurological views, by those of Charcot, Breuer, and others on psychopathology and its cure and implications for the nature of mind. It is this side of the model that Freud later expanded, through his own work and observations, into a psychology of the abnormal. Freud accepted psychological ideas, such as repression, the unconscious, and associationist learning principles. He then provided an explanation for these in concepts compatible with the neurology of his teachers. As we shall see, Freud went beyond this inheritance, and indeed discarded much of the actual neurological terminology, but nonetheless it is the foundation of his theory of motivation, and he never abandoned it.

Motivational Aspects

Following the classification of motivational notions that I made earlier, we can set out the themes of the prepsychoanalytic model in a more clearly motivational form, separating out the precipitating, energizing, and directing hypotheses in Freud's theoretical inheritance.

PRECIPITATING FACTORS

In the prepsychoanalytic model, the precipitation (initiation) of behavior comes from two sources: endogenous stimuli (instincts or drives); and exogenous stimuli, through the externally directed sense organs. There are structural as well as dynamic aspects to this system. The precipitating stimuli can be translated into action only because the system is organized reflexively and acts under the pleasure principle to divest itself of tension. In addition, for any behavior to be triggered, the drive stimulation underlying it has to be high; only drives can provide enough energy to effect an action. Stimulation from an external source is not sufficient to effect behavior. Multiple cues from internal and external sources act together to precipitate behavior, but they can do this only when the organism is appropriately energized.

ENERGIZING FACTORS

Except where there is an excessive amount of stimulation impinging on an individual organism from without (pain), it is the energy of endogenous sources that powers behavior, even though such energy must ultimately be derived from external sources through nourishment. Energy is from somatic sources, and is related to somatic needs—hunger, thirst, sex, and so on. The fundamental tendency is that of the organism to divest itself of excitation. Drive energy is transferred through brain pathways to effect behavior. This behavior may, through learning or because of the presence of some caretaking other, be effective in bringing about a change in the conditions that originally gave rise to the drive tension. The individual may eat or be given food, for example. Where it is effective, it brings to a conclusion the motivated behavior by restoring the optimum tension levels within the system. It operates in an equilibratory way.

This is only a crude outline. Both Freud and his predecessors realized the complexities of the nervous system and the associated complexities of motivated behavior. In spite of its general discharging tendency, the nervous system can store, release, and redirect energy in myriad ways. The behavior that results may be a long way from simple eating and copulating.

DIRECTING FACTORS

The pleasure principle gives the direction of all behavior in its most general sense. This primary direction is, however, modified by accommodation of the system to reality for survival purposes. This is achieved by various complications of the system's structures, of its operations, and by the learning an individual does. The first "exit" path for an individual (an infant) in a state of arousal (say, hunger) is in emotional expression such as screaming and kicking (see Freud, 1895a, pp. 317–318). These discharge paths are built into the organism. Then another person, his or her actions, and some object—say, the breast, aided by the reflex swallowing and sucking actions of the infant—bring about a removal of the endogenous stimulation. This effects changes in the neural pathways, thus associating the perception of the object, the drive sources, and the behavior that led to satisfaction. These changes in neural pathways constitute learning. Memories are the records of that learning, and are "grooved" into the neural system by means of permanent facilitations between neurons. Behavior is directed because of the subsequent tendency for excitation to pass along these facilitated pathways (memory traces). This action reproduces behaviors that lead to tension reduction.

Again, this is only a crude outline of the directing factors in the prepsychoanalytic model. The complexity of the natural and social environments demands a very sophisticated directing of behavior. These demands are accommodated by the nervous system through the refinement of learning and the associated establishment of an ego that acts as an executive agency, directing and controlling the transfer of energies in the nervous system.

THE CONCEPT OF MOTIVATION

The concept of motivation inherent in this prepsychoanalytic model treats the determinants of human behavior as mechanistic, as neurological as much as psychological in character, and as hierarchically ordered.

The theory of motivation is mechanistic in a biological sense. It sees that what motivates human behavior is part of the natural world, as is any biological process, and that it is explicable in causal terms. What motivates behavior is not irreducibly purposive. No final causes are at work here, only the forces and structures at work in the physical world.

The concept is neurological as much as psychological because it holds that whatever is describable in psychological terms—purpose, intention, wish, sensation—is a function of neural processes and may be explained as a consequence of those processes. This is the way that psychological qualities are assimilated to the mechanistic, biological world. They are stripped of their vitalism and made subject to the causal laws of nature.

This conception of motivation is hierarchical in the sense that one can describe the motives for an action on a number of different levels. The motive for some particular behavior might, for instance, be described at its most basic level as the tendency to discharge excitation (the pleasure principle); or it might be at a slightly more specific level (the constancy principle); or still more specific, as an instance of the operation of some drive; or as some drive-related wish; or as the excitation of some cortical trace, and so on.

This concept of motivation and the principles of the pre-psychoanalytic model remain part of all the reformulations of psychoanalytic theory by Freud, a point I shall argue in the chapters that follow. Similar points have of course been argued by a number of authors over the years, for example, MacIntyre (1958), Holt (1965, 1976), Gill (1976), Sulloway (1979). I differ from most of them in that I do not see Freud's retention of these prepsychoanalytic themes as a philosophical aberration, the unfortunate residue of a nineteenth-century scientism, nor as inimical to the real aims of psychoanalysis.

3

EARLY THEORIES OF MOTIVATION

THE ABREACTION MODEL

In the first properly psychoanalytic motivation theory, the "abreaction" theory, Breuer and Freud (1895) attempt to give theoretical coherence to a striking clinical phenomenon: that forgotten memories in hysterical patients appear to motivate current hysterical behavior and symptoms. In the introductory pages, the following statements give the core of the theory:

> *Hysterics suffer mainly from reminiscences* [p. 7] . . . *these memories correspond to traumas that have not been sufficiently abreacted* [p. 10]. . . . [Abreaction is where] *there has been an energetic reaction to the event that provokes an affect* [p. 8] . . . *ideas which have become pathological have persisted with such freshness and affective strength because they have been denied the normal wearing-away processes by means of abreaction and reproduction in states of uninhibited association* [p. 11].

Where the affect aroused by a traumatic event has not been abreacted, it may persist in an unconscious idea, later to be diverted into a hysterical symptom. Although at this stage Freud and Breuer are not attempting a general psychology, merely an account of hysteria, both the general physicalism and a number of principles of the prepsychoanalytic model may be discerned in it.

General Physicalism

The physicalism in this model of motivation shows itself in Freud and Breuer's use of the explanatory categories of natural science, in particular that of energy. "Affect" is the energy concept. It obeys the laws of physical energy: it has quantity and direction; it is conserved; it is fluid in nature, moving from higher to lower potentials; it operates reflexively within the system.

> . . . in mental functions something is to be distinguished—a quota of affect or sum of excitation—which possesses all the characteristics of a quantity (though we have no means of measuring it), which is capable of increase, diminution, displacement and discharge, and which is spread over the memory-traces of ideas somewhat as an electric charge is spread over the surface of a body.
>
> This hypothesis . . . can be applied in the same sense as physicists apply the hypothesis of a flow of electric fluid [Freud, 1894, pp. 60–61].

Affect, as the term "abreaction" suggests, is reflexively discharged:

> By 'reaction' we here understand the whole class of voluntary and involuntary reflexes—from tears to acts of revenge—in which, as experience shows us, the affects are discharged. If this reaction takes place to a sufficient amount a large part of the affect disappears as a result. Linguistic usage bears witness to this fact of daily observation by such phrases as 'to cry oneself out', and to 'blow off steam.' If the reaction is suppressed, the affect remains attached to the memory [Breuer and Freud, 1895, p. 8].

Specific Physicalism

The physicalism, and the similarity with the prepsychoanalytic model, is also shown in the specific structure of the abreaction model, and in the language it uses. The functional units of the mental model are termed by Breuer "psychical elements"

(1895, p. 193). In this usage Breuer is apparently keeping his early promise that "In what follows little mention will be made of the brain and none whatever of molecules. Psychical processes will be dealt with in the language of psychology" (p. 185). Later (p. 193), however, the phrase "psychical elements" is immediately qualified by "(? cortical cells)." Breuer illustrates the nature of the system into which these elements fit by discussing nerve cells, excitation, and the discharge of energy. Still later he uses the phrase "cerebral elements" to replace "psychical elements" (p. 199). The "element" is clearly the psychological equivalent of a neuronal cell, and events and processes involving the element have parallel events and processes involving the neuron. We merely have a transposition of terms from the neural to the psychical side of the brain-mind parallel.

The system is built, then, on the pattern of the prepsychoanalytic model. The first property of the element is its capacity to become charged: to be in a state of "tonic excitation" (p. 192). Raised tension brings "paths of conduction into a state of high facilitation" (p. 196). Hysteria is explained by the passing over of affect into paths that have been established by associative learning. This leads to "somatic innervation," which occurs when, for some reason, the normal paths for discharge are closed and the affect has not been "abreacted."

The system also works on an equilibratory ("constancy") principle. Somatic needs result in a rise in tension and unpleasure. This tension can be dissipated, functionally, in actions that bring about change in somatic need conditions.

> . . . cerebral elements . . . liberate a certain amount of energy even when they are at rest; and if this energy is not employed functionally it increases the normal intracerebral excitation. The result is a feeling of unpleasure. Such feelings are always generated when one of the organism's needs fails to find satisfaction. Since these feelings disappear when the surplus quantity of energy which has been liberated is employed functionally, we may conclude that the removal of such surplus excitation is a need of the organism. And here for the first time we meet the fact that there exists in the organism a *tendency to keep intracerebral excitation constant* [p. 197].

There are close parallels between the psychological and the neurological notions used. The neurological story is that neural elements become charged by excitation from instinctual sources (p. 199). This is directed along facilitated conduction pathways, because of previous excitatory activity in the elements. Ultimately it discharges via these paths. The equivalent psychological story is that instinctual sources of excitation charge memories with affect, giving rise to an idea. This "affective idea" (p. 200) is a wish. It normally leads to motor, sensory, or ideational activity as a way of discharge.

The abreaction model is relatively crude by Freudian standards. It is also designed, not as a general theory of mind, but as an account of hysteria. Yet it possesses the major elements of the prepsychoanalytic model in its operative principles. It is in Freud's *Project for a Scientific Psychology* (1895a) that the prepsychoanalytic inheritance is shown at its clearest and most complete.

THE PROJECT

Its Place in Psychoanalysis

The *Project for a Scientific Psychology* is an important document for understanding psychoanalysis, its metapsychology, its motivation theory, and the roots of its major concepts.

First, even though it is highly condensed and often elliptical, the work does give the clearest statement of a number of major psychoanalytic propositions. For example, in it may be found accounts of the energy principles (pp. 296–297), Freud's conception of the basic unit of the psychic apparatus (pp. 297–302), and the importance of survival value in determining the form of the mental apparatus (pp. 302ff.).

Second, the Project throws light on basic hypotheses that are puzzling and obscure in the manner in which they appear in later works. For example, Freud sets out and justifies the notions of primary and secondary processes (pp. 324–327) and places them in relation to the evolving organism and to its behavior. He discusses wish fulfillment (p. 340), bound and free energy forms (pp. 368ff.), reality testing (pp. 325ff.), and defensive functions (pp. 351–352) in a detail missing from later treatments.

Third, the Project outlines psychoanalytic approaches to topics that make up modern experimental psychology—topics such as learning, memory, attention, thinking, and reinforcement. As psychoanalysis became more a theory of psychopathology, these topics were neglected, or only considered inasmuch as they are of importance to clinical matters.

Fourth, as the Project is couched in the language of Freud's neurological education, it shows quite clearly the legacy of Meynert, Brücke, Exner, and the tradition to which they belonged.

Finally, and most important for present purposes, the Project sets out the form, or logical structure, of psychoanalytic theory. This form persists through many changes in Freud's theory. It is the clue to the underlying unity of the many psychoanalytic presentations that Freud made.

General Physicalism

The Project is a model where psychological functions, from rational thought to dreams and psychopathology, are explained as consequences of neural processes. It is a neuropsychology. Freud starts with a statement of his physicalist assumptions: "The intention is to furnish a psychology that shall be a natural science: that is, to represent psychical processes as quantitatively determinate states of specifiable material particles [neurons]" (1895a, p. 295). Q, the energy notion, is "neuronal excitation . . . quantity in a state of flow" (p. 296), and is "subject to the general laws of motion" (p. 295). The neurons' fundamental property follows the inertia principle: they "tend to divest themselves of Q" (p. 296). Upon these basic hypotheses—about the physical determinants of psychological processes, and the reflexive, discharging nature of nervous tissue—is constructed the remainder of the elaborate model. All of the organism's activity is ultimately traceable to the reflexive passage of energy through the nervous system.

THE EVOLUTIONARY SETTING

An increasingly complex organism has to live and function in the world. An organism has to feed itself, reproduce, flee noxious stimuli, and so on. Flight requires that some energy be retained (pp. 296–297), rather than immediately discharged by the system. Similarly, an organism's needs for food, sex, and so on require energy-consuming activity by the organism if the needs are to be fulfilled. The system evolves so that the needs give rise to endogenous stimuli. The organism cannot escape from these by flight, and a store of energy is required so that "specific actions" (for example, taking in nourishment) may be performed. These alter the somatic conditions associated with needs, and so remove stimuli.

PRIMARY AND SECONDARY PROCESSES

There are two aspects to the modifications necessitated by the "exigencies of life" (p. 297). First, in the energy processes, the primary mode of discharge gives way to a secondary mode:

> . . . the nervous system is obliged to abandon its original trend to inertia (that is, to bringing the level [of φ'η] to zero). It must put up with [maintaining] a store of φ'η sufficient to meet the demand for a specific action. Nevertheless, the manner in which it does this shows that the same trend persists, modified into an endeavour at least to keep the φ'η as low as possible and to guard against any increase of it—that is, to keep it constant [p. 297].

In this way Freud's model uses both the reflexive "inertia" principle and a derivative form, the constancy principle.

Second, a corresponding structural change takes place. This is based in the neuron. He says that neurons, as well as tending to discharge φ, may retain ("cathect") energy because of resistances to energy outflow at their points of connection with other neurons.

> A single neurone is thus a model of the whole nervous system with its dichotomy of structure, the axis-cylinder being the organ of discharge. The secondary function [of the nervous system],

however, which calls for the accumulation of φ'η is made possible by the assumption of resistances which oppose discharge [p. 298].

The Subsystems and Their Interactions

Freud partitions the neural system into the ψ and φ groups of neurons, and further differentiates the latter, adding a ω group. These neural subsystems are distinguished largely according to psychological function. He explains the capacity of these subsystems to carry out their functions by appealing to both the properties of the neurons involved and to their anatomical position, specifically, where they stand in relation both to incoming stimulus paths and to efferent motor pathways. The system details are not of importance here; they have been well covered by a number of commentators, notably Pribram and Gill (1976). However, some account of the workings of the model needs to be given because Freud's conception of the determinants of behavior, implicit in these workings, is important.

Freud sets out a model of the structures required to supply the basic functions of an intelligent, sentient organism of the complexity of the human. He constructs this out of the properties of nervous tissue as understood at the time, and manages a model sophisticated even by more recent standards, though the language is archaic. The differential facilitatory capacities of neurons—that is, the variations in ease and impedance of conduction of excitation—accounts for the ability of the nervous system to underwrite the major psychological functions. Memory and learning are achieved by the longer-term registration of passages of excitation through the permanent lowering of facilitatory barriers of some groups of neurons, the grooving of memory traces. Perception is accounted for by the capacity of other groups of neurons to transmit excitation without permanent change (pp. 298–302). Consciousness is explained by the distinction between the registration of quantity of excitation and the registration of its quality or patterning (pp. 309, 311–312). This distinction is also used to account for the capacity of the system to monitor the levels of tension deriving from within the system—instinctual drive demands (p. 320). Energy from drive demands presses for, and may achieve, immediate discharge in undirected motor action. This, however, has no long-term value for the system because the undirected motor activity would not alter the sources of tension, the somatic needs (pp. 297, 317).

The Secondary Processes and Structures

These are a matter of great importance. For longer-term discharge to take place, it must result in "specific actions" (ones that stop the somatic source of tension, by, say, taking in food in the case of hunger; p. 318). The organism has to develop this capacity in the early part of its life. It (1) has to develop a means of learning from experience what activities and objects are instrumental in reducing somatic needs, and (2) learn to inhibit discharge in action until it can be directed, in the correct ways, onto appropriate objects. On these rides nothing less than the development of all secondary processes—thought, judgment, repression (and the possibility of pathology)—and ultimately communication, social values, and all the qualities we consider distinctively human.

MOTIVATED LEARNING: THE "EXPERIENCE OF SATISFACTION"

Freud discusses the beginnings of such learning. The system initially discharges through inborn pathways, relatively well facilitated neuronal tracks. At first, discharge paths lead to "*internal change* (expression of the emotions, screaming, vascular innervation)" (p. 317). The achievement of a specific action then:

> takes place by *extraneous help*, when the attention of an experienced person is drawn to the child's state by discharge along the path of internal change. In this way this path of discharge acquires a secondary function of the highest importance, that of *communication*, and the initial helplessness of human beings is the *primal source* of all *moral motives*.

When the helpful person has performed the work of the specific action in the external world for the helpless one, the latter is in a position, by means of reflex contrivances, immediately to carry out in the interior of his body the activity necessary for removing the endogenous stimulus. The total event then constitutes an *experience of satisfaction,* which has the most radical results on the development of the individual's functions [p. 318].

Freud goes on to articulate these changes in terms of the neuronal subsystems and facilitation. This process provides the links—the facilitatory paths—between the neurons that correspond to the perception of the satisfying object, those that correspond to the to-be-satisfied drive, and those that lead to the effective discharge of the drive tension. The precipitating factors in motivation (the perception of the object) and the motive force (the endogenous drive stimuli) are linked and are directed into specific motor activity. Subsequent perception of the object (incoming excitation from external sources) will release the cathexes (supplied from somatic sources) of the relevant neurons more easily by facilitating their discharge paths. Importantly, Freud also allows for endogenous φ to fill these same neurons, and then φ will tend to pass over into the neurons corresponding to the perception of the originally satisfying object. Under special circumstances this constitutes a hallucination, but generally the cathexis results only in a "wishful state" for the object (pp. 321–322), and a distinction between wish and reality is maintained until appropriate action can take place. There then must be processes that delay discharge until the time is right. This is the second essential aspect of the secondary processes. It is achieved by the development of ego.

THE EGO AND THE DELAY OF DISCHARGE

Freud postulates that there is a group of neurons, once again specialized by virtue of their facilitatory qualities and their position in the discharge routes of the system, that grows in the life of the individual. This is the ego. These neurons have the property of becoming constantly cathected with a store of energy (p. 323), and energy entering the system becomes "drained off" into the ego. This process has important consequences: it acts to inhibit immediate motor discharge of energy and provides a reservoir of energy in the system, ready to be redirected by higher processes. The draining off of the endogenously supplied cathexes into a system of temporary storage, the ego, delays ineffective and immediate discharge. It binds cathexes, and so defends the organism against unpleasure.

Upon this delaying process are predicated all ego functions: defense (p. 324), inhibition (p. 323), repression (p. 322), thought and cognition (pp. 327ff.), reality testing (p. 325), attention (pp. 360ff.), and even dream and symptom formations (pp. 322ff.). For example, this defensive, delaying capacity of the ego system operates as a reality tester (pp. 325–326). It only releases the drive energy cathecting some wish when certain feedback signals from that system indicate a match between the cathected, wished-for memory and the current percept. That is, the drive energy is only released into activity when the wished-for object really is there. Until then, appropriate action upon that object—action that previously led to satisfaction in similar circumstances—is inhibited by the draining off of cathexes by the ego. This matching of signal and wish is an aspect of thought processes. Where there is a mismatch, activity or thought may result. These are productive if they result in a reorientation of the individual that reduces the incongruity between wish and percept.

Attention and thought are explained in similar ways, by elaborate feedback mechanisms dependent on discharge delay. Attention (pp. 337, 360ff.) involves a special reinforcing cathexis of perceptions, achieved by a feedback system. Thought is small-scale experimental action, achieved by very small energy displacements (pp. 334–335). These warn, by the release of small amounts of unpleasure, of the dangers involved in a particular path of action. Dreams (pp. 336ff.) and hysteria (pp. 347ff.) are explained by temporary and pathological loss of ego functions, respectively. This loss results in the discharge of energies through pathways established previously, often by accidental associations of circumstances and correspondingly of ideas.

Relation of the Project to Earlier Models

The Project clearly contains the major elements of the pre-psychoanalytic model. It adopts its physicalism, its use of force and energy concepts, and its reflex view of nervous processes and argues the evolutionary necessity in the transition from primary to secondary processes. In the Project, Freud develops the inertia principle into an equilibratory process, and goes into considerable detail concerning the energic aspects of neuronal activity.

The Project, however, goes beyond the prepsychoanalytic and abreaction models. Many changes are made to help the model account for clinical observations, but others simply represent a sophistication of Freud's model of human motivation. Freud elaborates the mechanisms by which the inertia principle operates, and also the secondary modifications to which these mechanisms, and the principle itself, are subjected by the "exigencies of life." Freud develops the inertia principle into a series of subprinciples responsible for the finer regulation of the system. In the Project, not merely the constancy principle but also other regulatory mechanisms are spawned by the inertia principle: for example, a complex of feedback mechanisms (as in the attention process), and a delaying mechanism (primary ego defense). These mechanisms depend on the learning process, which enables the organism to maintain tolerable levels of tension (the theory of ego-directed specific actions).

Freud also develops the notion of ego, presents a theory of consciousness, and discusses the roles these two play in the regulation of the motivational system. He outlines the ego's defensive function, its links with consciousness, with perceptual and attentional processes, and he puts forward a theory of thinking as small-scale experimental action. Freud also makes a sharp and explicit distinction between primary and secondary processes.

On the clinical side, Freud uses the model to account for defense and hysteria. He links these with other, characteristically psychoanalytic, views: the importance of repression for pathology, and the significance of sexuality—especially pre-pubertal sexual experience—in psychopathology.

Overall, the Project represents a remarkable synthesis of ideas: Freud's own innovations, his clinical insights, and views present in his earlier models. The themes he deals with read like a catalog of the major psychoanalytic hypotheses. Jones (1953, p. 392) lists the themes of the Project:

Principles of Inertia and Constancy
Primary and Secondary Processes
Unconscious and Preconscious
Urge towards Wish-Fulfilment
Hallucinatory and real fulfilment of Wishes
Criteria of Reality
Inhibitory function of the ego—Mobile and bound energy
Separation of function between perception and memory
Relation of Memory to contact-barriers and facilitations
Three conditions for the arising of consciousness
Significance of Speech
Thought as experimental small-scale action
Traumas and pain as excessive stimuli
Protective screen against them and concentration of cathexes to deal with irruptions
No screen against internal stimuli
Signals of unpleasure instead of full doses
Dreams: wishful, hallucinatory, regressive, distorted—No motility during sleep
Parallelism of dreams and neurotic symptoms
Importance of sexuality in neuroses
Hysteria: defense, repression, displacement, distortion
Significance of Attention
Analysis of intellectual processes, including logical errors, etc.
Connection between repression and retardation of puberty

And Jones comments: "All except the last three were developed further in Freud's later writings, often thirty years later."

THE PROJECT AND MOTIVATION

The Project presents the person as a system with a primary discharge tendency. This is determined by the laws of nature, and the specific properties of nervous tissue. The latter in turn are a consequence of evolutionary exigency. This is overlaid, and regulated, by both the structural and dynamic modifications of the secondary process. All this constitutes its crude motivational form. In the last analysis, behavior is energized by instinctual drives and is given direction by the primary and then secondary process; the factors that precipitate action are found in the relationship between the state of the organism and the environment.

First, there are changes in the postulates about the energizing factors. The Project emphasizes endogenous stimuli (instincts) as the power source for behavior. No longer does the system function simply by carrying exogenous stimuli through the system toward motor discharge. Further, the system stores and directs these quantities of endogenous energy to effect specific actions. These are the basic goal-directed actions of humans. Freud's emphasis on the internal sources of motivation became even more pronounced after he abandoned the infantile seduction theory of hysteria, two years after the writing of the Project. He discovered that the "memories" of hysterical patients were in fact fantasies: they were internally based and not determined by external factors. Associated with this is Freud's emphasis on sexual instinct as the main motivating factor that brings into play anxiety, repression, and psychopathology (pp. 354ff.).

Second, there are also changes in the theory of how behavior is directed and precipitated. The bulk of the Project is devoted to detailing how secondary processes redirect the tendency of the primary process, and how, through learning, various configurations of external and internal stimuli precipitate action.

In contrast to the usual textbook presentation of Freud's theory as a simple instinct or drive reduction theory, the Project shows it to be much more complex. In particular it has a strong cognitive orientation; most of the directing factors in behavior are, for Freud, cognitive ego processes. Jones (1953) was one of the first to note this in Freud's work, and he does so in a discussion of the Project. He says:

> It does not pertain to a Biography, but I would throw out the suggestion that an interesting study could be made of a comparison and contrast of Freud's sketch of cerebral physiology

sixty years ago, one he discarded as worthless, with the recent electrotonic theories of cerebral functioning as expounded by Hebb, Lashley, Penfield and Rasmussen, Wisdom, Wiener, Young, and others. Freud's conceptions of 'unpleasure' producing neuronic disorder, the order being restored by pleasure, of the significance of varying electrical resistances at the synapses, the nature of memory traces, his views on the association areas, etc., would seem to be of special interest in this connection [p. 393].

This is a hint that Freud's model here is what modern psychologists might term "a biological cognitive control theory." A number of authors (for example, Erdelyi, 1985; Farrell, 1972; Innes, 1971; Peterfreund and Schwartz, 1971; Peterfreund, 1980; Pribram and Gill, 1976) have since treated Freud's theory as a control theory.

CONCEPTUAL ASPECTS OF THE PROJECT MODEL

I noted earlier that the motivational concept of the prepsychoanalytic model is mechanistic, hierarchical, and as much neurological as psychological. The same can be seen in the Project. We also get a further clue as to how Freud conceived of his explanatory model from his own discussion of "biological" and "mechanical" categories of explanation.

MECHANISM, CAUSE, AND PURPOSE

In the Project, Freud adopts two criteria for the assessment of his explanations: a "biological" criterion and a "mechanical" one. The biological one is that the hypotheses he puts forward have to make evolutionary sense. As the structures underlying human behavioral capacities are part of an evolving organism, they must have some survival function. Some hypothetical process or posited structure might not be locatable anatomically, and might not make the most parsimonious of explanations. Yet, if it is evolutionarily feasible, it has satisfied an important criterion of explanation. Freud says, in talking of the distinction between the contact barriers of two of the subsystems, that "morphologically . . . nothing is known in support of the distinction" (p. 302). However, he goes on to ask if "the two classes of neurones can have had a different significance biologically" (p. 302). He argues that "it would be possible to follow a Darwinian line of thought and to appeal to the fact of impermeable neurons being indispensable and to their surviving in consequence" (p. 303).

In another example, Freud discusses his hypothesis about the mechanism of primary defense, or repression. He argues:

> . . . the explanation should lie in the fact that the primary experiences of pain were brought to an end by reflex defence. The emergence of another object in place of the hostile one was the signal for the fact that the experience of pain was at an end, and the ψ system, taught *biologically,* seeks to reproduce the state in ψ which marked the cessation of the pain. With the expression *taught biologically* we have introduced a new basis of explanation, which should have independent validity, even though it does not exclude, but rather calls for, a recourse to mechanical principles (quantitative factors) [p. 322].

The mechanical basis of explanation is described by Strachey in a footnote (p. 305): "By 'mechanical' (for which he sometimes uses 'automatic' as a synonym) he means that the phenomenon in question is determined directly by contemporary physical events." In seeking for a mechanical explanation of some phenomenon, Freud is looking for an account that establishes causal links with physical events and processes. To be adequate, such an explanation must be coherent and the hypothesized mechanism must be self-sufficient and of a physical kind. The mechanical conception of his Project model is contained in a well-known statement by Freud in a letter to Fliess:

> Now listen to this. One strenuous night last week, when I was in the stage of painful discomfort in which my brain works best, the barriers suddenly lifted, the veils dropped, and it was possible to see from the details of neurosis all the way to the very conditioning of consciousness. Everything fell into place, the cogs meshed, the thing really seemed to be a machine which in a moment would run of itself. The three systems of neurones, the "free" and "bound" states of quantity, the primary and secondary processes, the main trend and the compromise trend of the nervous system, the two biological rules of attention and defence,

the indications of quality, reality, and thought, the state of the
psycho-sexual group, the sexual determination of repression,
and finally the factors determining consciousness as a perceptual
function—the whole thing held together, and still does. I can
naturally hardly contain myself with delight [Freud, 1887–1902,
p. 129].

This conception of the determinants of behavior is a causal one.
There is no room for teleological factors to intrude into the
lawlike events of the psychic system.

There are a number of concepts that Freud uses which are
not only psychological, but are also intentional or subjective—for
example, wish, idea, will, affect, experience of satisfaction, unpleasure. The use of these same concepts in later psychoana-
lytical work seems to indicate that psychoanalysis attempts to
explain behavior by reference to the (unconscious) intentions
and purposes of the individual, rather than by reference to the
causal conditions that give rise to the behavior. However, the
way that these concepts are introduced and used in the Project
shows that it is otherwise. These experiential and purposive
concepts are part of a causal theory of motivation and may be
defined nonpurposively.

Wish, for example, is a major motivational concept in psychoanalysis. In ordinary nonpsychoanalytic contexts wish is the
epitome of an intentional concept. However, for Freud, to be
in a wishful state is to be in a certain physical condition. It
means that certain neurons are cathected. These are neurons
associated (by means of facilitated barriers) both with the neurons that correspond to the percepts of the wished-for object,
and with those that were previously involved in the discharge
of similar excitation. To say an individual wishes for some object
is a shorthand way of saying that certain neurons corresponding
to previous perception of that object are excited.

PSYCHOLOGY OR NEUROLOGY?

Earlier I stressed that the beginnings of psychoanalysis were
as much neurological as psychological. In the context of the
Project it needs to be said that Freud's hypotheses are as much

psychological as neurological. In fact, the Project is a neuro-psychology. Freud builds his model out of apparently neuro-logical concepts. This is why the Project has something of an alien look to it for many psychoanalysts. However, most of the functions he wishes to account for are behavioral (though, in turn, any psychological explanations he gives are constrained by his views on the operation of the nervous system). The terms of the Project refer to the nervous system *as Freud conceives of it.* Freud is talking about brain processes, but he is talking of what psychologists have come to call the "conceptual nervous system" (for example, Hebb, 1955). The working parts of the conceptual nervous system are differentiated according to psy-chological as much as neurological criteria. They are hypotheses about the sorts of internal machinery required to account for behavior rather than about actual nervous tissue. Inasmuch as these hypotheses are constrained by the then current knowl-edge of the properties of the nervous system, Freud's model is neurological. Inasmuch as it is constrained by knowledge of human behavior and experience, it is psychological (more is said on this important point in Parts II and III).

MOTIVATIONAL HIERARCHY

A hierarchy of motivational concepts exists in the Project model, just as it does in the prepsychoanalytic model. This means that explanations of psychological phenomena can be given in a number of different ways, some using specific and some more general psychoanalytic concepts. Appealing to needs or instincts means using very broad explanatory concepts. Freud, for example, explains the delayed effects of infantile sexual experiences by the pubertal upsurge of sexual instincts. On a case of hysteria in an adolescent girl, who was sexually assaulted prior to puberty, Freud comments: "Here we have the case of a memory arousing an affect which it did not arouse as an experience, because in the meantime the change [brought about] in puberty had made possible a different understanding of what was remembered" (Freud, 1895a, p. 356).

However, Freud's model also provides much more specific explanatory concepts, such as wish. Wishes are cathexes of groups of neurons and are object-specific. In a different context the sexual etiology of some symptoms may already be known. In that case a more specific wish or idea can be given as the explanation for the symptom.

4

LATER THEORIES OF MOTIVATION

THE TOPOGRAPHICAL THEORY

The first full statement of the "topographical" version of psychoanalytic theory is given in Chapter 7 of *The Interpretation of Dreams* (1900; hereafter Interpretation). The last major theoretical work of the topographical model is *Beyond the Pleasure Principle* (1920). Between these are several papers dealing with the metapsychology (1915a, 1915b, 1915c). Other writings dealing with general psychoanalytic theory also occur between 1900 and 1920, but the main aspects of the topographical theory are present in the mentioned works. Most of Freud's remaining writings during this period are clinical, though they are clearly informed by the topographical conception that Freud used at the time.

This presentation of psychoanalysis is designated as "topographic" because of the emphasis Freud places on mental topography during this period. The topographical metaphor is literally that—a model that relates the parts of the mind in a hypothetical mental space. It draws on an analogy between mental and physical space. Freud (1900) introduces his model by saying he is concerned in it with "the idea of *psychical locality.*" He goes on to say:

> I shall entirely disregard the fact that the mental apparatus with which we are here concerned is also known to us in the form of an anatomical preparation, and I shall carefully avoid the temptation to determine psychical locality in any anatomical fashion.

I shall remain upon psychological ground, and I propose simply
to follow the suggestion that we should picture the instrument
which carries out our mental functions as resembling a compound microscope or a photographic apparatus, or something
of the kind. On that basis, psychical locality will correspond to
a point inside the apparatus at which one of the preliminary
stages of an image comes into being. In the microscope and
telescope, as we know, these occur in part at ideal points, regions
in which no tangible component of the apparatus is situated. . . .
   Accordingly, we will picture the mental apparatus as a compound instrument, to the components of which we will give the
name of 'agencies', or (for the sake of greater clarity) 'systems'.
It is to be anticipated, in the next place, that these systems may
perhaps stand in a regular spatial relation to one another, in the
same kind of way in which the various systems of lenses in a
telescope are arranged behind one another [pp. 536–537].

The posited systems are designed to account both for the
psychological functions discovered in the analysis of dreams
and in the treatment of neurotics (defense, inhibition, repression, displacement, condensation of symbols, and so on), and
for normal psychology. The principal structures are the unconscious (*Ucs.*) and the preconscious (*Pcs.*). Freud also includes
a sensory reception system (*Pcpt.*), and one responsible for consciousness (*Cs.*). The system names are abbreviated because,
Freud says, "We . . . attempt to avoid confusion by giving the
psychical systems which we have distinguished certain arbitrar-
ily chosen names which have no reference to the attribute of
being conscious." Otherwise, Freud (1915c) says, "we cannot
escape the ambiguity of using the words 'conscious' and 'unconscious' sometimes in a descriptive and sometimes in a systematic sense, in which latter they signify inclusion in particular
systems and possession of certain characteristics" (1915c, p.
172). So the system *Ucs.* is distinguished from the simply "non-
conscious." It is part of a theory of the mind and not merely
a descriptive category. The topographical theory treats symptoms, dreams, behavior, and experience as the compromise
outcome of an internal dynamic involving the interaction between these systems, energized by drive forces.
   On two important points the topographical model differs
from that of the Project. First, it divides the mind along clinically

relevant lines. Freud, by this stage, is particularly interested in accounting for clinical material. He needs a way of articulating the conflicts that underlie clinical and dream processes. Accordingly, he is less interested in giving the fine details of the mental processes, and he is less concerned to make his theory "mechanically" consistent than he was in the Project. About the Project model he was pleased, he had said, because it "really seemed to be a machine which . . . would run of itself" (Freud, 1887–1902, p. 129). By contrast, his approach into the topographical period is more holistic. Second, he has abandoned any explicit neuropsychology. He says that he wants to "remain upon psychological ground" (1900, p. 536). Because of this, the physicalism of the topographical model is not as apparent as that of the Project. However, as we shall see, the formal structure of the prepsychoanalytic and the earlier models remains intact, with its physicalism, conceptions of energy and structure, and so on.

Physicalism and Reflexive Operation

The physicalism of psychoanalytic theory does not consist in specifying the material of the mental processes—the "wetware" of the system. It consists of a set of principles. One of these is that the characteristics of human behavior are a function of man's evolutionary past—of environmental exigencies effecting change in the organism. A second principle is that mind is lawful and natural; behavior is the product of the interplay of wholly natural forces in and through the structures of the system. In this interplay of forces the energies involved obey the laws of physics. This means the energy is quantitative, and its quantity is conserved within any isolated system.

EVOLUTIONARY SETTING

An evolutionary perspective is clearly a part of the topographical theory. Freud (1915a, pp. 119–120) introduces an exposition of the topographical theory by saying: "Let us imagine ourselves in the situation of an almost entirely helpless living organism, as yet unoriented in the world, which is receiving stimuli in its nervous substance." From this point he goes on to discuss the development of flight from noxious stimuli. He contrasts these external stimuli, "which can be avoided by muscular action (flight)" with "stimuli against which such action is of no avail and whose character of constant pressure persists . . . ; these stimuli are the signs of an internal world, the evidence of instinctual needs." Consideration of these kinds of stimuli leads Freud to a "biological" postulate: "the nervous system is an apparatus which has the function of getting rid of the stimuli that reach it." Now, "if it were feasible" the nervous system "would maintain itself in an altogether unstimulated condition." However, "the simple pattern of the physiological reflex is complicated by the introduction of instincts." Instincts, though, are themselves, at least in part, precipitates of the effects of "external stimulation," and "are the true motive forces behind the advances that have led the nervous system . . . to its present high level of development." A later introduction to a theoretical exposition of the topographical theory (Freud, 1920) is almost identical, and both are similar to that of the Project.

In short, the nervous system, operating according to the primary discharge principle, undergoes structural modification due to the exigencies of life.

ENERGY CONCEPTION

The energy operating in the system is "quantity" (1900, pp. 561, 599, 616ff.), or later "psychical energy" (1915b, p. 152). As the term "quantity" implies, energy exists in "definite quota[s]" (1915b, p. 152), and it is conserved unless more energy is added from outside the system (stimulation) or energy is discharged from it (motor activity). The transfer and distribution of set quantities of psychic energy is the basis of all mental activity in the topographical model. Having ideas, wishing, repressing, feeling, and simply behaving are effected by "the displacement of quantities" (1900, p. 616) in the mental system. Thus he says (1915c) "ideas are cathexes" (p. 178); "emotions correspond to processes of discharge" (p. 178); and repression is a "*withdrawal* of cathexis" (p. 180).

The "economic point of view" encapsulates Freud's energic views. Freud (1915c) mentions this as a part of his metapsychology:

> We see how we have gradually been led into adopting a third point of view in our account of psychical phenomena. Besides the dynamic and the topographical points of view, we have adopted the *economic* one. This endeavours to follow out the vicissitudes of amounts of excitation and to arrive at least at some *relative* estimate of their magnitude [p. 181].

THE SYSTEM AS A REFLEXIVE MECHANISM

As in earlier models, the system is reflexive:

> The first thing that strikes us is that this apparatus, compounded of ψ-systems, has a sense or direction. All our psychical activity starts from stimuli (whether internal or external) and ends in innervations. Accordingly, we shall ascribe a sensory and a motor end to the apparatus. At the sensory end there lies a system which receives perceptions; at the motor end there lies another, which opens the gateway to motor activity. Psychical processes advance in general from the perceptual end to the motor end. . . .
>
> This, however, does no more than fulfill a requirement with which we have long been familiar, namely that the psychical apparatus must be constructed like a reflex apparatus. Reflex processes remain the model of every psychical function [Freud, 1900, pp. 537–538].

Later (1915a) Freud says, "the nervous system is an apparatus which has the function of getting rid of stimuli that reach it, or of reducing them to the lowest possible level" (p. 120).

The material of the structures in the system is not specified in detail by Freud. He does not discuss the electrochemical nature of the energy involved; nor does he discuss neurons. Rather, he is content to use an extended analogy in which psychic energy, psychic structures, and psychic space are formally the same as physical energy, structure, and space. He does not commit himself to saying exactly how these relate to material processes: "The mechanics of these processes are quite unknown to me." Yet he still employs the concepts intimately associated with the earlier nervous energy model: he talks of stimuli, excitation, energy, discharge, cathexis, reflex, and so on. And he does go on to say, "anyone who wished to take these ideas seriously would have to look for physical analogies to them and find a means of picturing the movements that accompany excitation of neurones" (1900, p. 599).

Primary and Secondary Processes

The primary reflexive tendency of the system differentiates, for evolutionary reasons, into primary and secondary processes, with their associated structures. In this the topographical model follows the earlier models. The secondary processes and structures have the function of retaining (binding) a certain amount of energy within the system. This energy is, in turn, used to subserve the primary process.

> The *first* ψ-system is directed towards securing the *free discharge* of the quantities of excitation, while the *second* system, by means of the cathexes emanating from it, succeeds in *inhibiting* this discharge and in transforming the cathexis into a quiescent one, no doubt with a simultaneous raising of its potential. I presume, therefore, that under the dominion of the second system the discharge of excitation is governed by quite different mechanical conditions from those in force under the dominion of the first system. When once the second system has concluded its exploratory thought-activity, it releases the inhibition of damming-up of the excitations and allows them to discharge themselves in movement [1900, pp. 599–600].

These "two systems are the germ of what, in the fully developed apparatus, we have described as the *Ucs.* and *Pcs.*" (p. 599). Shortly after this, Freud names the processes by which the two systems operate: "I propose to describe the psychical process of which the first system alone admits as the 'primary process' and the process which results from the inhibition imposed by the second system as the 'secondary process' " (p. 601).

The secondary process evolves in conjunction with the instincts. Freud (1915a) comments:

The instincts themselves are, at least in part, precipitates of the effects of external stimulation, which in the course of phylogenesis have brought about modifications in the living substance . . . Instinctual stimuli, which originate from within the organism, cannot be dealt with by this mechanism [the simple discharge mechanism]. Thus they make far higher demands on the nervous system and cause it to undertake involved and interconnected activities by which the external world is so changed as to afford satisfaction to the internal source of stimulation. Above all, they oblige the nervous system to renounce its ideal intention of keeping off stimuli, for they maintain an incessant and unavoidable afflux of stimulation. We may therefore well conclude that instincts and not external stimuli are the true motive forces behind the advances that have led the nervous system, with its unlimited capacities, to its present high level of development [p. 120].

FUNCTIONS OF THE PRIMARY PROCESS

The pleasure principle and wish fulfillment are the two main functions of the primary process. Freud writes that "the accumulation of excitation [from somatic sources] . . . is felt as unpleasure" (1900, p. 598). The importance of this is that the whole mental apparatus "is automatically regulated by feelings belonging to the pleasure-unpleasure series" (1915a, p. 120), and "These feelings reflect the manner in which the process of mastering stimuli takes place—certainly in the sense that unpleasurable feelings are connected with an increase and pleasurable feelings with a decrease of stimulus" (1915a, pp. 120–121).

The pleasure principle is then the tendency of the organism to discharge accumulating tension. Freud (1920) states it thus:

In the theory of psycho-analysis we have no hesitation in assuming that the course taken by mental events is automatically regulated by the pleasure principle. We believe, that is to say, that the course of those events is invariably set in motion by an unpleasurable tension, and that it takes a direction such that its final outcome coincides with a lowering of that tension—that is, with an avoidance of unpleasure or a production of pleasure [p. 7].

This is an economic principle. It relates to the fact that the pleasure principle is an aspect of the "primary process," and that all mental events have to do with the distribution of energy within the mental system. Thus Freud says of the pleasure principle: "In taking that course into account in our consideration of the mental processes which are the subject of our study, we are introducing an 'economic' point of view into our work" (p. 7). He specifies the pleasure principle as a primary process: "We know that the pleasure principle is proper to a *primary* method of working on the part of the mental apparatus" (p. 10).

Wishing, closely connected with the pleasure principle, is a function of the *Ucs.* (the "first ψ-system"): "As a result of the unpleasure principle, then, the first ψ-system is totally incapable of bringing anything disagreeable into the context of its thoughts. It is unable to do anything but wish" (1900, p. 600).

Wishes are, however, more specific than simple unpleasurable currents. They are linked to external objects through "experience of satisfaction." This is, as before in the Project model, the registration in a memory trace of both a tension diminution, and of the conditions instrumental in bringing it about. This is important for the system. This capacity of the individual to learn what satisfies is the first step in the transition to full secondary-process function.

The child's first such learning is achieved through the agency of a caretaker. The following passage, closely resembling that of the Project (1895a, p. 318; quoted above in Chapter 3), describes the process:

> The excitations produced by internal needs seek discharge in movement, which may be described as an 'internal change' or an 'expression of emotion'. A hungry baby screams or kicks helplessly. But the situation remains unaltered, for the excitation arising from an internal need is not due to a force producing a *momentary* impact but to one which is in continuous operation. A change can only come about if in some way or other (in the case of the baby, through outside help) an 'experience of satisfaction' can be achieved which puts an end to the internal stimulus [1900, p. 565].

Freud (1900) goes on to discuss further the nature of this experience of satisfaction, linking it with wishing and the establishment of a perceptual identity between the wished for and the perceived object:

> An essential component of this experience of satisfaction is a particular perception (that of nourishment, in our example) the mnemic image of which remains associated thenceforward with the memory trace of the excitation produced by the need. As a result of the link that has thus been established, next time this need arises a psychical impulse will at once emerge which will seek to re-cathect the mnemic image of the perception and to re-evoke the perception itself, that is to say, to re-establish the situation of the original satisfaction. An impulse of this kind is what we call a wish; the reappearance of the perception is the fulfilment of the wish; and the shortest path to the fulfilment of the wish is a path leading direct from the excitation produced by the need to a complete cathexis of the perception. Nothing prevents us from assuming that there was a primitive state of the psychical apparatus in which this path was actually traversed, that is, in which wishing ended in hallucinating. Thus the aim of this first psychical activity was to produce a 'perceptual identity'—a repetition of the perception which was linked with the satisfaction of the need [pp. 565–566].

This wishful activity, attempting to produce the "perceptual identity," must, however, fail to yield genuine satisfaction of needs. There has to be a delay until conditions are such that a real, and not just a temporary, discharge can take place. Correspondingly, there has to be a mechanism that matches the wish to reality. This ensures that the result of a wish is not a mere hallucinatory fulfillment, not some random and functionless behavior, and not the recathexis of an unpleasurable memory. Instead a lasting discharge can take place through an action that effects appropriate changes in the environment. This comes on top of the learning capacity, and is the second of the two steps to a fully functioning system. It is the essential function of the secondary process.

FUNCTIONS OF THE SECONDARY PROCESS

Freud (1900) takes up the above point about the wishful attempt to cathect a percept of previous satisfaction:

The bitter experience of life must have changed this primitive thought-activity into a more expedient secondary one. The establishment of a perceptual identity along the short path of regression within the apparatus does not have the same result elsewhere in the mind as does the cathexis of the same perception from without. Satisfaction does not follow; the need persists. An internal cathexis could only have the same value as an external one if it were maintained unceasingly, as in fact occurs in hallucinatory psychoses and hunger phantasies, which exhaust their whole psychical activity in clinging to the object of their wish. In order to arrive at a more efficient expenditure of psychical force, it is necessary to bring the regression to a halt before it becomes complete, so that it does not proceed beyond the mnemic image, and is able to seek out other paths which lead eventually to the desired perceptual identity being established from the direction of the external world. This inhibition of the regression and the subsequent diversion of the excitation becomes the business of a second system [p. 566].

All the complex secondary processes arise out of this delaying inhibition of discharge. Thinking, repressing, judging, and the other higher-order cognitive processes are all functions of the secondary system, the *Pcs.*:

The second system . . . is in control of voluntary movement—[and] for the first time, that is, makes use of movement for purposes remembered in advance. But all the complicated thought-activity which is spun out from the mnemic image to the moment at which the perceptual identity is established by the external world—all this activity of thought merely constitutes a roundabout path to wish-fulfilment which has been made necessary by experience. Thought is after all nothing but a substitute for a hallucinatory wish; and it is self-evident that dreams must be wish-fulfilments, since nothing but a wish can set our mental apparatus at work [pp. 566–567].

Freud gives similar accounts of the secondary processes in later topographical works (1915c, p. 188; 1920, p. 10). In the latter he points out that these secondary processes are oriented toward reality:

The pleasure principle is replaced by the *reality principle*. This latter principle does not abandon the intention of ultimately obtaining pleasure, but it nevertheless demands and carries into effect the postponement of satisfaction, the abandonment of a number of possibilities of gaining satisfaction and the temporary toleration of unpleasure as a step on the long indirect road to pleasure [1920, p. 10].

He also identifies the secondary process as the binding of energy, and similarly points out that this subserves the primary process: "The binding of an instinctual impulse would be a preliminary function designed to prepare the excitation for its final elimination in the pleasure of discharge" (p. 62).

Memory, Learning, and Association. The secondary process works to bring the organism into a relationship with the environment that satisfies its needs. Underlying this is the capacity to learn and remember. As in the earlier models, association and the laying down of memory traces are the mechanisms of learning:

> A trace is left in our psychical apparatus of the perceptions which impinge upon it. This we may describe as a 'memory-trace'; and to the function relating to it we give the name of 'memory'. If we are in earnest over our plan of attaching psychical processes to systems, memory-traces can only consist in permanent modifications of the elements of the systems. But . . . there are obvious difficulties involved in supposing that one and the same system can accurately retain modifications of its elements and yet remain perpetually open to the reception of fresh occasions for modification. In accordance, therefore with the principle which governs our experiment, we shall distribute these two functions on to different systems. We shall suppose that a system in the very front [system *Pcpt.*] of the apparatus receives the perceptual stimuli but retains no trace of them and thus has no memory, while behind it there lies a second system which transforms the momentary excitations of the first system into permanent traces. . . . Our perceptions are linked with one another in our memory—first and foremost according to simultaneity of occurrence. We speak of this fact as 'association'. . . . The basis of association lies in the mnemic systems. Association would thus consist in the fact that, as a result of diminution in resistances and of the laying down of facilitating paths, an excitation is transmitted from a given *Mnem.* element more readily to one *Mnem.* element than to another [1900, pp. 538–539].

The close parallels of the topographical model and that of the Project are clear. In both we see

1. The system is built out of units—simply named "elements," not "neurones" in the topographical model—which can transmit or retain excitation (see also 1915c, p. 178; 1920, pp. 24ff.).
2. The transmission of excitation depends on the facilitation of junctions between elements (see also 1920, p. 26).
3. Memory associations (see also 1915c, pp. 175–178) work through the permanent facilitation of elements, forming a network of associations based primarily on simultaneity. Given this network, one idea can be substituted for another by displacement along a chain of connections (see also 1915b, p. 155).
4. The system divides into subsystems that depend on the capacity of its elements to be either only temporarily facilitated, or to be permanently facilitated.
5. Accordingly, one subsystem, that for perception, receives and passes on perceptual excitations, and one for memory retains records of these (see also 1920, pp. 24–25).

All this relates to the experience of satisfaction. The latter involves the association of (1) the traces left by perception of an object (its memory), with (2) elements cathected by incoming drive energy, with (3) element paths along which excitation lead to specific actions (1900, p. 565).

Reality Testing, Attention, Quality, and Consciousness. Following upon the delay of wish discharge, there must be a process that first tests to see if the wish may reach satisfaction in reality, and only after this process it releases its energy. The process is discussed in some detail in the Interpretation, and is also referred to later (for example, 1915c, 1920). Freud says:

> The primary process endeavours to bring about a discharge of excitation in order that, with the help of the amount of excitation thus accumulated, it may establish a 'perceptual identity' (with

the experience of satisfaction). The secondary process, however, has abandoned this intention and taken on another in its place—the establishment of a *'thought* identity' [1900, p. 602].

The establishment of this "thought identity" is in fact reality testing: checking that the wished-for object is actually being perceived. Freud does not give a comprehensive, nor a consistent, account of this function. However, it is clear that here, as in the Project, it is made possible by a combination of factors: the existence of information feedback loops in the system; the fact that discharge has qualitative as well as quantitative aspects; the existence of groups of elements in the system that are responsive primarily to quality; the fact that sections of the system exist in a state of general cathexis, and of course the interrelations and interactions of the several psychic structures.

Thus Freud describes the function of the system *Cs.* as *"only that of a sense-organ for the perception of psychical qualities"* (1900, p. 615), and he goes on to sketch its place in the mental system:

> Excitatory material flows in to the *Cs.* sense-organ from two directions: from the *Pcpt.* system, whose excitation, determined by qualities, is probably submitted to a fresh revision before it becomes a conscious sensation, and from the interior of the apparatus itself, whose quantitative processes are felt qualitatively in the pleasure-unpleasure series when, subject to certain modifications, they make their way to consciousness [p. 616].

The conditions under which "the excitatory processes . . . [wishes] can enter consciousness [which 'is at the same time the system which holds the key to voluntary movement']" are stated by Freud: "provided that . . . they reach a certain degree of intensity, [and] that the function which can only be described as 'attention' is distributed in a particular way" (p. 541). Attention is due to "hypercathexis" (p. 594), the addition of a special facilitating cathexis to a wish.

Consciousness serves the function of monitoring important aspects of wishes and of their relations to the environment, and of directing these relations. Of *Cs.* Freud (1900) says:

> By perceiving new qualities, it makes a new contribution to di-

recting the mobile quantities of cathexis and distributing them in an expedient fashion. By the help of its perception of pleasure and unpleasure it influences the discharge of the cathexes within what is otherwise an unconscious apparatus operating by means of the displacement of quantities [p. 616].

Thinking is related to this process: "All thinking is no more than a circuitous path from the memory of a satisfaction . . . to an identical cathexis of the same memory which it is hoped to attain once more through an intermediate stage of motor experiences." This is achieved by trial displacements of energy. These are very small so that they restrict "the development of affect . . . to the minimum required for acting as a signal" (p. 602).

Repression. Despite its importance for psychoanalysis, the process of repression is cloudy in Freud's writings. However, we do know some things about it. It is closely related to the inhibition of primary processes and is a defense against the release of anxiety.

Repression is either the withdrawal of hypercathexis from an idea (wish) or the refusal of hypercathexis to an idea. Just as wishes or thoughts may become conscious through the addition of hypercathexis, so conversely, "a train of thought which is 'suppressed' or 'repudiated' is one from which this cathexis [the hypercathexis] has been *withdrawn*" (1900, p. 594). And again (1915b), withdrawal of a cathexis is a defining characteristic of repression: "the mechanisms of repression have at least this one thing in common: *a withdrawal of a cathexis of energy*" (pp. 154–155).

The initial repudiation of an idea or wish is what Freud terms "primal" repression (1915b, p. 148). However, an idea may yet remain the vehicle of an instinct: "the representative [idea] in question persists unaltered from then onwards and the instinct remains attached to it" (p. 148). In this way an idea may be kept repressed while fed by instinctual energy. Under these conditions the cathexis of the repressed idea flows over into other associated ideas. These also press for discharge. This leads to further repression:

The second stage of repression, *repression proper,* affects mental derivatives of the repressed representative, or such trains of thought as, originating elsewhere, have come into associative connection with it. On account of this association, these ideas experience the same fate as what was primally repressed [p. 148].

Repression of the originally unacceptable idea and of closely associated ones is maintained by "anticathexis." Some idea, distantly associated with the original, receives the cathexis from the original idea, and it also receives additional cathexis. This maintains a substituted idea as capable of becoming conscious while keeping the first idea, and close associates, unconscious:

The cathexis that has taken flight attaches itself to a substitutive idea which, on the one hand, is connected by association with the rejected idea, and, on the other, has escaped repression by reason of its remoteness from that idea. This substitutive idea—a 'substitute by displacement'—permits the still uninhibitable development of anxiety to be rationalized [1915c, p. 182].

Freud's distinction between repression, which we normally think of as a mechanism of pathology, and simple inhibition, which is necessary for normal psychological process, is not clear. So it is not clear if there can be successful repression. However, the paradigm of repression is the unsuccessful form. It is economically inefficient, and it often breaks down and releases anxiety. The economic inefficiency is clear:

The process of repression is not to be regarded as an event which takes place *once,* the results of which are permanent, as when some living thing has been killed and from that time onward is dead; repression demands a persistent expenditure of force, and if this were to cease the success of the repression would be jeopardized, so that a fresh act of repression would be necessary. We may suppose that the repressed exercises a continuous pressure in the direction of the conscious, so that this pressure must be balanced by an unceasing counter-pressure. Thus the maintenance of a repression involves an uninterrupted expenditure of force, while its removal results in a saving from an economic point of view [1915b, p. 151].

The process whereby anxiety is released is problematic. It is another mechanism not satisfactorily explained by Freud in the topographic model. Indeed, this issue, like that of repression, was one motive for the changes in the theory that led to the later, structural, formulation (see Gill, 1963). In outline, Freud (1915c) holds that the cathexis of the repressed wish gets converted to anxiety in some neuroses. In anxiety hysteria, anxiety appears

> without the subject knowing what he is afraid of. We must suppose that there was present in the *Ucs.* some love-impulse demanding to be transposed in the system *Pcs.;* but the cathexis directed to it from the latter system has drawn back from the impulse (as though in an attempt at flight) and the unconscious libidinal cathexis of the rejected idea has been discharged in the form of anxiety [p. 182].

STRUCTURAL THEORY

Changes from the Topographic Model

The final version of psychoanalytic theory produced by Freud is the "structural" model. In this the major components of the mind are "id," "ego," and "superego." This replaces the earlier division into *Ucs., Pcs.,* and *Cs.* The main reason for the change is that the topographical model's terms, "unconscious," "preconscious," and "conscious," have several different senses. These different senses were recognized by Freud as early as 1912. However, he did not present the structural model itself until *The Ego and the Id* (1923). It is further illustrated and amplified in a number of theoretical writings after this—for example, *The Economic Problem of Masochism* (1924), *New Introductory Lectures on Psychoanalysis* (1933), and finally *An Outline of Psycho-Analysis* (1940a).

UNCONSCIOUS, PRECONSCIOUS, AND CONSCIOUS

First, there is a descriptive sense to the terms "unconscious," "preconscious," and "conscious": ". . . let us call 'conscious' the conception which is present to our consciousness and of which we are aware, and let this be the only meaning of the term 'conscious'. As for latent conceptions, if we have any reason to suppose that they exist in the mind . . . let them be denoted by the term 'unconscious' " (Freud, 1912, p. 260).

Second, there is a dynamic sense to the terms. Freud revises the uses of these terms a little further on in the same text: "The term *unconscious*, which was used in the purely descriptive sense before, now comes to imply something more. It designates not only latent ideas in general, but especially ideas with a certain dynamic character, ideas keeping apart from consciousness in spite of their intensity and activity" (p. 262). However, unlike a descriptively unconscious idea, "the [dynamically] unconscious idea is excluded from consciousness by living forces . . . while they [the forces] do not object to other ideas, the foreconscious [preconscious] ones" (p. 264).

Third, there is a systematic sense, in which these terms name postulated mental systems or structures. In this case, particular unconscious acts are indications of a mental system "we designate by name 'The Unconscious'. . . . And this is the third and most significant sense which the term 'unconscious' has acquired in psycho-analysis" (p. 266).

Freud (1923) came to believe that the topographical model's means for making distinctions between the systems were inadequate:

> . . . these distinctions have proved to be inadequate. . . . This has become clear in more ways than one; but the decisive instance is as follows. We have formed the idea that in each individual there is a coherent organization of mental processes; and we call this his *ego*. It is to this ego that consciousness is attached; the ego controls the approaches to motility—that is, to the discharge of excitations into the external world; it is the mental agency which supervises all its own constituent processes, and which goes to sleep at night, though even then it exercises the censorship on dreams. From this ego proceed the repressions. . . . We find during analysis that . . . [the patient's] associations fail when they should be coming near the repressed. . . . He is dominated by a resistance. . . . There can be no question but that his resistance emanates from his ego and belongs to it. . . . We have come upon something in the ego itself which is also unconscious, which behaves exactly like the repressed—that is, which produces pow-

erful effects without itself being conscious and which requires special work before it can be made conscious [p. 17].

So Freud made corrections to the model, postulating the ego as a system, part of which is dynamically unconscious:

> We recognize that the *Ucs.* does not coincide with the repressed; it is still true that all that is repressed is *Ucs.*, but not all that is *Ucs.* is repressed. A part of the ego, too—and Heaven knows how important a part—may be *Ucs.*, undoubtedly is *Ucs.* And this *Ucs.* belonging to the ego is not latent like the *Pcs.;* for if it were, it could not be activated without becoming *Cs.*, and the process of making it conscious would not encounter such great difficulties [p. 18].

ID, EGO, SUPEREGO

Thus the topographic systems are replaced by id and ego (superego is a special development of the ego). Freud (1940a) defines the characteristics of these two systems: "[The id] contains everything that is inherited, that is present at birth, that is laid down in the constitution—above all, therefore, the instincts, which originate from the somatic organization and which find a first psychical expression here [in the id] in forms unknown to us" (p. 145). Id operates according to the primary process and contains everything previously ascribed to the *Ucs.* The ego is a "portion of the id (which) has undergone a special development" (p. 145). Its characteristics were given in the quote above. It is the secondary-process instrument of the mental apparatus. But, unlike the *Pcs.*, a part of the ego is dynamically repressed—for example, that part which effects repression.

The remaining system of the structural model, the superego, is of more consequence clinically than metapsychologically. It is a development out of the ego (1940a, p. 146) and shares its metapsychological characteristics. The structural position, the condition of energy, and the mode of operation of the superego are similar to those of the ego. Like the ego, the superego has a conscious part and a repressed, unconscious part. It is involved in repressing, providing the motives for much repression. Structurally, it is a secondary-process system, developing from the ego. Its economics and mode of operation are also according to the secondary process.

Another sort of change takes place over the time of the topographical and structural models, and it is in the theory of the instincts. This warrants a brief separate discussion (below, at the end of this chapter).

Form of the Structural Model

In spite of the change from the topographic to the structural means of describing the mental apparatus, the underlying principles remain the same. Instead of discussing Freud's final model in detail, I shall adopt a more economical way of demonstrating their basic similarity, selecting quotations which show that the structural model contains the same principles we have seen in the previous theories.

PHYSICALISM

We know two kinds of things about what we call our psyche (or mental life): firstly, its bodily organ and scene of action, the brain (or nervous system).

We assume that mental life is the function of an apparatus to which we ascribe the characteristics of being extended in space and of being made up of several portions [1940a, pp. 144–145].

EVOLUTIONARY SETTING

Under the influence of the real external world around us, one portion of the id has undergone a special development. From what was originally a cortical layer, equipped with the organs for receiving stimuli and with arrangements for acting as a protective shield against stimuli, a special organization has arisen which henceforward acts as an intermediary between the id and the external world. To this region of our mind we have given the name of *ego* [p. 145].

The hypothesis we have adopted of a psychical apparatus extended in space, expediently put together, developed by the exigencies of life, which gives rise to the phenomena of consciousness only at one particular point and under certain conditions—this hypothesis has put us in a position to establish psychology on foundations similar to those of any other science, such, for instance, as physics [p. 196].

FORCE, ENERGY, AND STRUCTURE

We have reckoned as though there existed in the mind . . . a displaceable energy [1923, p. 44].

Internal processes . . . represent displacements of mental energy which are effected somewhere in the interior of the apparatus as this energy proceeds on its way towards action [p. 19].

PRIMARY PROCESS

Reflexive Discharge

Displaceable libido is employed in the service of the pleasure principle to obviate blockages and to facilitate discharge. In this connection it is easy to observe a certain indifference as to the path along which the discharge takes place, so long as it takes place somehow. We know this trait; it is characteristic of the cathectic processes in the id [1923, p. 45].

[We] have . . . attributed to the mental apparatus the purpose of reducing to nothing . . . the sums of excitation which flow in upon it [1924, p. 159].

Instinctual Sources of Energy

The forces which we assume to exist behind the tensions caused by the needs of the id are called *instincts*. They represent the somatic demands upon the mind . . . they are the ultimate cause of all activity" [1940a, p. 148].

Pleasure Principle

Every unpleasure ought thus to coincide with a heightening, and every pleasure with a lowering, of mental tension due to stimulus [1924, pp. 159–161].

SECONDARY PROCESS

The *pleasure* principle represents the demands of the libido; and the modification of the latter principle, the *reality* principle, represents the influence of the external world [1924, p. 160].

We seem to recognize that nervous or psychical energy occurs in two forms, one freely mobile and another, by comparison, bound; we speak of cathexes and hypercathexes of psychical material, and even venture to suppose that a hypercathexis brings about a kind of synthesis of different processes—a synthesis in the course of which free energy is transformed into bound energy [1940a, p. 164].

The Ego and the Delay of Discharge

Here are the principal characteristics of the ego. In consequence of the pre-established connection between sense perception and muscular action, the ego has voluntary movement at its command. It has the task of self-preservation. As regards *external* events, it performs that task by becoming aware of stimuli, by storing up experiences about them (in the memory), by avoiding excessively strong stimuli (through flight), by dealing with moderate stimuli (through adaptation) and finally by learning to bring about expedient changes in the external world to its own advantage (through activity). As regards *internal* events, in relation to the id, it performs that task by gaining control over the demands of the instincts, by deciding whether they are to be allowed satisfaction, by postponing that satisfaction to times and circumstances favourable in the external world or by suppressing their excitations entirely. It is guided in its activity by consideration of the tensions produced by stimuli. . . . From time to time the ego gives up its connection with the external world and withdraws into the state of sleep, in which it makes far-reaching changes in its organization. It is to be inferred from the state of sleep that this organization consists in a particular distribution of mental energy [1940a, pp. 145–146].

Thought

The activity of thought . . . after taking its bearings in the present and assessing earlier experiences, endeavours by means of experimental actions to calculate the consequences of the course of action proposed. In this way the ego comes to a decision on whether the attempt to obtain satisfaction is to be carried out or postponed 1940a [p. 199].

Reality Testing

It (the ego) makes use of the sensations of anxiety as a signal to give a warning of dangers that threaten its integrity. Since memory-traces can become conscious just as perceptions do, especially through their association with residues of speech, the possibility arises of a confusion which would lead to a mistaking of reality. The ego guards itself against this possibility by the institution of *reality-testing* [1940a, p. 199].

DEVELOPMENTS IN THE THEORY OF MOTIVATION

I have been arguing that there is a fundamental continuity in form throughout the development of Freud's psychoanalytic theory. The same principles shape the early versions of his theory, as do the later versions: there are general principles, such as Freud's physicalism, that represent a philosophy of science; and there are more specific principles, for example, that thought is trial action carried out by minute displacements of energy. Before I go on to dicuss some of the changes that take place across his successive formulations, I want, briefly, to point to another similarity between the early and later theories. In the topographical and structural models may be identified those factors that Freud considers to energize, to precipitate, and to direct action: that set of factors that mark it as a motivation theory. These are very similar to those of his earlier models, though the language within which they are described has changed.

Energizing, Precipitating, and Directing Factors

There are still two identifiable sources of stimuli, endogenous and exogenous. The instinctual drives belong to the former group. The basic pattern for this brand of stimulation is laid down in the prepsychoanalytic model and persists throughout the development of the theory. Instincts are endogenous stimuli related to needs such as sex, hunger, and respiration. The needs themselves are constituted by somatic, chemical processes. Changes in the somatic chemistry associated with one of these needs can produce excitation in the system that automatically builds up pressure to discharge.

Now, there are changes in the theory of instincts between the early and later versions of Freud's theory that can be confusing here. These have a brief separate treatment below. For example, Freud talks of "ego-instincts," and later of "life instincts," the "death instinct," and so on. However, these classifications are of secondary importance. The basic form of instinctual activity is as described: somatic needs give rise to mental tension and a pressure to discharge. Thus Freud says of the instincts: "They represent the somatic demands upon the mind. . . . They are the ultimate cause of all activity" (1940a, p. 148).

Behavior is precipitated, as for earlier models, when external stimuli impinge on the system and are matched with the wishes current in the system. Where a genuine match is achieved, specific actions can take place. This means that certain internal and external stimulus conditions have to obtain for motivated action to take place. In this sense, endogenous and exogenous stimuli precipitate or "cue" behavior, and these factors, which precipitate activity, are dependent on learning.

The basic direction of all behavior is determined by the tendency to discharge tension. In the psychological terms that dominate the topographical and structural theories, this means that the pleasure principle is the primary director of behavior. A slight specificity of direction comes about from the source of the particular energy pressing for discharge. However, the objects of specific instincts (for example, sex) have to be learned. The major modification to the primary direction comes from the secondary process, which is responsible for the vicissitudes the instinctual energy can undergo. The secondary process is the inhibition of the immediate discharge of instinctual energy. The redirection of the upheld energy takes place in accordance with learned ways of achieving experiences of satisfaction (lasting discharges of tension). In turn, the learned ways depend on environmental conditions. The structures involved in this directing are complex. However, they include the network of associated memory traces. The pattern of this network aids in giving direction to energy passing through it. It is then the secondary process mechanisms, with their matching of wishes and perceptions, that give the system its flexible, goal-directed character. This character marks purposive human activity.

Change in Freud's Theory

I have stressed that sense in which Freud's theory does not alter in any basic way. Freud's conception of how the mind works (his mental model), and how motivated action can be explained (the metapsychological points of view) remain the same across the several versions of the theory. On the other hand, there are considerable changes between both the earlier and the later formulations of psychoanalysis, and within the formulations themselves. There are changes in Freud's theoretical and clinical ideas; and there are even changes in which the unchanging aspects, the metapsychological principles, are expressed.

CLINICAL CONTENT

The period of the topographical and the structural theory is the main period of growth in Freud's clinical and other empirical hypotheses. Freud applies his theory to more and more situations. He develops his ideas on dreams—their meaning, their interpretation, their motives, and their mechanisms. He develops, too, his ideas on transference, resistance, and psychotherapeutic technique. He expands his understanding of the sexual motivation of dreams, neuroses, psychoses, and character traits, and later emphasizes the role of aggression as a motive. He applies his theory to the variety of neuroses, to psychosis, to aspects of social behavior, and to normal development. He also introduces the oedipal theory, as well as his views on infantile sexual development, on the nature of perversions, and on many other topics. Indeed, much of what we normally consider to be distinctively psychoanalytic is developed during this period.

There are also changes of a different order during this period. As psychoanalysis is applied to new areas, and as Freud's clinical ideas proliferate, new hypotheses are added to the theory. For example, there are several changes in the theory of instincts. In addition, Freud changes his theory of affects and anxiety, of symptom formation, and of other mental mechanisms. The most important changes have been detailed: changes in the structural arrangement of mental processes, first into the topographical systems, then into the structural. Yet, it must be stressed, all this change is assimilated into the motivational model whose form changes little from the earliest of Freud's theories.

CONCEPTUAL CHANGES

For present purposes the most important changes are not changes in the clinical and theoretical hypotheses, but those in the language in which the theory is expressed. These are conceptual changes.

Mechanism, Cause, and Purpose. The language in which the topographical and structural theories are expressed does differ from the Project, from the prepsychoanalytic model, and even from the abreaction model. However, the language of the later theories, like that of the Project, is mechanistic. Now, classing a system as mechanistic implies two things. The first is that the system can be thought of as a series of structures through and upon which forces operate. The second is that any behavior that issues from this system, and any transactions that take place within it, are causally explicable. In his topographical and structural models theory, Freud is again concerned with forces and structures. His writings of the later period abound with reference to forces, and the very designations "topographical" and "structural" are structural, albeit psychologically so. In and through these psychological structures (which are in turn made up of lesser structures, elements) operate the forces.

In this deterministic, causal system, where does purpose fit? For Freud does treat individuals as motivated by wishes and desires, and as striving toward objects. The answer lies in Freud's theory of the directors of behavior. Freud's model of the mind is purposive in the sense that it accounts for the goal-directedness of behavior. In fact, Freud identifies the primary purposive element in his system as contained in the reflex postulate:

> This postulate is of a biological nature, and makes use of the concept of 'purpose' (or perhaps of expediency) and runs as follows: the nervous system is an apparatus which has the function of getting rid of the stimuli that reach it, or of reducing them to the lowest possible level; or which, if it were feasible, would maintain itself in an altogether unstimulated condition [1915a, p. 120].

In all of Freud's successive models the reflex tendency gives the direction of behavior at its most general.

Wishes are also goal-directed and purposive: they "seek" to repeat experiences of satisfaction. This purposive terminology is not irreducible, and the ascription of purpose (conscious or unconscious) is not for Freud the end to explanation. Explanations may be carried further. In more mechanistic terms, wishes tend to discharge automatically, in ways that maintain a tension equilibrium. The regulation of wish discharge depends on the secondary system and its capacity to match wish and reality. The "object" of the wish is not, of course, any future goal; it is merely the registration in the memory system of a previous perception. Ultimately, there is no teleology involved, despite the confusion Freud causes with his mixture of mechanistic, purposive, and even anthropomorphic language.

Consciousness is often associated with human purposiveness. However, for Freud, conscious reflection and the consciousness of wishes and emotions are not part of the actual constitution of purposive activity. Rather, they are offshoots of the processes of the secondary process regulation of wishes. Freud regards conscious thought as a part of the fine-tuning of the regulatory mechanism (for example, 1900, pp. 606–607). Thinking itself is, for Freud, merely an efficient means of securing discharge of wishes. Thus consciousness, like all of Freud's postulated mental structures, has a function. Consciousness is not necessary for purposeful, motivated action, nor is the conscious awareness of some "motive" for an action sufficient to guarantee that it is the motive for that action.

Ultimately all psychological theories must come against the problem of the "mental executive"; all psychologies need to account for the means by which behavioral choices are finally selected. The danger for any mechanistic theory is that it ends up in an explanatory regress. This can happen when purposiveness is not treated as a property of the total organism, but is referred back to some specific part of the organism. The theory is then faced with a problem similar to the original. What makes this specific part of the system capable of directing behavior and choice? The issue is, Can goal-directed behavior be reduced to, or explained in terms of, purely causal processes? In the Project, Freud makes a clear attempt to set out a system that can go by itself. Using his term, such a system would be "mechanically" self-sufficient. In this system the ego is the executive process. Freud does not, of course, solve the problem of the executive once and for all. However, his attempt is comparable to those of modern cognitive theorists (see Pribram and Gill, 1976, pp. 76–82), and it is a model that deliberately "deteleologizes" purposive behavior by using a complex of feedback and other control mechanisms.

The topographic and structural models place less emphasis on the micromechanics of the mental system than the Project. They do not try to set out the basis of the automatic regulation of behavior with consistency and completeness. So it is harder to see exactly how these later models could be made fully automatic. It is especially difficult when Freud, talking loosely, treats the separate subparts of the system as independent operatives, as though they are homunculi battling for the control of the mind. However, Freud's intention is to create a system whose purposiveness can be explained in natural-science terms. Even the homuncular qualities often ascribed to mental subparts are merely shorthand, metaphorical ways of treating complex mechanisms.

PSYCHOLOGICAL AND NEUROLOGICAL LANGUAGE

In the topographic and structural models, Freud has almost entirely dropped direct reference to neural processes. In the

Project, Freud accounted for psychological functions by discussing the neural processes he thought might cause them. The later Freud still accounts for psychological phenomena by discussing the internal processes that might cause them, but he uses terms that are psychological and that do not refer directly to material processes. There are several reasons for this change.

One is that internal processes may be described in "micro" or "macro" terms. They may be the passage of quantities of energy along neuron fibers (or elements). Or they may be the interactions of the major mental subparts. Freud favors the latter in the later theories, and for the most part he explains psychic phenomena by appealing to the interactions of the topographic or structural systems as wholes. In doing this, his views about the actual material basis of the mental processes are obscured. The systems themselves may even appear as homunculi, rather than as automatically regulated systems.

Another reason for the change is that during this period the clinical application of psychoanalysis expanded very quickly. More and more phenomena were covered by the theory. Under these circumstances a precise mechanical consistency, such as motivated the Project, was no longer a major goal in Freud's theorizing. He wished to give holistic accounts of clinical phenomena, and the topographical and structural models enabled him to do this.

However, the most important reason for the change was that, as Freud's theory developed, he simply became agnostic about the actual neural realization of the mental processes (see Chapter 8 for more detail). At first, Freud took issue with Meynert on the latter's precise localization of mental processes in the brain. Later (1900) he declares he wants to "avoid the temptation to determine psychical locality in any anatomical fashion," and says that he will "remain on psychological ground" (p. 536). He even goes so far as to say that attempts to "discover a localization of mental processes, every endeavour to think of ideas as stored up in nerve-cells and of excitations as travelling along nerve-fibres, has miscarried completely" (1915c, p. 174).

As Freud dealt with more and more complex psychological processes, he realized that giving a neurological explanation of these processes is, "for the present" (p. 174), impossible. This agnosticism about the actual localization of mental functions always remained with Freud, but it does not mean that he abandoned materialism. He stayed committed to the idea that "all our provisional ideas in psychology will presumably some day be based on an organic substructure" (1915c, p. 78). Indeed, as I have tried to show in these chapters, Freud's physicalist philosophy of science continued to determine his mental model and the kind of explanations he gave.

A NOTE ON INSTINCT THEORY

As psychoanalytic theory changed and developed, Freud gave several different versions of instinct theory. The successive versions of the instinct theory are, however, not closely coordinated with the successive versions (abreaction, Project, topographical, structural) of the general theory. The received view of the theories of instincts derives from a footnote added by Freud to *Beyond the Pleasure Principle* (1920, pp. 60–61), and most commentators (for example, E. Jones, 1955; Fancher, 1973) keep to this view. This says there are three different versions of the instinct theory in Freud's writings, and that these succeed and supplant each other. More even than in the case of Freud's general motivation theory, the common emphasis is on changes in instinct theory over time, rather than on the underlying formal similarity of the three different versions.

The first "theory" usually identified is one first made explicit during the topographical period (Freud, 1910). In it instincts are divided into two classes, the libido and ego-instincts. The former comprises the sexual instincts, the latter the self-preservative ones. The second formulation is also introduced by Freud during the topographical period (1914). The instincts are similarly classed in two groups. One is termed the "object-libido," the other the "ego-libido." Both are subdivisions of "libido" in general. The third version is also introduced in the topographical period (1920), and elaborated during the structural (1923). In this Freud states there are "only two basic instincts, *Eros* and *the destructive instinct* . . . the *death instinct"* (1940a, p. 148).

However, the striking changes in *content* across Freud's different instinct formulations belie an underlying, and largely unstated, unity of *form* or *process,* and the different formulations are not really different theories of instinct—rather they are revisions of aspects of the theory, addressing themselves to only a part of the theory of instincts. In these respects, the changes in instinct theory are similar to those in the theory of motivation—of which, of course, instinct theory is an essential part. Instinct theory must be considered in relation to the whole theory of motivation. The process of instinctual drive is given by Freud (1915a):

> By the pressure of an instinct we understand its motor factor, the amount of force or the measure of the demand for work which it represents. . . .
> The aim of an instinct is in every instance satisfaction, which can only be obtained by removing the state of stimulation at the source of the instinct. . . .
> The object of an instinct is the thing in regard to which or through which the instinct is able to achieve its aim . . . [p. 122].
> By the source of an instinct is meant the somatic process which occurs in an organ or part of the body and whose stimulus is represented in mental life by an instinct. We do not know whether this process is invariably of a chemical nature or whether it may also correspond to the release of the other, e.g. mechanical, forces. The study of the sources of instincts lies outside the scope of psychology. Although instincts are wholly determined by their origin in a somatic source, in mental life we know them only by their aims [p. 123].

This definition of instinct fits his early and late theories of motivation, and holds across the variations in what are usually called the different "theories" of instinct. It even applies after Freud has introduced the death instinct. The notion of the death instinct was introduced to satisfy the requirements of this definition. It was not obvious that there is any somatic need to which aggression can be linked. However, Freud stuck to his appetitive model. He posited the death instinct as an explanation for aggression, and as a biologically bedded need of the organism (1920). This gave aggression a somatic function and source equivalent to the sexual instincts.

PART II

THE PSYCHOANALYTIC CONCEPT OF MOTIVATION
AS A THEORETICAL CONSTRUCT

5

PRELIMINARIES

Part I set out the general theory of psychoanalysis and traced its development. The psychoanalytic concept of motivation is a central part of this theory. Indeed, psychoanalytic theory is above all a theory of motivation.

I argued that the *content* of the theory changes over time; new hypotheses are added to the theory, old ones are removed or changed. Freud changes the theory of instincts, emphasizes aggression in mental life, changes the theory of anxiety, and so on. Freud also becomes more clearly psychological in his approach; he abandons the attempt to analyze mind in directly neurophysiological terms. Yet, behind all these changes in content are a number of major principles that remain stable. These determine the *form* of psychoanalytic theory and establish its motivational structure. This form persists throughout the development of Freud's thought. His mental model is always given in terms of forces acting on and through structures, involves a theory of associationist learning, treats mental actions as complex, modified reflexes, retains a theory of primary and secondary processes, and so on.

As a theory of motivation, psychoanalysis contains a principle of multiple causation. Energizing, precipitating, and directing factors all count as causes of behavior. In fact, the full motivational explanation of any given behavior or experience consists in the specification of the internal processes that energize, that precipitate, and that direct the behavior. The motivation concepts that psychoanalysis employs—wishes, intentions, ideas, and others—are to be understood as causal notions that derive their full meaning from the theory within which they are set.

Philosophical Questions about the Mental Model

The treatment of the psychoanalytic concept of motivation goes beyond the treatment of just the theory of motivation. It concerns the various conceptual and logical relations that hold between the notions that make up the theory. My concern is not only with what the processes are which Freud postulates to explain behavior, but with the *explanatory, epistemological,* and *ontological status* of the motive constructs he postulates, i.e., with the philosophical viability of the model of the mind.

The main philosophical questions to be answered about the psychoanalytic concept of motivation are:

1. What is the explanatory status of the concept?—How are motive concepts employed in motive ascriptions, and what are their functions?
2. What is the epistemological status of the concept?— How does the theory account for the way in which we gain knowledge of motives, and what kind of knowledge do we achieve?
3. What is the ontological status of the concept?—Are motives biological, psychological, material processes? Are they the kinds of entities that could cause behavior?

While these questions are being answered, we must keep in mind that there are a number of objections to the causal-motivational approach to the explanation of human action that psychoanalysis embodies. Some objections are made by philosophers who oppose causal explanations of human actions on various grounds, or who object to the appeal to hypothetical mental processes in explanations of behavior. Other objections come from psychoanalytic theorists who want to rewrite psychoanalysis as a different sort of theory from the kind I outlined in Part I. They want to render psychoanalysis as a theory of phenomenological meanings and as irreducibly intentionalist in character, or as a hermeneutic science. These matters will be dealt with in more detail in Part III.

These questions, and the objections to the causal-motivational analysis of psychoanalysis mentioned above, can be dealt with by taking a particular philosophical approach to the concept of motivation. This approach starts with the point that the psychoanalytic concept of motivation is an explanatory concept set within a theory: it is a theoretical construct. From this it is possible to go on to gain an understanding of the explanatory, epistemological, and ontological status of the concept.

The theoretical construct analysis argued for here says that (1) theoretical constructs get their meaning and explanatory worth from the theory within which they are set; (2) being a theoretical construct is fully compatible with being real —theoretical constructs are attempted characterizations of real and existent entities, processes, and states; and (3) these entities, states, and processes are the causes of behavior. The analysis offers a contextualist, realist, and causal analysis of the concept of motivation in psychoanalysis. This approach to theoretical concepts contrasts with other nonrealist views that have been common in positivist philosophies of science. I stress that calling the psychoanalytic motive concept a "theoretical construct" is not to classify it as some insubstantial and watery concept. It is to point up the ways in which it is established as a real process.

WHAT IS A THEORETICAL CONSTRUCT?

The paradigm of the theoretical construct is the concept that is introduced into use by a scientific theory. It is the concept of some process, state, or entity postulated by the theory but of which there is, at least at the time of introduction, no direct confirmation. It is a "construct" in the sense that it is constructed on analogy to some known process, often by inference from observed effects. Of course, there is a great variety of theoretical constructs. Any one may be more, or less, similar to this paradigm. Further, the very notions of "theory" and of "observed effects," used here to introduce the paradigm, are notoriously difficult to define. But it does give a rough initial idea of "theoretical construct," and this will be elaborated below.

FEATURES AND FUNCTIONS OF THEORETICAL CONSTRUCTS

There are a number of different aspects to the concepts that appear in theories. For our purposes these may be classed under three headings: theoretical/explanatory, epistemological, and ontological.

Theoretical/Explanatory Features. Among these features are:

1. The statement of a theoretical construct abridges a large number of data statements; it provides an economical systematization of a large amount of information.
2. A theoretical construct has a heuristic function in that it leads to new hypotheses and theoretical ideas. These can be used to further systematize knowledge, to test the theory, and to predict.
3. Such a construct has a "conceptual" function in that a postulated theoretical construct mediates between external causes and observed effects. It sets up a mechanism whereby a past cause may have a future effect, establishing a spatio-temporal continuity between otherwise separated events.
4. Theoretical constructs belong to theories, though there often is an ordinary language counterpart out of which the construct grew. And the constructs themselves change with the changes in the theory within which they reside.

These are the features that might be emphasized by pragmatists in their assessment of the functions of theoretical constructs. They point to what theories, with the concepts they involve, actually enable us to do. They enable us to systematize data, predict, expand understanding, and form conceptually satisfying accounts of observed phenomena.

Epistemological Features. Among these features are:

1. Theoretical constructs are, in the first place, postulated on the basis of evidence.
2. Our means of gaining knowledge of theoretical constructs is indirect.
3. Knowledge gained of theoretical constructs is, in the first place, less sure than that which we may gain of observables.
4. Knowledge claims about theoretical constructs are justified by testing the consequences that flow from their postulation.

The first of these epistemological features has to do with the setting up of theoretical constructs; the second with our means of gaining knowledge of them; the third with the quality of our knowledge of them; the fourth with their justification.

Ontological Features. Among these are:

1. Theoretical constructs are set up as characterizations of the processes that cause observed phenomena.
2. They are, in the first place, less secure than observables in the order of real, existing things.
3. Their reality becomes assured when independent confirmation of their existence is given.
4. They are often the postulated structural counterparts to groups of related functions.

These features point out the way in which the reality of such constructs is usually perceived. Initially they are little more than guesses about what might cause observables. But, as confirmation of the theory grows, it comes to be accepted that there really are such entities as the theory postulates.

A group of "logical features" could be added to these, covering, for example, that theoretical constructs cannot be exhaustively defined in terms of observables. However, logical aspects are not the current concern.

A point to note is that the phrase "in the first place" occurs several times in the description of the features. It was stressed that "in the first place" the constructs are only indirectly known and so on. One means for the recognition of theoretical constructs is by the way they are introduced into the language (as parts of theories). But, because they are not static concepts, and they change in ontological and epistemological status as the theories grow, this is not the only means. We may also recognize theoretical constructs by the way they organize knowledge. We do not identify and classify theoretical constructs in terms of single, simple, criteria such as knowable/unknowable, directly known/indirectly known, real/hypothetical, as some philosophers suggest. What may first appear in a theory as simply hypothetical, a guess about a mechanism underlying observed phenomena, may gain a cognitive and ontological status as firm as any "observable."

A second point to note is that these are only a few of the features and functions of theoretical constructs. These are not exhaustive lists, and the statements of the features would need a lot of qualification to be complete and accurate. As this essay continues, more will be said about the various features of theoretical constructs.

6

MEANING AND THEORETICAL CONSTRUCTS

GIVING THE MEANING OF A SCIENTIFIC CONSTRUCT

The theoretical constructs of science are postulates in the sense that they are processes or mechanisms postulated as responsible for the phenomena requiring explanation. Thus the concept of the germ, developed by Pasteur and others, was a hypothesis about the mechanisms involved in the degeneration of wine and milk, as well as in human diseases. It was postulated as responsible for various observed phenomena. Subsequent direct observation of the mechanisms involved, perhaps using new instruments and depending on other theories, can consolidate our knowledge of the mechanisms, and secure our postulated explanation as the best available. The observation through the microscope by Van Leeuwenhoek (long before Pasteur) has become accepted as an observation of germs. And of course Pasteur and others isolated and observed germs in diseased substances.

In spite of the considerable knowledge we now have about bacteria and disease, and in spite of the confidence we have in what we know about the existence and operation of bacteria, we still talk of the germ "theory" of disease. The general concept of the germ is still a postulate in a theory, and in particular cases we postulate that germs of one kind or another are responsible for certain diseases.

Simple direct observation of postulated processes is not always, perhaps not usually, forthcoming in science. It is, however, doubtful whether any theoretical construct is in principle nonobservable; criteria for making the distinction between observables and nonobservables have proved elusive. There are examples of processes that are confidently known to exist, yet not on the grounds that scientists have observed them. Electromagnetic waves, for example, have not been observed, but we do have a large amount of reliable evidence about them, and there is a vast body of good theory that is consistent with the postulation of their existence. This point has been made by a number of critics of the traditional observation-theory distinction (for example, Feyerabend, 1975; Hanson, 1958; Hesse, 1970; Putnam, 1962), and a particularly clear statement is given by Maxwell (1962).

In the absence of direct observation, and of ostensive definition, the meaning of a term that appears in a theory can be given, in part, by listing some of the hypotheticals that link that term with observable conditions and with other theoretical terms. The general form of such a hypothetical is, *If a body X possesses property P then, under conditions of type C, it will display behavior B*. Now, taking the example of the eighteenth-century theory of electric charge, we might get the following:

A1. If a body X is electrically charged, then a certain kind of substance Y, when placed closed to X, will be attracted to it.

A2. If . . . , then any such attracted body will be repelled by X on contact with it.

A3. If . . . , then, when brought close to an earthed body in the dark, sparks will fly between X and the body.

A4. If . . . , then it will repulse bodies charged in the same way.

A5. If . . . , then, when X is connected to another chargeable substance by a metal rod, the substance will display the properties of charged objects.

Of course, the more that is known about the theoretical construct, the more likely it is that the statement of the hypotheticals will include other concepts that themselves are theoretical, and in need of "unpacking." Electricity was, for example, quite quickly seen as fluid in nature; it was divided into positive and negative forces (discovered to be subject to the inverse square law), and found to be closely related to magnetism, light, and heat. Concepts like force, magnetism, electric fluid, and positive and negative charges are themselves not simple observables and require explication. So, if reference to them appears, as it must in any fuller account, in the hypotheticals explicating "electric charge," then the latter's meaning can be given only by means of a large, perhaps infinite, number of hypotheticals.

GIVING THE MEANING OF A PSYCHOLOGICAL CONSTRUCT

A similar unpacking can be applied to psychological terms to make their meanings clear. Consider, for example, "wish" (in its stronger sense of "desire" rather than merely "idle dream"). If we take the ordinary use of "wish" to begin with, not specifically the psychoanalytic use, then we might unpack it thus:

B1. If a person P has a wish for a state of affairs X, then he will behave in ways that usually lead to X.

B2. If . . . , then, if he believes that behavior Y will lead to X, he will carry out Y.

B3. If . . . , then, if P is prevented from achieving X, he will show negative emotions (anger, disappointment, and so on).

B4. If . . . , then he will show an interest in X-related matters.

B5. If . . . , then his talk about X and X-related matters will become more frequent.

B6. If . . . , then he will contemplate the thought of X with pleasure.

B7. If . . . , then, if X should be achieved, he will be pleased.

B8. If . . . , then, if he wishes equally for another state of affairs, Z, which is incompatible with X, he will show hesitation in acting toward X, will vacillate emotionally, and so on.

B9. If . . . , then, when asked, he will say he wants X.

As with the A list, these B hypotheticals contain terms that themselves are in need of unpacking. Notions like "belief" are not any more (or less) observable than "wish" itself is. (That is, the meaning of "wish" is to be found in a network of psychological terms including "belief," "contemplate," "pleasure," and so on.) Further, the B list contains statements that are more obviously tendency statements than those in the A list. There is a tendency for persons to show these various behaviors when they have a wish for X. But there is no certainty about it. For example, sometimes a person will not talk about something that he or she wishes for. Even so, we do often learn about others' wishes because they talk about the objects of their wishes.

Individuals do not only have one wish at a time. B1 says that if a person has a wish for X, then he or she will behave in ways that usually lead to X. However, there is nothing in these hypotheticals to prevent an opposing and stronger wish from prevailing. This condition could be written into the hypotheticals. B8 deals specifically with the case where there are two equal and conflicting wishes. Here the achievement of X would bring about a state of affairs "not-Z," where not-Z is aversive to P. This is obviously important for psychoanalytic theory. In particular, the clinical application of psychoanalysis deals almost entirely with instances where there are conflicting wishes. In fact, psychological theories of wishing (motivation) have to take into account the relative strength of motives, so that a person acts toward the state of affairs most strongly wished for at that moment. It is widely recognized that approach-avoidance conflict (an important element in neurotic behavior) may result where the achievement of a desired object is also associated with aversive consequences.

THE PSYCHOANALYTIC CONCEPT OF WISH

The foregoing use of "wish" has much in common with the psychoanalytic concept of wish. After all, psychoanalysis is a general theory of motivation, not merely of psychopathology. However, the psychoanalytic concept goes beyond the ordinary concept in at least two important respects. First, it is explicitly part of a theory of motivation, and this makes it closer to the case of electric charge mentioned above. Second, it emphasizes the unconscious nature of much motivation, or rather it deemphasizes the conscious aspect of wishing. Taking the notion of unconscious wish, we might unpack it thus:

C1. If a person has an unconscious wish for a state of affairs X, then he will behave in ways that usually lead to X.

C2. If . . . , then, if he believes (consciously or not) that behavior Y will lead to X, he will carry out Y.

C3. If . . . , then, if P is prevented from achieving X, he will show negative emotions (anger, disappointment, and so on).

C4. If . . . , then he will show an interest in X-related matters.

C5. If . . . , then his talk about X and X-related matters will become more frequent.

Up to C5, the hypotheticals unpacking the term "unconscious wish" are virtually identical with those for "wish" as sketched above in B. That is to say, the ascription of an unconscious wish in the psychoanalytic context has, up to this point, the same meaning as the ordinary ascription of a wish.

There are more hypotheticals:

C6. If . . . , then he also possesses a wish for Z, where Z is a state of affairs incompatible with X.

C7. If . . . , then, as P approaches the achievement of X, he will manifest neurotic symptoms, ambivalence, anxiety, and other negative emotions, and so on.

C8. If . . . , then he will manage to achieve X or X-related states of affairs, ostensibly by accident.

C9. If . . . , then he will think and talk much about X-related matters without realizing their relation to X.

C10. If . . . , then, when asked, he will deny any wish for X.

C11. If . . . , then he will express a strong wish for states of affairs that clearly preclude X.

This second group of hypotheticals differs from the first. It emphasizes that unconscious wishes are unconscious because they are in opposition to other wishes. Their manifestation, while not essentially different from "ordinary" wishes, is complicated by the expression of the opposing wishes. So P will show ambivalence toward the achievement of X, will act toward its achievement while denying to himself and others that he wishes for it, will show an exaggerated interest in X-related matters while actively denying any interest in X, and so on.

Thus far, little has been mentioned of the clinical conditions associated with the ascription of unconscious wishes. There are still further hypotheticals:

C12. If . . . , then, when in psychotherapy a wish for X is suggested by the therapist, P will resist that suggestion by denial, change of subject, rationalization, and so on.

C13. If . . . , then, any approach toward an interpretation that P wishes for X will arouse anxiety in P.

C14. If . . . , then an alternative wish—a substitute for the wish for X—will be maintained in consciousness. This alternative wish—say, for state of affairs Y—will be such that Y is symbolically linked to X through forgotten associations.

C15. If . . . , then, if X involves a person E, P will transfer the affect toward E onto both his or her therapist and others similar to, or associated with, E.

C16. If . . . , then P will dream about X in a disguised way, such that symbolic equivalents of X appear as salient points in the dream.

This group of hypotheticals is more clearly part of the theory of psychoanalysis. It states the clinical manifestations of having an unconscious wish.

However, in psychoanalytic theory, to have a wish (conscious or unconscious) is to be in a certain mental state. This state is that described by the mental model. Thus further hypotheticals are generated:

C17. If . . . , then, registered in the memory system, are traces corresponding to both the perception of X and to experiences of satisfaction associated with the achievement of X.

C18. If . . . , then these traces have been energized from instinctual sources, giving rise to a pressure to discharge along paths that previously led to X-achieving actions.

C19. If . . . , then the trial displacements of small amounts of this energy have signaled the release of unpleasure associated with achievement of X.

C20. If . . . , then the traces have been prevented from discharge by the withholding, or withdrawing, of ego cathexis.

C21. If . . . , then other traces linked to X traces in the memory network will become energized.

C22. If . . . , then, if these secondary traces are not too closely linked to X, the conscious perceptions associated with them will become hypercathected, and appear as substitute wishes.

This group of hypotheticals, expresses the psychoanalytic theory that wishes are states of the individual. That is, an unconscious wish is an energized group of psychic elements pressing for discharge in a particular direction. What appears consciously is a compromise between ego and id processes. This is designed to prevent the release of unpleasure in the uncontrollable quantities that would result from the open expression of the wish.

Wolf Man's Unconscious Homosexual Wish

An example of an unconscious wish ascription from psychoanalysis is provided by the Wolf Man case (1918). (The Appendix contains an account of this case, from which I will be

drawing illustrations in this and later chapters.) The unconscious wish is that of Wolf Man for sexual relations with his
father. One must note that this is put forward as an explanation
of a wolf phobia and is not merely the ascription of a single
simple wish. Rather, it is a series of hypotheses about the Wolf
Man's mental processes: that he has a wish for the father, that
he believes that the consequence of the fulfillment of this wish
is castration, that he reacts to this with fear, and that a substitute
object appears in consciousness.

It is clearly possible, but unnecessary here, to generate hypotheticals for this unconscious wish by applying each of the
C-list hypotheticals to the Wolf Man case. This would result in
an equivalent list of D hypotheticals. In this case D1–5 would
express the fact that Wolf Man acted toward his father in a way
that was at times seductive, at times provocative; that he showed
anger when his father did not provide him with the right kind
of attention; that he was keenly interested in matters associated
with receiving things from his father, in anal sexuality, and
other passive or homosexual matters; and that he talked about
such things, particularly in therapy. D6–11 would express the
conflict of wishes in Wolf Man's behavior, and the unconsciousness of the homosexual wish. D12–16 would express the clinical
manifestations of the wish: the resistance to interpretation; the
maintenance of substitute ideas in consciousness such as the
wolf fear itself; the transference in analysis; and the dream
symbolism. D17–22 would be the "theoretical" hypotheticals in
that they would express the psychodynamics of the wish: that
sexual energy is displaced through associated networks, and so
on. The details of the psychodynamics of wishing were discussed in Part I.

MEANING AND "SPELLING OUT"

Analyticity and Meaning

We need to look closely at the relation between "giving meaning" and "spelling out in hypotheticals." It often seems as

though the only statements involving a particular term that actually give its meaning are those which are analytic. This would mean that the hypotheticals that spell out the concepts of charge and wish, given above, would only count as giving a part of the meaning of "charge" or "wish" if they were true by definition.

Consider this example:

E1. If a person scores a goal in football (soccer), then he propels the ball through the posts while the ball is in play.
E2. If . . . , then the crowd roars.
E3. If . . . , then he gets a bonus on his pay that week.
E4. If . . . , then he gets hugged by the captain.

E1 gives the meaning of "goal," and is true by definition; that is what we mean by "goal." E2–4, however, do not give the meaning of goal. They indicate the usual, contingent, consequences of the goal. To someone outside the stadium the roar of the crowd may well indicate that a goal has been scored, but there is no necessary link between the roar and the goal.

But with other kinds of concept it is not possible to get hypotheticals that are, individually, analytically true. For example, wish as explicated above in the B list only generates nonanalytic hypotheticals. As the hypotheticals stand, none is true by definition. Each expresses the fact that the person wishing for some state of affairs tends to behave in some manner. Thus B1 says that a person with a wish for X will behave in a manner that usually leads to X. Yet it is quite conceivable that a person wish for something (his thirst to be quenched) yet not act toward that (he continues to run in the marathon and does not turn off to the nearest bar) because he has other commitments (winning the race). Or he may not behave appropriately simply because he is incapacitated. As a second example, consider B2: it is possible that a person believes that an action (turning on a tap) will lead toward X (quenching his thirst) but he does not perform that action; instead he performs some alternative (he goes to the nearest bar).

The B list contains no single hypothetical that is necessarily true. All the behaviors mentioned in the hypotheticals are likely to occur, and are associated with having a wish, but they are not necessary to having a wish. B9 is controversial. It states that a person can avow his wish. And it often seems as though being in a particular mental state, such as having a wish, and being able to avow the mental state are connected in a special way; that is, a person has privileged access to his mental state. It appears indeed that it is impossible to sincerely avow a wish and be wrong. Now if this argument were correct (which it is not), it would not, of course, make B9 analytically true. The entailment in B9 as stated is from wish to avowal. The above argument goes from avowal to wish. I shall return to the problem of avowal later (Chapter 8). For the present, let me take the position that a person might not, even to himself, be able to admit a wish. Then no one behavior is a necessary criterion for the ascription of a wish to someone; it is not necessarily true that having a wish entails behaving in any one particular way.

There is no entailment in the reverse direction either; there is no one behavior whose occurrence would necessarily mean that a person had a particular wish. No behavior is sufficient criterion for the ascription of a wish.

Yet, in contrast to the fact that no one behavior is either a necessary or a sufficient criterion for the ascription of a wish, some behaviors are more central to the notion. For example, that a person behaves in ways that usually lead to X is more basic to the notion than that the person is interested in X-related matters.

A Statement on Meaning

The position I shall take on meaning is, then: *The meaning of a theoretical term consists of the totality of the hypotheticals it generates.* That is, while no one hypothetical provides the necessary nor the sufficient criterion for the application of the particular term, the conjunction of all the hypotheticals does.

There are some points to note about this:

First, I have been using as an example a motivation term, "wish," that is not obviously theoretical. But, as we will see, there are good grounds for treating it as such.

Second, there are several categories of hypotheticals in the unpacking of a term like "unconscious wish." Each category corresponds to a different aspect of the content of the concept. Some hypotheticals give the common-sense meaning of the term (C1–11). Some give the more theoretical side (C12–22). Some give the material process that the theory regards as underlying the state of wishing (C17–22). Some hypotheticals link "wish" to observables, some to other theoretical terms. For example, C1 states that a particular (observable) behavior is likely to ensue from a wish. But C2 introduces the notion of belief; a person will carry out act Y if he believes it will lead to X. "Belief" is quite as much in need of unpacking as "wish." In psychoanalytic theory a belief is also a particular mental state, with various conditional, behavioral consequences.

Hypotheticals that link theoretical terms to observables would, in a more traditional description of theoretical structure, be termed "correspondence rules." Hypotheticals that link theoretical terms to other theoretical terms would be called "theoretical statements" and "postulates."

It is not only mental state or motivational concepts that separate into various aspects in this way. For example, in giving the meaning of "magnet," we would have a common-sense meaning expressed in a hypothetical: "if a body is a magnet, then iron filings will be attracted to its ends." The material basis of magnetism would be contained in hypotheticals, saying, for instance: "if . . . , then each of its individual molecules will be polarized." And "magnet" would be linked to other theoretical terms, as where a hypothetical says, "if . . . , then its movement through a solenoid will generate an electric current."

Third, each hypothetical gives a partial criterion for the application of the theoretical term. Any one behavior or conjunction of behaviors specified by the hypotheticals is indicative of a wish. The number of hypotheticals may be infinite, since any one that contains a further theoretical term itself requires spelling out in terms of hypotheticals. This point has been covered by writers such as Braithwaite (1953), Craig (1956), and Hempel (1965) in their work on theoretical statements. What emerges from this work is that a statement containing a theoretical term may be replaced—without loss of empirical content—by a set of statements containing only observational terms. However, the set of observation statements is generally infinitely large.

Fourth, and perhaps most important, the meaning of a term (the content of a concept) may change. Hypotheticals that are at first purely speculative or marginal to the concept of the concept may become central to it. Conversely, other hypotheticals may diminish in significance. This is illustrated and discussed below.

Meaning Change

Concepts like those of electric charge and atom have changed greatly in a few hundred years of use. So the hypotheticals of list A, giving the eighteenth-century meaning of the term "electric charge," are out of date. It is now part of the meaning of "electric charge" that, when a charge is propagated, it displays wave characteristics and is part of the electromagnetic wave spectrum. Similarly, it is part of the modern meaning of "atom" that an atom is divisible into subatomic particles. Yet originally atoms were the basic and indivisible units of matter.

What happened was that the original, primitive versions of these concepts were used in an everyday or marginally scientific context. But as more was discovered about electricity and microphysics, the new knowledge was incorporated into the concepts. So initially "atom" meant "indivisible particle." Later it meant "a particle of matter divisible into protons, neutrons, electrons."

These changes in meaning can be represented by additions, deletions, and changes to the hypotheticals. Some additions convey that the concept is linked to other theoretical concepts—for example, that a charge in flow will create a magnetic field. Others link it with observables—for example, that a charged body will part the leaves of an electroscope.

Returning to "wish," the term does not initially belong to any scientific theory, but Freud incorporates it into a psychology of motivation. He thereby changes the content of the concept, and these changes to the meaning of "wish" are represented in the hypotheticals generated. The B list gives the ordinary meaning of "wish." The C list gives the ordinary meaning together with the changes. C6–11 are not critically psychoanalytic. They articulate the fact, known before Freud, that wishes may be unconscious. But C12 and onwards incorporate an explicit theory about wishes. They try to tell us what wishing is all about. They tell us of the relation of wishes to other mental states and to behavior.

There are apparent differences between the wish case and that of electric charge and atom. Electric charge and atom are concepts that belong mostly to scientific theory. It is science that has specified and explained the properties of electricity and of atoms. But "wish," though used in psychological theory, is primarily an ordinary language term. So it might be thought that the meanings of "atom" and "electric charge" are given by their scientific, theoretical use and, in contrast, the meaning of "wish" is given in its everyday use. Ordinary language philosophers have assumed this to be so, and treated the everyday use of mental terms as having legislative force over the meaning of the terms.

However, the differences between the two cases are relative. In both, the change in meaning of the terms comes about because of a growth in theory about the processes concerned, and in both cases the change in meaning is embodied in new hypotheticals generated. The difference is that the growth of theory in physics is greater, more systematic, and more informative than in psychology. This makes it tempting to restrict the meaning of psychological terms to their common-sense usage. But there is no reason why a theory cannot change our motivation concepts. Psychoanalysis tries to characterize wishes and other mental states. That it does not match up to physics' characterization of electricity does not make its attempt illegitimate. Indeed, psychoanalysis has already affected the common-sense meaning of "wish": since Freud we accept more easily that a person may be deceived about his own motives.

Theoretical Context and Meaning

The context in which a term is used bears on its meaning. First, when a theoretical term is invoked—say, in ascribing an unconscious wish to someone—the user means to convey information, appraisal, and so on. In the everyday context the user does not mean to convey anything about mental energies or any other psychoanalytic hypothesis. (There may be, however, a variety of tacit assumptions in his use of the notion.) This latter use only shares some meaning with Freud's use of "unconscious wish." For Freud clearly does mean to say something about mental energies and the like when he ascribes an unconscious wish. The same applies to other theoretical concepts. The man in the street does not mean to say anything about the electromagnetic wave spectrum when he warns his child not to play with electricity. In this his use of "electricity" is only a limited version of the physicist's use.

Second, the meaning of a theoretical term is the totality of the hypotheticals it generates. So the meaning of the term is made up of the various relationships described in the hypotheticals between, say, "having a wish" and "behaving in manners such and such," or "being in mental state so and so." "Wish" is then located in a network of terms, both theoretical and observable. This network, or context, gives the meaning of "wish." This applies both to the common-sense version and the psychoanalytic version. It means they are both theoretical, the former in an implicit sense.

Dispositions

For general science, positivists have often given explications of science's hypothetical constructs in purely dispositional terms; that is, to say a body is electrically charged is to say nothing more than that it has a disposition: a tendency to exhibit certain characteristics under certain conditions. The main thrust of such analyses was to demonstrate that theoretical statements were merely ways of making disguised reference to observables, and that there was really nothing above and beyond the data that was causally responsible for the observables. Here I am equating a dispositional analysis of mental concepts with a purely behaviorist, reductionist account. Under such a definition, dispositional statements say nothing categorical about an individual, and nothing about the mental causes of behavior. Ryle (1949) uses "disposition" in this way. However, there are philosophers who use "disposition" in a way that makes a dispositional analysis compatible with the sort of realism for which I am arguing (for example, the collection in Tuomela, 1978, especially Alston, 1971; Armstrong, 1973b; and Tuomela, 1977). Smythe (1972), whose analysis of the Freudian concept of desire is otherwise similar to mine, also regards his treatment of theoretical concepts as dispositional.

In the dispositional way of dealing with theoretical constructs, both causes and effects belong to the realm of the observable. Strictly speaking, laws do not hold between theoretical properties and observable consequences, but between sets of observables. Thus, in explicating a term like "electric charge," what is lawlike about the hypotheticals is not that they link being charged to, say, attracting neutral bodies, but rather that they link certain procedures, such as being rubbed with a glass rod, to attracting neutral bodies.

In the case of psychological concepts, it is the behaviorist who would give a purely dispositional analysis, saying that predicating a psychological quality of someone is nothing more than saying that person would behave in certain ways under certain conditions. To have a wish is nothing more than to respond in certain ways, under certain conditions.

What then distinguishes the way I have set out the concept of wish from a purely dispositional one? There are a few distinctions.

First, I have argued that there is an indefinitely large number of hypotheticals associated with such a concept. A dispositional analysis, however, looks less and less dispositional the larger and more complex the string of hypotheticals gets. This is because the core of the dispositional analysis is that the statement of a theoretical (mental) concept reduces to a series of statements about observables. And it makes nonsense of the idea of "reduction" if the reduction is to an indefinitely large set of observation statements. The paradigm case of a dispositional concept is perhaps that of brittleness. It might be explicated in this way:

F1. If a body is brittle, then it will fracture on an impact of X dynes or greater.
F2. If . . . , then it will neither fracture nor dent nor bend under a force of less than X dynes.

A dispositional analysis of the concept would say that this short list of hypotheticals exhausts the meaning of "brittle." If F1 and F2 are true of a body, then a body simply is brittle by virtue of the way we use the words. Also, if a body is brittle, then F1 and F2 are true.

Second, a purely dispositional analysis gives a series of hypotheticals that only mention behaviors, or simply observable properties, as being indicators of the ascribed state. But, once the list lengthens and hypotheticals include nonobservable terms, terms that themselves need spelling out, the hypotheticals are no longer dispositional. It is, for example, dispositional that a charged body will part the leaves on a gold-leaf electroscope. It is not dispositional that a charged body is in a state of ionization, or is otherwise depleted of its normal number of electrons. The more that the hypotheticals mention properties of bodies that require further spelling out, the less dispositional that spelling out becomes. For example, a hypothetical that says if a person is thirsty, that such and such a neural mechanism will be active, is a long way from saying that if presented with a drink the thirsty person will drink it.

It is in going beyond predictions about immediate behavioral properties that a concept becomes nondispositional and states something categorical about some body or process. This is true in spite of the fact that the cash value of any statement about a body is observational; that is, there is nothing known about any body or process that is not manifest in observations of one sort or another. Even the properties of subatomic particles are only known because of things that we can observe.

The laws that are expressed by the hypotheticals, and which are part of the meaning of the term, are not then purely dispositional. They say more than merely that a body that exhibits behavior Y1, under conditions C1, is also a body that exhibits behavior Y2 under conditions C2. The laws say that there is a systematic relation between a state of a body, say, having a wish for X, and behaviors such as doing Y, if Y usually leads to X.

7

THEORETICAL ASPECTS OF THE PSYCHOANALYTIC CONCEPT OF MOTIVATION

In Chapter 5, I outlined three main features of theoretical constructs: explanatory/theoretical, epistemological, and ontological. The next three chapters deal with these three, using the method of unpacking for illustration. This chapter deals with explanatory features of theoretical constructs: their role in systematizing data, their heuristic function, and the conceptual functions they perform.

SYSTEMATIZATION

The statement of a theoretical construct provides an economical systematization of a large number of data statements. This quality of theoretical statements has been singled out by positivist philosophers of science and treated as the essence of explanation in science. Logical empiricism argued that theoretical statements were only a logical abridgment of statements containing theoretical terms. Here no strict reducibility of theoretical statements is implied. It is merely that the statement of a theoretical concept—as in the ascription of a motive to someone—does convey a large amount of information about observables and other theoretical states. In doing this the theoretical concept can be said to "systematize" a large number of data. It does function as a shorthand for the data statements, though this is not the sole function of theoretical constructs.

A theoretical concept such as that of unconscious wish achieves a systematization of data in two senses, specific and general.

Specific Case

The concept of unconscious homosexual wish as Freud uses it in the Wolf Man case (1918; also my Appendix) can be unpacked in the following way:

D1. If Wolf Man has an unconscious homosexual wish for his father, then he will act toward his father in ways that usually encourage affectionate and other physical attentions.

D2. If . . . , then, if he believes certain actions (for example, being naughty or coy) will bring about the attention of his father, he will act accordingly.

D3. If . . . , then, if he is prevented from receiving attention from his father, he will show negative emotions—anger, frustration, and so on.

D4. If . . . , then he will show an interest in matters related to passive homosexuality (for example, anality, the "absence" of genitals in females, and so on).

D5. If . . . , then his talk about matters related to homosexuality will be greater than in most persons.

D6. If . . . , then he also possesses a wish for a state of affairs incompatible with passive homosexual relationships (viz., the narcissistic wish for intact masculinity and for union with the opposite sex).

D7. If . . . , then, as Wolf Man approaches the achievement of a passive homosexual relationship with his father, or persons similar to his father, he will manifest neurotic symptoms (for example, intense anxiety, obsessive rituals).

In general the D list of hypotheticals parallels the C list. So it covers the fact that Wolf Man will deny the unconscious wish (equivalent to C10); that he will find himself "by accident" in situations congruent with passive homosexuality (equivalent to C8); and so on.

Note: the wish ascribed to Wolf Man is an explanation of the phobia. It is more than just the attribution of a single, simple wish. It is a complex hypothesis about a wish (for the father); about Wolf Man's interpretation of its consequences (castration); a reaction to this (fear); and a consequent substitution in consciousness (the wolf phobia). The behavioral consequences of this ascribed wishful state are equally complex. For this reason this wish results in, and is indicated by, some behaviors characteristic of homosexuality, some of passivity, some directly indicative, some indirectly. It is the totality of behaviors that indicates the complex wish.

The D hypotheticals mentioned thus far correspond to the C1–11 hypotheticals. I have not yet mentioned hypotheticals that cover the clinical manifestations of having an unconscious homosexual wish. Nor have the "theoretical" hypotheticals been mentioned, those that cover the theoretical implications of Freud's mental model (corresponding to C17–22). Further hypotheticals, for example, might be:

D12. If . . . , then, when in psychoanalysis Freud inter- prets Wolf Man's behavior as a homosexual passive wish for his father, Wolf Man will resist this by denial, changing the subject, superficial acceptance, and so on.

D16. If . . . , then Wolf Man will dream about passive homosexual satisfaction in a disguised way, so that symbolic equivalents of passivity, of homosexuality, and of the father appear as salient points of the dream.

These cover clinical matters. The following are psychoanalytic-theoretical:

D17. If . . . , then, registered in Wolf Man's memory sys- tem, are traces corresponding to the perception of satisfaction associated with a passive sexual attitude toward the father.

D20. If . . . , then the above-mentioned traces, when energized, have had their discharge prevented by the ego's withdrawl of cathexis.

When Freud ascribes this unconscious homosexual wish to Wolf Man, he implies all the information contained in the D hypotheticals. He is predicting that Wolf Man will act seductively toward his father, will be jealous of his sister's place in his father's affections, will be anal in his preoccupations, will tend toward obsessional forms of neurosis, and so on—all the things contained in the hypotheticals. Freud also implies the various goings-on in the mental system as postulated by the mental model—for example, that the ego's hypercathexis is withheld from the memory traces. The ascription is an "economical systematization" of all the information contained in the hypotheticals.

But one must be careful about in what exact sense it is a systematization. I pointed out in the last chapter that no hypothetical specifies either a necessary or sufficient condition for the ascription of a wish. This is both because hypotheticals describe only tendencies to behave, and also because it is always possible to think of exceptions. It is therefore not possible to reduce the ascription of the wish to one statement, or a finite number of statements, about observable behaviors without loss of empirical content. Yet the wish ascription does condense a great deal of information about behaviors and about mental properties. The occurrence of any one such behavior, or the presence of any one such property, is a partial criterion for the correct ascription of the wish. When Freud does ascribe this wish to Wolf Man, anyone who understands Freud's theory understands the large number of behavioral predictions that are implied. Indeed, an examination of the Wolf Man case (see Appendix) shows that the wish hypothesis ties together a huge amount of data about Wolf Man. In this it is aided by the various supplementary hypotheses. The wish hypothesis links the childhood wolf phobia, the obsessional neurosis, the child's change of character, his anal symptoms, and so on. Each of these facets of Wolf Man's life consists of many and diverse activities. Freud's use of the wish concept in this particular context draws all these unlikely bedfellows together.

General Case

There is another aspect to the systematizing quality of theoretical constructs. Consider the notion of unconscious wish in abstraction from its particular application to Wolf Man. Wish is the major motivation concept in psychoanalysis. It stands astride the boundary between clinical and metapsychological explanation. Because it is a motivation concept, it has a tripartite structure. Whenever the term "wish" is used in psychoanalytic explanation, it implies that there are three factors responsible for the phenomenon explained: energizing, precipitating, and directing factors. The mental model itself incorporates these factors and this marks it as a motivational model. Wish, as the central explanatory concept in the mental model, brings the whole of the mental model to bear on the phenomena to be explained. This, then, is the second sense in which wish concentrates a large amount of information; it draws together the different aspects of the mental model of which it is a central notion.

Freud on Systematization

Freud himself (1915c) makes briefly two of the points for which I have been arguing. First, he recognizes that unconscious processes are postulates, and that they are posited for the purposes of explanatory utility. He defends his "right to assume the existence of something mental that is unconscious and to employ that assumption for the purposes of scientific work" (p. 166). Second, he argues in justification of postulation of unconscious mental processes that it (1) systematizes the data, and (2) brings meaning into them: "It is *necessary* because the data of consciousness have a very large number of gaps in them . . . [certain] psychical acts often occur which can be explained only by presupposing other [unconscious] acts." And,

> conscious acts [alone] remain disconnected and unintelligible
> . . . on the other hand, they fall into a demonstrable *connection*
> if we interpolate between them the unconscious acts which we
> have inferred. A gain in *meaning* is a perfectly justifiable ground
> for going beyond the limits of direct experience [p. 167; italics
> added].

Freud has more to say on the inferential nature of unconscious mental processes and on their ontology. These are discussed in Chapters 8 and 9, to follow.

HEURISTIC FUNCTIONS

It is commonly recognized that theoretical constructs have a heuristic function. This is independent of the truth of the theories in which they reside. The use of theoretical constructs leads us from the data that the construct originally was intended to explain to novel hypotheses. In this way theoretical constructs are part of a "theoretical imperialism," ever trying to extend the theories' power to account for data. Theoretical constructs both accommodate data they were not originally designed for and actively lead us to predictions about unexpected states of affairs.

Freud's motivational constructs are of various levels of generality, from specific hypotheses about unconscious wishes to very general ones about the ultimate determinants of human action. Correspondingly they serve both general and specific heuristic functions.

Two General Examples

THE STRUCTURAL HYPOTHESIS

Even the most abstract aspects of the motivation theory have heuristic value. They serve to establish expectations about mental phenomena and provide a means for accommodating them. Consider, for example, the structural hypothesis. Early in his work Freud follows the practice of postulating structures to correspond to functions. It is the same for his psychology as for his neuropsychology. He notes, for example (1895a, pp. 299–300), that there are two functions of cognition: (1) the ability to register rapidly changing stimuli in the field of attention; and (2) the ability to retain the impression of some stimuli for a long period of time. He postulates two structures to correspond to these two functions. He calls these the "ω system" of neurons and the "ψ system." (These are essentially the perceptual and the memory systems.) These postulated structures tie in with the rest of his mental model. It is the same structural approach that, more than twenty years later, leads Freud to the idea of the superego. Once again he makes the assumption that a structure (this time a fully mental one) must correspond to a function. So he postulates a superego as the structural counterpart to moral and other functions of the person (1923).

The structural hypothesis is not heuristic in the sense that it leads directly to data. Rather, at this abstract level, it sets the stage for a whole range of hypotheses about behavior. The superego is an extremely fruitful notion for psychoanalysis, helping to explain identification (for example, 1933, pp. 63–64) and other matters. Its heuristic value consists in establishing new theoretical hypotheses rather than directly empirical ones.

MOTIVATIONAL ACCOUNT OF HYSTERIA

There are other quite general aspects of Freud's motivational model that have heuristic worth. What is novel about Freud's explanation of hysteria is largely that it says hysterical symptoms are motivated. This contrasts with pre-Freudian accounts of the phenomenon. But once Freud has adopted this it leads him to expect that all sorts of other behaviors, previously unexplained, are motivated. It also enables him to accommodate the new data in his theory. So, not long after the *Studies on Hysteria* (Breuer and Freud, 1895), he starts treating dreams as motivated phenomena and goes on to do the same with parapraxes, with psychoses, and so on. Eventually almost all behavior is reinter-preted in his motivational terms.

There are many other examples from Freud's motivation theory that could be used to show its heuristic value. In each case, some aspect of the psychoanalytic concept of motivation can be seen to lead Freud forward in his theorizing, to allow him to incorporate more phenomena into the theory. One should note that usually there is an interaction of theoretical concepts and data. The use of the theoretical concepts leads to expectations about psychological phenomena. As these phe-nomena are incorporated into the theory, the theory and its concepts change. This is how the theory develops. In this way, for example, the superego notion develops. Initially, it is merely an aspect of the ego assigned self-evaluative functions and is called the "ego-ideal" (1914, p. 94). But it is a fruitful notion. It helps Freud understand the motives of repression, allows him to incorporate the facts of aggression into psychoanalysis, and enables him to assimilate cultural and social factors to the theory. As this happens, the concept itself changes until it is a major psychic structure.

Specific Example: The Wolf Man's Wish

It is not only the very general and abstract aspects of the motivation theory that have this heuristic function. Specific motive ascriptions show the same quality. For an example, we may return to the Wolf Man case (1918; see also Appendix). Freud is originally called in to understand and help Wolf Man in an adult breakdown. His approach, however, takes him back to the patient's childhood. He gathers from Wolf Man memories of childhood pathology. Freud sets out three riddles to be re-solved: "[1] What was the origin of the sudden change in the boy's character? [2] What was the significance of his phobia and of his perversities? [3] How did he arrive at his obsessive piety?" (p. 17).

Much of the solution to these riddles about the data is pro-vided by the hypothesis that Wolf Man is motivated by a passive unconscious wish for sexual satisfaction from his father (see Appendix).

EXTENSION OF THE WISH HYPOTHESIS

The wish ascription, however, does much more than provide an account of these three riddles. It also provides, as we shall see, information about a fourth riddle: "How are all these phenomena interrelated?" (p. 17), and it runs throughout the case study. It is a focus for the many hypotheses Freud makes about the unconscious mental life of Wolf Man. Just how complex and intricate is Freud's explanation is hard to convey here. The case study itself is a condensation of four years of analysis. Yet even in the case study Freud ties together a huge number of facts and hypotheses using the wish concept, together with various auxiliary hypotheses. But something of the heuristic character of this wish hypothesis can be illustrated. It can be shown how the hypothesis goes beyond the three riddles to help explain, for example, the wolf dream and also Wolf Man's anality.

THE WISH AND THE WOLF DREAM

The wish hypothesis explains the dream of the still wolves. Freud approaches the dream with the wish hypothesis to guide him, and he has auxiliary hypotheses to help in this, such as the clinical rules-of-thumb. He is looking for symbols and associations that indicate the elements of the ascribed wish, and he hopes that in the course of this, further information will emerge. So he looks for signs that indicate passivity, sexuality, the father, the castration that is the condition of being satisfied by the father, and for the relations between these elements. Moreover, he expects that these elements will be disguised and in places represented by inverted symbols (see Appendix).

In explaining the dream, Freud does find a support for the wish hypothesis and, importantly, he finds something else: pointers to a new and related hypothesis about a "primal scene." This is an early event, a scene witnessed by Wolf Man when very young, and is a source of significant memories. Now the postulated primal scene itself forms an explanatory nucleus to which many pieces of the case are attached. It is thus that the wish hypothesis both aids the dream interpretation and leads to a new and also heuristically valuable notion.

THE WISH AND ANALITY

A striking feature of Wolf Man's mental life is his anality. This is shown in his obsessive ruminations about Christ's behind and eliminative functions (1918, p. 63); in his sexual preferences for women with large buttocks (p. 41); in his compulsive attraction to women he discovers bending over (p. 94); his chronic constipation and the relief (psychological as well as physical) that enemas afford him (pp. 74–75); and so on.

Once again it is the wish hypothesis, originally constructed to explain other matters, that leads to an account of the anal symptoms. Once again, the links between the hypothesized wish and the symptoms to be explained are many and extremely complex, and employ auxiliary hypotheses. Some links are indirect, others more direct. I shall sketch only a few.

The wish hypothesis helps elucidate the dream (see Appendix). From this the primal scene emerges with its anal themes: the mother bending over receiving the father's penis from behind (Freud, 1918, p. 39). In his wish for the father, Wolf Man identifies with his mother in the primal scene, receiving his father's penis from behind. There is thus an erogenization of his anus. But, inasmuch as his heterosexuality is dominant, he identifies with the father. This too results in anal attitudes; he is attracted especially to women similar to the mother in the primal scene, bending over and/or with buttocks prominent. This connection between the anus and sexuality is reinforced from other quarters. Wolf Man's childish understanding of his mother's ill health was that it has to do with blood in her stool (the result, he fears, of anal intercourse? p. 77). Further, there is the common children's theory of birth, that babies are born from the anus (pp. 78–80).

The wish hypothesis is also connected to the anality through another link, or rather set of links—the obsessional neurosis. Underlying Wolf Man's obsessional thoughts and behaviors is a regression from genital to anal sexuality (p. 25). The regression occurs under a threat of castration, and this is a blow to his heterosexuality. His sexuality then takes on an anal form, wavering between sadism and masochism (pp. 26–28). The wish for the father is, unconsciously, the wish to gain sexual satisfaction from the father anally. In his symptoms this becomes the rumination: Does Christ (the son) have a behind? Could he be used by his father like a woman (p. 64)? Indeed, Freud points out here (p. 117) and elsewhere (for example, Freud 1913a, pp. 320ff.) that obsessional neurosis and anality are closely linked.

WISH HYPOTHETICALS AND THE HEURISTIC FUNCTION

If we look back to the unpacking of the "unconscious homosexual wish," we get another perspective on the heuristic functions of this concept. The concept itself spawns a large, possibly infinite, number of hypotheticals. Yet the wish is only ascribed on the basis of a limited amount of data. These data are the three riddles Freud mentions: puzzles about Wolf Man's character change in childhood, his phobia, and his perversities. The D hypotheticals state that displaying certain kinds of behavior is consistent with having an unconscious homosexual wish. For example, D1 states:

> D1.　If Wolf Man has an unconscious homosexual wish for his father, then he will act toward his father in ways that usually bring about affectionate and other physical attentions.

Now, Freud sees Wolf Man act in ways that usually bring about the physical, sometimes punitive, attentions of the father. This, in Freud's eyes, is consistent with having an unconscious homosexual wish for the father. The wish explains the actions. Of course, a fair number of behaviors and experiences mentioned in the hypotheticals have to occur before Freud makes the inductive inference to the wish. Each hypothetical gives only a partial criterion for the ascription of the wish.

Once the wish hypothesis has been established on this basis of a set of data, further hypotheticals serve as predictions. They tell us where to look for new data. For example, Freud's wish concept is set in his theory, a network of clinical and theoretical hypotheses. One clinical hypothetical is D16.

> D16. If . . . , then Wolf Man will dream about passive homosexual satisfaction in a disguised way, so that symbolic equivalents of passivity, of homosexuality, and of the father appear as salient points of the dream.

Because D16 is a part of what Freud means by "Wolf Man's unconscious homosexual wish," Freud is led from the wish to the dream interpretation. "Unconscious homosexual wish" also generates theoretical hypotheticals. For example, one might go something like:

> Dn. If . . . , then the sexual instinct will be redirected toward activities and objects associated with anally mediated pleasure.

Because Dn is part of what Freud means by "unconscious homosexual wish," Freud is led to explore Wolf Man's anality.

COMPLEXITY OF THE EXPLANATION

It is worth emphasizing again how complex is the account Freud offers of Wolf Man. The above few paragraphs, and the discussion in the Appendix, show only a fraction of the connections Freud makes between the "wish" hypothesis and the other elements of the case. Freud's method is to use the idea of the unconscious wish for the father to probe more and more of the patient's story. He adds auxiliary hypotheses where he feels the need to, and offers supporting evidence for those. He draws upon the case history itself, upon clinical generalizations, and upon his general theory of motivation to justify the wish hypothesis, the method of investigation, and the auxiliary hypotheses.

The result of all this is that the wish hypothesis is truly heuristic, gathering to itself more and more material. It is the center of an immensely complex web of facts and hypotheses. The unconscious wish is linked by Freud to many other aspects of Wolf Man's life—for example, to his sexual preferences and attitudes, to his pathology and experiences. And then again, Freud traces multiple connections between each of these other aspects, and tries to show new links that go back to the wish. In this way Freud seeks to support and justify the wish hypothesis, and uses it to dig out further information.

CONCEPTUAL FUNCTIONS

There is a further and most important function served by the motive construct. This is a conceptual function.

For purposes of examination, theories are often treated as series of statements and are analyzed formally. However, theories are items that have to be understood and communicated. We actually have to apprehend and think in terms of a theory if we are to explain anything with it. Any concept introduced to explain things must conform to notions already in use. It must be acceptable to current means of conceptualizing. If this were not so, the new theoretical concept would not be intelligible. In this way an adequate theoretical construct serves a conceptual function. That it does so is not an accident. It is an essential part of the explanatory process, of what makes an explanation an explanation. One type of conceptual function is modeling.

Models

Part of explaining something consists in linking the explanation to something familiar. This does not mean that explanation is a matter of reducing the unfamiliar to the familiar. Obviously, many of the best explanations science offers are not, in any simple way, familiar. But the theoretical constructs that we postulate are modeled on constructs that are accepted as useful in other fields. Explanation is based on the assumption that if the phenomena in two different fields are similar, then their explanations will also be similar (see, for example, Harré, 1970, 1972; Hesse, 1966, 1967). If in one of the fields we have a good explanation of the phenomena, then we can construct an explanation for similar phenomena in a different field. The construct will be an analogy to, or modeled upon, the explanation in the first field. This not only provides a heuristic device for opening up new explanations, it also renders the to-be-explained phenomena intelligible and "familiar" to concepts in use.

FORM AND CONTENT: POSITIVE AND NEGATIVE ANALOGY

A simple example comes from social psychology. The activities of players in a theatrical production are, within bounds, set and predictable. This is intelligible because we know that they have roles to perform. The roles govern the actions and interactions of players in set positions in the production. In society at large we can also predict the behaviors of persons in set positions of occupation, status, and so on. Priests, students, and union officials, for example, are predictable because they hold those positions. They have styles and rules of behavior they generally follow. This is often explained through the use of the construct "social role." This concept is constructed on analogy with "theatrical role." It is similar in form, though it differs in content.

Inasmuch as social role is similar to theatrical role, we may say that there is "positive analogy" between the two concepts. "Negative analogy" also exists in modeling. For example, there is no literal or set script for a social role. And, most important for the growth of knowledge, there is something that may be termed "neutral analogy," a gray area where the phenomena in the second field may, or may not, be similar to these in the first (see Hesse, 1967).

The modeled concept effectively predicts that the phenomena in this gray area will be similar to those covered by the concept modeled. In the expectation that this is so, the new area is explored. In our role example, it may, or may not, be that the social role player's personality can bring an interpretation to the role to be played. The idea that personality and role do interact in this way is a constructive hypothesis. If it proves useful, then the analogy between theatrical and social phenomena is successfully extended. If it is not of use, then we have to remodel or even abandon the role concept in social explanation.

MODELS AND THE PSYCHOANALYTIC CONCEPT OF MOTIVATION

Freud constructs the psychoanalytic concept of motivation on several different models. It is a complex, hybrid notion. In Chapter 2, I have outlined the multiple conceptual influences on Freud's motivation concept. Freud also uses many analogies when he is explaining dreams and case histories. (The index to the *Standard Edition*, Vol. 24, gives a four-page list of analogies.)

The central and most striking models for the psychoanalytic motivation concept are: (1) the neuron with its reflex action; (2) the appetite, where stimulation through deprivation leads to consummatory action; and (3) the evolving animal, where structure and function alter to fit environmental contingencies. Freud notes that human actions are in essence the consequence of physical, biological processes. They resemble the effects of a biological machine. He sees that these effects are energized, organized, and directed. Further, their consequences are such that they enhance the animal survival of the human. In effect, Freud is arguing: since human behavior looks like the outcome of a biological machine, what motivates it must look like the workings of such a machine. So he builds a motivational system out of the neuron (eventually this is termed an "element"). He also says, in effect: human aggression and sexual behavior are directed and consummatory like appetitive acts, therefore what causes it must be like an appetite.

NO ACTION AT A TEMPORAL DISTANCE

A second conceptual function of theoretical constructs can be dealt with more briefly, yet it is a significant one. Theoretical concepts like motive help achieve a spatio-temporal continuity between the causes of behavior and the behavior itself. Behaviorists, such as Skinner (1950), argue that environmental causes and behavioral effects are functionally related. The statement of these functions, he argues, may be given without mention of intervening and mediating processes such as mind or motive. Another, and essentially similar, argument is presented by psychoanalytic theorists such as Schafer (1976; see also Part III, below). He argues that we need no mental substantives ("feelings," "id," "ego," "cathexis," "motive," "wish") to explain action. We merely require a description of the action itself.

In contrast to this, a theoretical construct such as motive in psychoanalysis effects a link between events in the history of the individual and his current activities. It represents some mechanism that is altered by earlier events such as childhood experiences, instinctual developments, and so on. This mechanism with its alterations persists in time and then is causally related to later activities. Motives are processes that mediate between what happens to the individual and what the individual does; whether such mediating variables are logically necessary does not matter. Factors affecting human action and experience are myriad and complex. Concepts like motive are needed to coordinate and organize the relationships between the causes and the effects to ensure that we do not have the conceptual discomfort of treating causes as acting at a temporal and spatial distance from their effects.

CONCLUSION

In this chapter I have been answering the question stated at the outset: "What are the explanatory functions of the psychoanalytic concept of motivation—how do motives explain actions?" I have argued that the concept is a construct and it systematizes the data to be explained. It brings together data that initially appear unrelated. It also works heuristically, extending the data, linking up new data, and assimilating the latter. Motives achieve conceptual functions as well. Characteristically, new explanatory concepts are modeled upon concepts already in explanatory use. Further, theoretical constructs achieve a spatio-temporal continuity between the past causes and current behavior.

A fundamental point made (Chapter 6) is that the very meaning of "motive" (in ordinary and psychoanalytic use) is constituted by its explanatory role. Motive is a concept set within a theory. Its relations to other concepts within the theory, and to behavioral and experiential concepts, give its content. I illustrated this by use of a device: unpacking the motive concept in terms of a series of hypotheticals. The hypotheticals give the conditions under which the term is used.

8

EPISTEMOLOGICAL ASPECTS OF THE PSYCHOANALYTIC CONCEPT OF MOTIVATION

My concern in this chapter is with the epistemological status of the psychoanalytic concept of motive: How does psychoanalytic theory say we get to know our own and others' motives, and what is the status of that knowledge?

Ascriptions of motives are explanations of behavior in the same way as postulations of the existence and operation of theoretical constructs are. It then follows that we get to know motives—particularly but not only the unconscious motives of which psychoanalysis speaks—in the same way we get to know the theoretical processes of science; that is, the knowledge we have of motives is indirectly gained. Further, knowledge claims about even one's own motives are corrigible and can be justified only indirectly. This approach accords with that of Freud. Psychoanalytic theory implicitly contains a theory of knowledge of minds, a characterization of how we know our own mental states. In some ways psychoanalysis is all about how we both know and often refuse to know what our motives are. In this it deals with two features that any adequate theory of motivation must concern itself with: (1) the apparent certainty with which a person can get to know his mental state; and (2) the fact that individuals may be unconscious of their motives.

In Chapter 5, I outlined the main epistemological features of theoretical constructs:

1. Theoretical constructs are, in the first place, postulated on the basis of evidence.
2. Our method of gaining knowledge of constructs is indirect.
3. Knowledge gained of theoretical constructs is, in the first place, less sure than that which we may gain of observables.
4. Knowledge claims about constructs are justified indirectly, by testing the consequences that flow from their postulation.

The first of these epistemological features has to do with the setting up of the constructs, the second with how we may gain knowledge of them, the third with the quality of our knowledge of them, and the fourth with our justification of the constructs. I will deal with these in turn.

EVIDENCE FOR MOTIVES

In the case of general science—for example, in physics—it is clear that we know about postulated processes via evidence. Returning to the example of "electric charge" (Chapter 6), we know that a body is charged if certain evidential criteria are met. The early and simple version of the theory of electricity stated that these criteria are a charged body's capacity to attract and to repel certain materials, to spark to earthed bodies, and so on. The hypotheticals state these evidential conditions. If a body does behave in these ways, then we know that it is electrically charged.

Motives, conscious and unconscious, are the same. When we ascribe motives to persons, including ourselves, we do so to explain behavior. We are saying that the state a person is in, called having such and such a motive, is responsible for the behavior we wish to explain. It is also taken to be responsible for phenomena that are often not strictly behavioral, and which are not currently open to third-person inspection. Phenomenological events associated with a particular motive are in this last category. So, too, are future behaviors about to ensue from having that motive. When, for example, we describe someone as jealous, there are various behaviors that we want to explain and that lead to this hypothesis. These are, say, that a person is angry and depressed, he argues with his partner, that he is hostile to his rival, and so on. Once we suppose on these grounds that a person is jealous, then other predictions flow from this supposition. We expect a person to admit, at least to a confidant, that he is jealous, and to say that he hates his rival, and we might expect his sexual performance to deteriorate, or that he loses his sexual appetite, and that he experiences a knot in his stomach.

As with the electricity case, we are not able to open up the body (the brain of the individual) and observe that he is in this motivational state. But, where there is no straightforward observation available of the postulated mechanism at work, we know that it is there through evidence.

Now, this fits the case of knowing another's motives quite easily. It also allows for the fact that in judging another's motives we do not have to rely on that person's awareness of the motive. For, as long as there is evidence, it does not matter if the owner of the motive perceives it or not. Indeed, in the case of an unconscious motive it is often the denial of that motive that serves as evidence for its presence. But the view that I am putting forward treats *first-person motive ascriptions as possessing basically the same logic as third-person ascriptions*. In both cases a logically corrigible explanation is being offered to account for behavior. When I say that I am jealous, this is an explanation of my behavior (and experience) in essentially the same way that another might explain my behavior by saying I am jealous. It is then not, as some have held, that though I can doubt another's motives, I cannot doubt my own. This means my knowledge of my own and others' motives is based on evidence, as is my knowledge of the processes postulated in other sciences.

Of course there are, as a matter of fact, some differences between the way I discover my own motives and the way another discovers them. If I am jealous then another will use my behavior—what I say (and what I deny), how I act toward my lover and my lover's lover—my distraction, and so on as evidence for my jealousy. I, too, may use some of these criteria in coming to the conclusion that I am jealous. But I do usually have other things to go on, for example, my feelings, and activities within me that are not normally available to others. This brings us to another part of the problem: What serves as evidence for motive ascriptions? For it is not obvious that when I attribute a motive to myself it is done on the basis of evidence, and if motives are to pass as theoretical constructs, there must be some sort of evidence involved in motive ascriptions. Now, it cannot be that it is simply my behaviors, or certain sensations, that serve as evidence for my recognizing my motive. However, the notion of evidence does not have to be taken simplistically. Here I want to take as evidence any *events, states, or processes upon the detection of which may be based knowledge of other events, states, or processes.*

The detection of evidential events, states, and processes does not have to be conscious. A person may come to the knowledge of some phenomenon without being aware of what it was that led him there. The practicing natural scientist will often talk about "seeing" something that is very much a theoretical entity. He will "see" a large molecule via an electron microscope, or "see" a subatomic particle pass through a bubble chamber. The scientist makes no conscious apprehension of, or inference from, evidence before him, but makes claims directly about theoretical objects. That he passes over conscious awareness of the evidence to the theoretical object is an indication of the trust he has in the theory that links the evidential with the inferred states. This in turn depends on, among other things, the demonstrated capacity of the theory to give good explanations of all sorts of physical phenomena. The psychological situation is similar. There are events, states, and processes that occur within the individual. These are detected and serve as the basis for knowledge of motives.

Having a Motive

Having a motive such as jealousy, anger, hunger, or an unconscious wish is not a simple unitary state of the individual. The complexity of the behavioral repertoire associated with even the simplest motive indicates this. Yet, so long as a person has a motive, there are going to be a variety of states and processes that mark the differences between having that motive and not having it. These states are both psychological and physiological. Experimental work indicates that at least for some basic motivational processes like aggression, hunger, and thirst, there are physiologically identifiable factors associated with them, albeit in a complex way. In the case of hunger, the peripheral cues of gastric motility, stomach distension, and blood sugar level are such factors. In addition, the lateral nuclei of the hypothalamus serve some part in the detection and processing of hunger cues that are carried neurally and in the blood. To these normally invisible factors we can add the behavioral ones associated with hunger. These then are the various sorts of factors that are candidates for evidence for motives.

Freud's theory of motivation does not, obviously, take into account modern research findings on the physiology of motivation. Yet the general theory is based on the idea that there are states of the organism—ultimately physiological—that mark the difference between having some motive and not having it. The actual physiological processes involved do not matter. The principle does.

A rough outline of what goes on when one has, and knows one has, a particular motive would be as follows: An individual is in a certain motivational state. This is a more or less complex state of his central nervous system and physiology. In his central nervous system he possesses a mechanism that receives information about the state. This information may be in the form of feedback from perceptions of his own behavior, or from sensations, or from his proprioceptors. It might be from blood-borne humoral indicators or from changes in the environment of the hypothalamic nuclei. None of these is singly sufficient to indicate the particular motivational state, but the information, synthesized by the mechanism and integrated with information from memory and other mental functions, is usually adequate to do so. As a result of this synthesis an individual may or may not, depending on his attention, become aware of his motive.

There are several points to note about this sketch of what it is to have a motive:

1. The individual's knowledge of his motive state is the outcome of a construction, and the foundation of this construction is the detection of various cues. This complex, constructive function is virtually a universal feature of human psychological processes. In simple visual perception, for example, there is construction even at the retinal stage. The individual is not necessarily, or even usually, conscious of the elements of the construction. This does not just apply to the introspection of motives. It also applies to perception where an individual sees "wholes" such as faces or even angry faces, but does not consciously apprehend the detailed features of the face. In addition, he may be unable to say what it was that gave rise to his total perception. He could see an angry face, but not consciously know that the rapid constriction of the pupils was a basic cue in gaining this piece of knowledge.

2. The construction of an individual's motive knowledge can depend on very complex processes, be influenced by a large number of factors, and hence be subject to error. One of Freud's contributions to the theory of motivation was showing just how some of one's motives affect the perception of other of one's motives. The individual may falsely perceive his own behavior, misled by his motives to do so. An example of the misrecognition of motives comes from the Wolf Man case. Wolf Man sees his state as a fear of wolves. His motive, Freud argues, is otherwise. It is a fear of castration, the consequence of adopting a feminine attitude toward his father.

Returning to experimental work on the recognition of mental states, Schachter and Singer (1962) studied the effects of different cognitions on subjects' reactions to injections of epinepherine (an adrenalinlike substance). Subjects in happy company perceived their drug-induced state of arousal as happy. Those in hostile company perceived it as angry. Schachter and Singer argue from this that motive perception is an intepretative process. One can at least say that perception of a motive is established on more cues than mere physical arousal, and that miscognition is possible.

3. There is a distinction between having a motive and con-

sciously knowing one has that motive. Having a motive consists of being in a particular state that produces energized and directed activities. Knowing one's motive is another matter. There are several types of discrepancy possible between having and knowing a motive. One is where the cues are misinterpreted because the individual has not been taught to identify his motives very well. Hunger and anxiety can be confused, for example. This happens with small children who may be fed by parents instead of being comforted by them, and then as adults eat when they are upset. In such cases the person believes himself to be hungry yet is really anxious. Another discrepancy arises in the case of simple repression. A person has a particular motive, say the unconscious homosexual wish of Wolf Man, and behaves accordingly. However, he does not know this, at least not in any conscious way. This is the case that Freud's theory emphasizes. In metapsychological terms, conscious hypercathexis is withheld from the wish and it does not reach conscious awareness.

So if I have a motive, I may or may not know it. And if I do know it, I may or may not know it consciously. There are degrees, and I may not be able to articulate it in that self-aware way that makes it conscious.

4. The confidence that we place in our self-perceptions derives not from the fact that we cannot be wrong about our motives, but from the fact that we are taught how to interpret the inner signs efficiently. For example, a child gets told that he is jealous when certain internal and external conditions obtain. His teachers do not know if and when a certain set of neurons in the central nervous system are firing, or what his blood chemistry is like at the time. However, they observe the behavior of the child and label it jealousy—they are using the "theoretical" concept of jealousy to explain the child's activities. The child perceives both the internal and external conditions as jealousy. He learns that a certain configuration of behavior perceptions, internal stimuli, and subjective states indicate jealousy. He can then identify his motive as well as he has been taught, providing other psychological processes do not lead to a misconstrual of the evidential configuration of stimuli.

5. The individual's motivational processes are essentially non-

conscious. Being aware of one's motives, or misreading them, does not constitute the motive. Consciously knowing one's motives is a secondary, reflective process. Knowing is, however, a psychological property just as much as is being motivated and, since psychological processes (such as knowing, hoping, believing, wanting) all interact, then knowing about a motive can affect one's motivations.

Freud on the Inferential Knowledge of Motives

The account I have so far given is not explicitly Freudian. Yet on examination it maps neatly onto Freud's account of motivation in a number of respects.

First, for Freud, having a motive is being in a particular state. This state is a compound of physiological factors, such as somatic needs, of memory structure, and of energy distribution in the brain. This state may be described in psychological terms, but ultimately it is a material one.

Second, Freud's account of motivation, like the outline above, is "constructivist." In this he is similar to modern cognitive psychology in his approach to higher-order mental functions. (This similarity is discussed at length by Pribram and Gill, 1976, especially Chapters 2 and 3.) This means that Freud, like modern cognitive psychologists, argues that lower-order input into the central nervous system is gathered and synthesized by higher-order mechanisms—such as an executive ego. For Freud, psychological functions such as thinking, judging, and attending take place in this manner. So too does motivation. This should be apparent from the discussion in Part I. For example, in the Project model, which is the formal basis for the later psychoanalytic models, the motivational process involves the energizing of various elements in the memory system. The energy comes from somatic sources. But, before these cathected memories (wishes) actually result in behavior, a complex regulatory process takes place. The wishes are detected, matched against reality, and tested for their anxiety-releasing properties. All this is done by an executive ego through a complex feedback system (a detailed discussion of this is given by Pribram and Gill, 1976,

Chapters 1, 2, and 3). This is in fact a synthesis of information by the ego mechanism. It has to take place before action ensues.

Third, consciously knowing the motive is distinct from having the motive. The whole motivational process is essentially aconscious. As discussed in Part I, for Freud consciousness is only an outgrowth of a mental system that is basically an aconscious motivational system. It is only when an attentional cathexis is given to the particular wish that it becomes conscious. This is a stage further than simple motivation. But similarly it is a constructivist account of attention that Freud gives. The person can be consciously aware of his motive only through appropriate synthesis of information by the attentional mechanism (above, Chapters 2, 3, 4; Freud 1895a, pp. 360ff.).

Fourth, Freud's own comments on our knowledge of mental states shows that this account is compatible with, and indeed very similar to, the theoretical construct account I am advocating. These comments are scattered throughout his writings. In the Project, for example, Freud argues that we cannot know everything about our psyche through the medium of conscious inspection, and what we do know about the unconscious mind must be known through inference:

> We at once become clear about a postulate which has been guiding us up to now. We have been treating psychical processes as something that could dispense with this awareness through consciousness, as something that exists independently of such awareness. We are prepared to find that some of our assumptions are not confirmed through consciousness. If we do not let ourselves be confused on that account, it follows, from the postulate of consciousness providing neither complete nor trustworthy knowledge of the neuronal process, that these are in the first instance to be regarded to their whole extent as unconscious and are to be inferred like other natural things [1895a, p. 308].

This approach, however, does not belong only to his early, neuropsychological, work. Later (1900) he makes the same point:

> The physician cannot learn of these unconscious processes until they have produced some effect upon consciousness which can be communicated or observed. But this conscious effect may

exhibit a psychical character quite different from that of the unconscious process, so that internal perception cannot possibly regard the one as a substitute for the other. The physician must feel at liberty to proceed by *inference* from the conscious effect to the unconscious psychical process. He thus learns that the conscious effect is only a remote psychical result of the unconscious process and . . . that the latter was present and operative even without betraying its existence in any way to consciousness [p. 612].

And a little later:

The unconscious is the true psychical reality; *in its innermost nature it is as much unknown to us as the reality of the external world, and it is as incompletely presented by the data of consciousness as is the external world by the communications of our sense organs* [p. 613].

In this latter quotation Freud is again saying that knowledge of unconscious processes is inferential. He is also going further to say that in this respect it is the same as our knowledge of the external world in general. Later still (1915c) he also argues that unconscious processes are postulates and, further, that it is quite normal to make such inferences even in our ordinary use of mental concepts:

The assumption of an unconscious is, moreover, a perfectly *legitimate* one, inasmuch as in postulating it we are not departing a single step from our customary and generally accepted mode of thinking. . . . That other people . . . possess a consciousness is an inference [p. 169].

Yet he adopts a realist view of inferred processes (see Chapter 9, below).

From these passages several points about Freud's philosophy of psychology are apparent: (1) he deliberately sets up his theoretical mental concepts as postulates to explain puzzles in the data—he considers these puzzles unresolvable without such assumptions because they bring meaning and order into the data; (2) knowledge of such theoretical processes is gained through inference—so, however, ordinary knowledge of minds is also inferential; (3) and it is normal for science to make such inferences beyond the immediate data.

INDIRECT KNOWLEDGE

If knowledge of motives is gained via evidence, it is mediate knowledge, knowledge based on inference. And when we infer we pass from knowledge of one state of affairs to knowledge of another. In this case we pass from knowing the evidential cues to knowing the motives. But at least superficially it seems doubtful whether the events, states, and processes that I have termed "evidence" can really be said to be "known" at all. In what sense does one know the various physiological cues on which the synthesis of motive perception is based?

There is a common, but mistaken, assumption here that has to be countered if this view (that knowledge of motives is indirect) is to survive. This assumption is that there is an important distinction to be made between what is causally indirect and what is epistemologically mediate. It is conceded that perceiving something—including one's motives—is causally indirect, simply because it is obvious that there are complex causal processes involved, and a great deal does go on between a stimulus and a percept. However, the assumption is that, whatever causal processes are involved in the introspection, there is no inference involved. There is no passage, it is assumed, from knowledge of the supposedly evidential states to knowledge of the motives. This is because the evidential states mentioned above cannot be said to be known. They may be detected by brain processor systems, but not known.

A look at this view shows up a weak presupposition within it. This presupposition says that what makes knowledge either mediate or immediate is how it appears in consciousness. It says that what makes an item of knowledge immediate is that it appeared immediately in consciousness. The converse is supposed, too: what would make it mediate would be that it is derived from something that is immediately in consciousness. In short, it holds that the criterion for something being knowledge is that it is conscious.

However, an individual does not have to be explicitly conscious of things that he knows. There are several kinds of counter example: an individual might reasonably be said to have a tacit knowledge of the rules of the language that he speaks, yet not be capable of articulating those. And where a person engages in self-deception, there is a real sense in which he knows something of which he is not aware. This is unconscious knowledge. Further, it is sensible to say that a person knows those features of a face that inform him that it is angry, yet he might be consciously unaware of these features. Such knowledge does not appear in consciousness, yet it is used in the perception of the angry face.

There is some philosophical argument that knowledge might be analyzable as justified true belief, or some variant of this. However, the property of "having knowledge of X," where X is the sort of phenomenon that is information for an individual about his motivational state, is a psychological property and must be analyzable as such. This means that the sort of thing that we should want to say about knowing is this: *To have knowledge of internal phenomena such as those I have termed "evidence" for motives is to be able to detect these phenomena and make complex responses to their presence.*

Of course, to give an adequate account of the psychology of knowing, we should have to refine this description a great deal and to specify what is the universal case of knowing. Simply responding to a drop in peripheral temperature with hair erection would, I think, not count as knowing the stimuli involved. Being able to correct one's balance on a tightrope from the proprioceptive stimuli perhaps would involve knowledge. What is crucial here is the notion of complexity. Ultimately it is a level and type of cerebral organization that characterizes the responses that one makes to internal phenomena as "knowledge of evidence," rather than simply "responses to stimuli." It does not have anything to do with consciousness, in the self-reflective sense of that notion.

We ascribe knowledge of certain states of affairs to individuals much as we do motives: to explain and predict their behavior with respect to the things of which they are said to have knowledge. We say a person "knew" that there was a cat in the road because we observed him maneuver his car around the animal. We thereby explain (at least in part) his behavior with respect to the cat. Similarly, it is a partial explanation of an individual's behavior with respect to internal processes when we say he has knowledge of them. As an explanation it tells us that he can make certain kinds of complex responses to those sort of stimuli, that they are situationally appropriate, capable of modification by learning, and so on, regardless of whether the knowledge is conscious or not.

Knowledge, like motive, may be treated as a theoretical construct. It is part of the theories that we entertain every day, and sometimes it is part of psychological theories such as Piaget's. The meaning of "knowledge" could be explicated by reference to the sort of behavior that we take as evidence for knowing, and the complex central nervous system processes involved in an act of knowing. The events, states, and processes upon whose detection our knowledge of our own motives is based are themselves possible objects of knowledge, even though this is not conscious. They count as such because we can learn to make the complex sort of responses to them that we would normally call "knowing," except for its unconscious nature.

Infinite Regress of Knowledge

A problem arises: If motives are inferred from knowledge of evidential phenomena, then are these evidential phenomena themselves known by inference? If they are, then what of the evidence for them? Is *that* evidence also known on inference? We seem threatened with an infinite regress of knowledge. The question is, are we forced to stay this threat by admitting that there is noninferential, direct, knowledge? There is no short and clear answer to this problem. But something of a solution may be found in a closer look at where the regress leads.

The approach I have taken, and this fits with the experimental evidence, is that the person comes to his knowledge through a complex processing of information that takes place in the brain and nervous system. This process may be considered to be an informational hierarchy. At each level, from the bottom to the top, information is taken and processed, and serves as data for the next level of processing. At some levels in this hierarchy the information is "known." For example, take the case where a person observes a face, and knows it is an angry face. He can be said to know, albeit unconsciously, the features of the face from which he inferred this knowledge, and this act of inference is a piece of information processing. However, as we move to a lower level in this hierarchy, we are less certain of ascribing to the person knowledge of the information being processed. For example, does the person "know," and then proceed to infer from, the angles subtended at the retina by the various facial features? I think not. Similarly the person cannot be said to be "inferring" in very basic levels of synthesizing in the nervous system—as, for example, when information on these angles and that from proprioceptors are integrated to give perceptual object permanency.

The same applies to the case of motivational knowledge. However, in that case, things are further complicated by the fact that, as we enter into the causal minutiae of the processes of knowing, we even lose sight of what is the known and who is the knower. This further degrades our ability to say when something is known in the ordinary sense of "know."

Thus it hardly matters whether or not the threatened infinite regress of knowledge is stopped by admitting a point where there is direct knowledge. The important point is rather that the basis of knowledge is not itself knowledge. And, at some low level in the information-processing hierarchy, we have to say that the passage from this basic information to slightly higher levels of information is not inference. This problem of "infinite regress" in mental explanation is perennial. It is a major part of Ryle's (1949) criticism of "intellectualism" (mentalism). Armstrong (1973a) also raises it. The solution I am suggesting is similar to those of Fodor (1968b) and of Dennett (1978b) in that I am arguing that the regress is stopped because each "regressive" step of explanation is to a level of simpler analysis, until basic and unanalyzable units are reached.

This matter is complicated further: the problem is part of a much wider one, that of the basis of scientific knowledge. There, too, we have to ask if anything is known noninferentially. Here we must say that every item of knowledge is contaminated with theory—a point often made in the philosophy of science literature (for example, Hesse, 1970; Feyerabend, 1975; Maxwell, 1962). So, at least in this sense, all knowledge depends on other knowledge for its establishment.

CERTAIN KNOWLEDGE

There is a puzzle about this theoretical construct analysis of motive knowledge, a puzzle often raised in considering psychoanalytic motive theory: motives can be known, at least sometimes, with a certainty that theoretical knowledge would seemingly preclude. Any analysis of motivation has to come to grips with this. Also, psychoanalysis presents us with the problem that motives can be unconscious and yet, when known, can be known with apparent certainty. The sense of certainty can be accounted for in the following way.

I emphasized above, in the preliminaries to Part II, in outlining the features of theoretical constructs, that they do not have a fixed epistemological status. In certain circumstances what we call a theoretical construct may be known with apparent certainty. In this sense, I simply know that there are molecules, and that the different properties of different molecules account in part for straightforward, observable qualities like elasticity and brittleness. Now, the certainty of knowledge a person may have of the presence and operation of a particular hypothetical mechanism (not logical certainty) depends, in general, on the power of the theory that posits it. In a particular case, it depends both on the power of the theory and the fit of the particular circumstances of the case with those that the theory has been shown to account for adequately. This concept of the power of a theory is intuitively easy to understand, but harder to specify exactly. Roughly, it is the capacity of the theory to organize the data, predict new facts, gel with other powerful theories, to perform various explanatory functions, and to perform certain conceptual functions. These latter conceptual functions are such things as giving "elegant" answers to problems and postulating mechanisms that bridge the temporal or spatial gap between cause and effects (see Chapter 6).

The certainty that I have of my own motives can be explained in similar terms. As a matter of fact, the kind of information I have about my own motives is usually reliable. I have learned to interpret the internal and external stimuli well. When I say I am jealous, for example, this self-explanatory statement sets the facts into a coherent whole and also predicts certain phenomena. It links my sensations of stomach clenching, weariness in my joints, flushes of anger, hostility toward my rival, and so on. It also predicts such things, perhaps, as sleeplessness and loss of sexual appetite. In addition, it coheres with other things about me—that I am in love, that I am possessive, and probably with my early experiences in coping with loss of loved objects. The capacity of past ascriptions of jealousy to self and others to bring coherence and understanding to otherwise diverse phenomena is the basis for my current certainty. Of course, the special range of information I have about my own jealousy—I am not dependent solely on observing my own behavior — reinforces the reliability of my self-knowledge. I am certain about my own motives, not because there is a logical guarantor to the truth of my self-knowledge claims, but because of the power of our everyday theory about motivation and the range of information available to me about my state.

The ascription of a motive in psychoanalysis is essentially the same. The psychoanalytic motive concept is continuous with the everyday concept. Both are equally explanatory in nature. The difference lies in the fact that the contexts for their uses are different. Also, since the use of motive attributions is so fundamental to our ordinary understanding of ourselves and others, we come to be very sure of our everyday "theory" of motivation. In fact, we get the sense of certainty that we have about our common motives. Psychoanalytic theory attempts a further characterization of motives, but of course it does not, in normal circumstances, achieve the same certainty in its characterization. It is more theoretical and less surely based on the everyday theory of motivation. There is, though, no necessity about this. There is no logical reason why a scientific theory should not displace or alter our everyday theory of motivation or of anything else. The ordinary person understands his physical and biological environment differently from his counterpart of a few hundred years ago. This is because physical and biological theory have affected our everyday concepts.

This bears on the matter of avowal raised briefly in Chapter 6. There is no certainty that a person who has a particular motive knows it, or is able to get to know it. So there is no necessity that if someone has a particular wish that he can avow it. In the spelling out of the term "wish" there were hypotheticals that made reference to the capacity of the owner of the wish to avow the wish. (B9: If a person wishes for X then, if asked, he will say he wants X.) Such hypotheticals cannot be analytically true. There is no logically guaranteed privileged access to the person's own motive state.

My argument here relates to a major debate in philosophical psychology springing largely from Wittgenstein's views on mental predicates and the "private language" argument (1958). My skeptical position on motivational predicates contradicts "Wittgensteinian" arguments that say a person simply knows (McGuinness, 1956–1957)—or at least can get to know (Dilman, 1972)—his own motives, and that to say otherwise makes no linguistic sense. Wittgenstein's analysis of the "pain" words is, I believe, an inadequate paradigm for analyzing motive ascriptions. I am arguing against any analysis that requires that there be behaviors, including utterances, whose occurrence logically entails ("expresses") the mental state. The whole thrust of the theoretical construct approach is that mental states are contingently related to behavioral expressions of them. This allows for unconsciousness of motives.

TESTING KNOWLEDGE CLAIMS ABOUT MOTIVES

The foregoing analysis asserts that we know motives indirectly. It follows that the truth of knowledge claims about motives must also be assessed indirectly, for we cannot inspect motives directly to verify or falsify knowledge claims about them. In a theoretical construct analysis, the truth of any claim about a theoretical process is measured by the capacity of that postulated process to explain the facts well. That is, we can justifiably say that a person has a particular motive—say, an unconscious homosexual wish—if this postulation performs well its explanatory role.

The sketch that I am giving of what it is to know a motive is a pragmatist one. The scientist (psychologist) attempts to characterize an aspect of reality, in this case motives. This happens in the general case, as where Freud develops a theory of motivation, and it happens in the particular case, where this general theory is used in giving a specific motive attribution to an individual like Wolf Man. The characterization might be better or worse. We only know how good it is by its explanatory performance—not an easy matter to judge. Inasmuch as it characterizes the motive well (explains the data well), we know something of that motive.

SUMMARY

At the beginning of this section I stated two features that any adequate theory of motivation must deal with. These were (1) the apparent certainty with which a person can get to know his mental state; and (2) the fact that an individual may be unconscious of his motives. These two would seem to be in contradiction. The first represents our ordinary experience; we do seem to know what we want with immediacy and certainty. The second represents another insight, greatly enlarged by psychoanalysis, that we may be unconscious of our motives. The psychoanalytic theory of motivation, considered within this theoretical construct approach, assimilates both the first and the second: we know our own and others' motives via evidence, just as we know theoretical constructs.

9

ONTOLOGICAL ASPECTS OF THE PSYCHOANALYTIC CONCEPT OF MOTIVATION

FREUD AND REALISM

In the material that I have so far presented, I have avoided explicit discussion of ontological questions about the motive concept in psychoanalysis. Instead, I have merely argued that the psychoanalytic concept of motivation is a "theoretical construct" both in the way it explains the data and in the way that it is known. Yet clearly the line I have pursued is a scientific realism; the theoretical terms of psychoanalysis name inferred mental states, and inferred mental states both exist and are causally related to behavior. The next step in this theory of causal inference is to make explicit and to justify the realism already implied. In this chapter I shall deal with questions about the ontological status of the psychoanalytic concept of motivation: Do such motives really exist? Do they cause behavior?

Theories as Descriptions

Theoretical constructs are descriptive in the sense that they are attempted characterizations of the (initially unseen) causes of observed phenomena. Returning to the example from biology that I used in Chapter 6, the germ concept was set up as a characterization of the entity that causes various observed phenomena—the souring of milks, degeneration of wines, septicity, and so on. The theory does not merely postulate that germs exist, it attempts to characterize them. Of course, the characterization may change—as it clearly has done in the bacteria case—without the existence of the entity coming into question. The germ concept was, and still is, a descriptive one. In addition to this existential assumption there is a second feature to note about such causal inference; the concept of the germ is a construction upon the basis of a model. The very term "germ" indicates the model: the postulated cause of the observed effects must be like organic individuals, living and, above all, reproducing. The physical sciences abound with examples where entities or processes are postulated in order to account for observed phenomena. They are modeled on familiar processes, on the assumption that like effect results from like cause. We may be equally realistic about psychoanalytic concepts, not in the sense that psychoanalysis necessarily gives the correct characterizations of mental processes, the causes of behavior, but that they are attempted characterizations of real processes.

FREUD ON EXPLANATION

Here we turn to the way in which Freud regards his own concepts:

1. How he regards them as scientific in the same way as the concepts of other sciences
2. How he recognizes them as conventional but not arbitrary
3. How he regards them as uncertain and subject to revision
4. How in spite of this he retains the view that they are descriptions of real, causal processes

All these views are part of Freud's realism.

On the Concepts of Science and Psychoanalysis

Freud often uses examples from physics to illustrate and justify the methods of psychoanalysis. Implicit in this is the idea
that they are both essentially the same: they are both sciences.
He tells us (1915a) that the basic concepts of psychoanalysis
may be conventional and subject to change, but then so are
those of other sciences: "Physics furnishes an excellent illustration of the way in which even 'basic concepts' that have been
established in the form of definitions are constantly being altered in their content" (p. 117). Yet, though he stresses the
hypothetical nature of the concepts in the above quote, he is
always ready to assert that the unconscious processes of which
psychoanalysis speaks are real. Thus he says, in criticism of
Janet's views, that Janet talks as though he "wanted to admit
that the unconscious had been nothing more to him than a
form of words, a makeshift, *une façon de parler*—that he meant
nothing real by it" (Freud, 1916–1917, p. 257). Since Janet
adopted this instrumentalist viewpoint, Freud declares, he has
"ceased to understand Janet's writings"!

In virtually Freud's last word on these metatheoretical matters (1940a), he makes the same equation between the concepts
of physics and those of psychoanalysis. He argues that the idea
that there can be a psychology of unconscious processes has
"enabled psychology to take its place as a natural science like
any other" (p. 158). Freud goes on to say that psychoanalysis'
" 'understanding' of the field of natural phenomena" could not
have been

> effected without framing fresh hypotheses and creating fresh
> concepts; but these are not to be despised as evidence of em-
> barrassment on our part but deserve on the contrary to be ap-
> preciated as an enrichment of science. They can lay claim to the
> same value as approximations that belong to the corresponding
> intellectual scaffolding found in other natural sciences, and we
> look forward to their being modified, corrected and more pre-
> cisely determined as further experience is accumulated and
> sifted. So too it will be entirely in accordance with our expecta-
> tions if the basic concepts and principles of the new science (in-
> stinct, nervous energy, etc.) remain for a considerable time no

less indeterminate than those of the older sciences (force, mass, attraction, etc.) [pp. 158–159].

Freud is arguing here that his mental model is a necessary and normal part of science. Its concepts are putative characterizations (approximations) of (natural) mental processes just as are those of physics. Yet at the same time Freud is quite clear on the hypothetical, tentative nature of his theoretical concepts. The concepts are "indeterminate," and further evidence is needed to bring about a more precise and accurate characterization. So Freud's perspective on his own theoretical formulations shows a balance between scientific realism and the realization that such concepts are only putative characterizatons of those real processes. This is the very essence of the "theoretical construct" approach I have been taking.

On Models

Freud arrives at these theoretical constructs—his characterizations of mental processes—through the use of models. In Chapter 2, I outlined the models he uses. Freud draws upon the then current theories of nervous functioning, and the theories of physics, chemistry, and evolutionary biology. At first he thinks that these theories do not have to be used analogously. At the time of the Project (Freud, 1895a), for example, he tries to refer directly to neural events to explain behavioral phenomena. But later he retains the formal, though not the substantive, similarities between the concepts of psychoanalysis and the natural sciences. His mental energy concept, for example, is modeled on the physical concept and is formally like the latter, but mental and physical energy are not the same thing. At times Freud is quite explicit about the way his concepts are built up through metaphor and analogy. When he first introduces the topographical version of his theory (1900, p. 536) he says he is going to "follow the suggestion that we should picture the instrument which carries out our mental functions as resembling a compound microscope or a photographic apparatus, or something of the kind. On that basis psychical locality will correspond to a point inside the apparatus." A little later he says: "Analogies of this kind are only intended to assist us in our attempt to make the complications of mental functioning intelligible by dissecting the function and assigning its different constituents to different component parts of the apparatus."

Elsewhere, discussing the theory of the instincts, he comments that psychoanalysis is obliged "to operate with the scientific terms, that is to say with the *figurative language,* peculiar to psychology" (1920, p. 60, italics added). He goes on to say, however, that the physical or chemical terminology that may one day replace this figurative terminology of psychology is also "only part of a figurative language; but it is one with which we have long been familiar and which is perhaps a simpler one as well." So he argues that the well-established physical sciences have to use models (figures) to construct their concepts no less than does psychology. He seems only a short step away from the more recent philosophy of science that says models are an essential and inevitable part of the scientific theory itself.

On Causation

The various models upon which Freud bases the construction of his theory are causal in the typical "hard science" way. They are theories about the causes of the phenomena they have to explain. This characteristic is carried over into Freud's theory. For Freud, mental processes postulated to explain behavior are causally related to that behavior. This is exactly as in those hard sciences from which Freud draws his models. The causal nature of psychoanalysis emerges often in a treatment of his basic mental models (see Chapters 2, 3, 4). It is an inherent part of the ideas that Freud incorporated into his theory, ideas such as that mind is lawful and determined in every aspect, that mind is a part of nature and to be explained by use of the concepts of force and energy, that the patterns of thought are based upon associations, that even the directionality of purposeful activity is derived from the directionality of a purely causal and intentionless process—instinct.

MULTIPLE CAUSATION

To understand Freud's theory of causation we must again recall the tripartite motivation concept, exemplified in the notion of wish that I have discussed already. In Freud's motivation theory all of three kinds of factor—directing, energizing, and precipitating—have to be given for a complete motivational account. Each of these is a causal factor.

Sometimes the mention of only one of the factors will suffice as an adequate explanation. This is because what makes an explanation adequate depends on the context in which it is given. An event has many causes, but one or more of these may be singled out as *the* cause(s). Which factor is elevated to the status of the cause depends on the context of the explanation and on what causal information is already known. Particular explanations, such as those that Freud gives in his case studies, are designed to resolve puzzles that arise out of the data.

At some stages of the clinical account the mere statement of the directing factor resolves the current puzzle. Thus Freud answers the puzzle about Wolf Man's dream by giving only a directional factor (the purpose that Wolf Man unconsciously entertains): "the wish for sexual satisfaction which he was at that time longing to obtain from the father" (1918, p. 35). For Freud's requirements at that moment, this unconscious aim can be said to be "the" cause. But clearly, in a slightly different context, Freud may select another of the causes as the focus of explanatory attention. In fact he does so, for at another point in the case study, when he is trying to deal with a different aspect of the dream's etiology, he gives an energizing factor as the dream explanation: what determines the dream is Wolf Man's "sexual organization (instinct)" in a masochistic form (p. 46). In each of these two cases Freud is addressing himself to a different problem, though they both form part of the overall clinical account. And in each case Freud offers, as "the" motivating cause of the anxiety dream, only one of the factor types involved in a full motivational explanation. These are ellipses that stand for the complete explanations.

Freud does not offer an explanation of the dream that mentions only the precipitating event (though he does mention some factors that precipitate the dream such as the anticipation of Christmas, an event of special psychological significance for Wolf Man; p. 35). However, he does explain the character change in Wolf Man by referring simply to an event that precipitated the change: "his sister had seduced him" (p. 20).

While it is true that Freud assumes multiple causation in his motivational explanations, it is also true that he explicitly argues for the view that psychological phenomena have multiple causes. The best-known example of this is his theory of the overdetermination of symptoms: "the principal feature in the aetiology of the neuroses . . . (is) that their genesis is as a rule overdetermined, that several factors must come together to produce this result" (Breuer and Freud, 1895, p. 263). By this Freud means that for a symptom there are generally two or more sets of causal conditions. These sets of conditions are jointly sufficient to produce the symptom. It is not, as psychoanalysts have often taken it, that an overdetermined symptom is one determined by several sets of singly sufficient causes.

Elsewhere, Freud explicitly sets out a theory of multiple causation, of what makes up the "aetiological equation" for neurosis. In this analysis he shows that he is clearly aware that (1) a psychological phenomenon may be multiply determined, and that (2) one may distinguish between a variety of combinations of causal factors: necessary, sufficient, sometimes necessary, jointly necessary, jointly sufficient, and so on. Freud's surprisingly sophisticated and philosophically subtle analysis of causation is thoroughly treated by Sherwood (1969, Chapter 5). But briefly, Freud (1895b) points to four types of causal factor:

> The *precipitating* or releasing cause [is] the one which makes its appearance last in the equation, so that it immediately precedes the emergence of the effect. . . .
> The factors which may be described as *preconditions* are those in whose absence the effect would never come about, but which are incapable of producing the effect by themselves alone. . . .
> The *specific cause* is the one which is never missing in any case in which the effect takes place, and which moreover suffices, if present in the required quantity or intensity, to achieve the effect, provided only that the preconditions are also filled.
> As *concurrent causes* we may regard such factors as are not

necessarily present every time, nor able, whatever their amount, to produce the effect by themselves alone [pp. 135–136].

These must jointly occur to make up a complete "aetiological equation" and hence produce the neurotic disturbance. The precipitating cause may be any of the other types, but it is defined by being the completing factor in the equation. As Sherwood (1969) points out, Freud is arguing that causes are

(1) complex, in the sense of there being a set of causal factors, and (2) multiple, in the sense of there being various possible sets of sufficient conditions. Furthermore, the causal factors, while being equally necessary, nevertheless can show variation in their quantitative strength or importance [p. 173].

FREUD AND THE MIND-BRAIN RELATION

For Freud the mental processes, events, and entities that psychoanalysis postulates are causes of behavior, and they are real. But in what does their reality consist? What *are* they? Freud's answer is a materialist one, though he comes to this view neither immediately nor unequivocally. There are several indications of his (changing) views on these matters. These range from his general physicalism to comments he makes specifically on the mind-brain relation and on his hopes that the physiological basis of mental processes may one day be discovered.

Freud's Physicalism

There is no need here to reiterate the details of Freud's physicalism; they are already given in Chapter 2. This physicalism is an essential part of psychoanalysis. It sets the stage for Freud's thinking, and underlies all his theoretical formulations, even where he is presenting them in an overtly mentalist language.

PSYCHOPHYSICAL PARALLELISM

A particularly striking indication of his views on the relation between mind and brain is the way he intermingles mental and physical terms. Freud, like his teachers and contemporaries in biological science, moves between a mental and a neurophysiological language without conceptual scruples (see Chapter 2). Freud's teachers assumed that the two languages may be accommodated, without any philosophical problems, in the same theory. This was because they adhered to a doctrine of psychophysical parallelism. Freud's teachers, and initially Freud himself, held that for each mental event, process, or entity there is a corresponding physical event, process, or entity. In his 1891 monograph on aphasia (in part reprinted as Appendix B to 1915c) he says:

> It is probable that the chain of physiological events in the nervous system does not stand in a causal connection with the psychical events. The physiological events do not cease as soon as the psychical ones begin; on the contrary, the physiological chain continues. What happens is simply that, after a certain point of time, each (or some) of its links has a psychical phenomenon corresponding to it. Accordingly, the psychical is a process parallel to the physiological—'a dependent concomitant' [p. 207].

And in the Project (1895a):

> No attempt, of course, can be made to explain how it is that excitatory processes in the ω neurones bring consciousness along with them. It is only a question of establishing a coincidence between the characteristics of consciousness that are known to us and processes in the ω neurones which vary in parallel with them [p. 311].

FREUD'S DEPARTURE FROM PARALLELISM

In a psychophysical parallelism it does not matter in what language one talks, since a simple one-to-one rule of correspondence exists between mental and neural terms. However, Freud's views on these matters change. First, he differs from

Meynert, from whom he otherwise derived much of his "anatomy of the mind." Even very early in his thinking he rejects Meynert's highly specific version of the parallelist thesis, that mental functions are exactly localized in the brain:

> We may recall that on the basis of Meynert's teachings the theory has grown up that the speech apparatus consists of distinct cortical centres in whose cells the word-presentations are contained, these centres being separated by a functionless cortical region, and linked together by white fibres (associative fascisculi). The question may at once be raised whether a hypothesis of this kind, which encloses presentations in nerve cells, can possibly be correct and permissible, I think not [1915c, p. 206].

Second, in spite of his avowed parallelism, Freud did not offer physical remedies for the mental disorders of his patients. His approach to therapy was psychological and not physiological, very different from that of his teacher Meynert. This was a source of Freud's estrangement from the medical world of the time. Freud operated, therapeutically, on the mental side of the mind-body dualism. Amacher (1965) comments that Freud had by 1890 already begun treating disorders similar to those Meynert was treating. Some of these Freud

> regarded as having physical causes and others mental causes, by working with the mental processes rather than with their physical concomitants. This was not inconsistent with Meynert's theory of concomitant mental and nervous functioning, although it was a radical departure from Meynert's and the orthodox ideas of proper therapy [p. 41].

By the time of the topographical formulation, Freud has explicitly abandoned psychophysical parallelism. He says: "The conventional equation of the psychical with the conscious is totally inexpedient. It disrupts psychical continuities, plunges us into the insoluble difficulties of psycho-physical parallelism" (1915c, pp. 167–168).

FROM NEUROPSYCHOLOGY TO PSYCHOLOGY

Freud also abandons the attempt to explain behavior in terms that refer directly to nervous functioning. As the theory of psychoanalysis develops, he becomes agnostic about the actual neurological instantiation of the mental processes. He wants to "avoid the temptation to determine psychical locality in any anatomical fashion." He says that "he will remain on psychological ground" (1900, p. 536) in the construction of his theory. In fact he goes so far as to say: "Every attempt to . . . discover a localization of mental processes, every endeavour to think of ideas as stored up in nerve-cells and of excitations as travelling along nerve-fibres, has miscarried completely" (1915c, p. 175).

But such comments should not be taken as a disavowal of materialism. His disavowals refer to (1) certain kinds of localization of psychical processes in the brain; and to (2) the identification of particular psychic processes with known neural processes in the present state of knowledge. In fact, the above quotation when given in full, including a prior sentence, is illuminating. Freud is involved in a discussion of the "relations of the mental apparatus to anatomy" (p. 174). He comments:

> We know that in the very roughest sense such relations exist. Research has given irrefutable proof that mental activity is bound up with the function of the brain as it is with no other organ. We are taken a step further—we do not know how much—by the discovery of the unequal importance of the different parts of the brain and their special relations to particular parts of the body and to particular mental activities.

It is only then that he makes the reference to the miscarriage of certain kinds of neurologizing, those that attempt the anatomical localization of psychological functions in the present state of science. But his materialist beliefs still remain. He continues:

> There is a hiatus here which at present cannot be filled, nor is it one of the tasks of psychology to fill it. Our psychical topography has *for the present* nothing to do with anatomy; it has reference not to anatomical localities, but to regions in the mental apparatus, wherever they may be situated in the body [pp. 174–175].

Freud always retains the hope that "all our provisional ideas in psychology will presumably some day be based on an organic substructure" (1914, p. 78). Even well into the period of the structural theory he can say: "We may look forward to a day when paths of knowledge . . . will be opened up, leading from organic biology and chemistry to the field of neurotic phenomena" (1926, p. 231).

The Mental, the Physical, and the Conscious

When Freud discusses the mind-brain issue it is almost always in the context of another and, for Freud, a closely related issue: that of the relationship between the mental and the conscious. Indeed, if there is one major conceptual issue with which Freud is always concerned it is this relation. His views on this matter are expressed in several places (for example, 1913b, pp. 178–179; 1915c, pp. 166–171; 1940a, pp. 157ff.). His presentation of these views always takes the same form: he argues that the mental and the conscious cannot be identical. Taking such a position, he holds, would either (1) ignore the fact of unconscious motivation, or (2) where some have defined the two as identical, then it would leave us *without a conceptual framework* within which to deal with the causes of the behavior that psychoanalysis has investigated.

It is worth going into this argument in more detail. It tells a lot about Freud's views on the mind-brain relation. Freud (1940b, pp. 281–286) wonders how one might answer the question, what is the "nature . . . the essence of the psychical?" (p. 282). He admits it is hard to answer. He says that if an analogous question had been asked of a physicist,

> his reply, until quite recently, would have been: 'For the purpose of explaining certain phenomena, we assume the existence of electrical forces which are present in things and which emanate from them. We study these phenomena, discover the laws that govern them and even put them to practical use. This satisfies us provisionally. We do not know the *nature* of electricity. . . . [This is] simply how things happen in the natural sciences [p. 282].

Returning to psychology, he comments "psychology too is a

natural science. What else can it be?" (p. 282). But in the case of psychology a "remarkable thing" happens:

> Everyone—or almost everyone—was agreed that what is psychical really *has* a common quality in which its essence is expressed: namely the quality of *being conscious*. . . . All that is conscious, they said, is psychical, and conversely all that is psychical is conscious; that is self-evident and to contradict it is nonsense.

But this equation has

> had the unwelcome result of divorcing psychical processes from the general context of events in the universe and of setting them in complete contrast to all others. But this would not do, since the fact could not long be over-looked that psychical phenomena are to a high degree dependent upon somatic influences [p. 283].

Therefore,

> to find a way out, the philosophers at least were obliged to assume that there were organic processes parallel to the conscious psychical ones, related to them in a manner that was hard to explain, which acted as intermediaries in the reciprocal relations between 'body and mind', and which served to re-insert the psychical into the texture of life. But this solution remained unsatisfactory [p. 283].

Psychoanalysis, Freud argues, gets out of this conceptual impasse by "denying the equation between what is psychical and what is conscious" (p. 283). It does this on the basis of psychoanalytic and other evidence of unconscious motivators. He then reiterates the view detailed over forty years before in the Project (1895a; see also above, Chapter 3):

> being conscious cannot be the essence of what is psychical. It is only a *quality* of what is psychical, and an inconstant quality at that—one that is far oftener absent than present. The psychical . . . is in itself unconscious and probably similar in kind to all the other natural processes of which we have obtained knowledge [p. 283].

Freud cites evidence for the existence of unconscious phenomena—latent memories, slips of the tongue, posthypnotic suggestion—and then he goes on to deal with "one further objection":

> We are told that, in spite of the facts that have been mentioned, there is no necessity to abandon the identity between what is conscious and what is psychical: the so-called unconscious processes are the organic processes which have long been recognized as running parallel to the mental ones. This, of course, would reduce our problem to an apparently indifferent matter of definition [p. 286].

There are really two parts to the objection that Freud is considering. The first is the idea that, whatever it is psychoanalysis investigates, it cannot really be reasons or any other sort of motives. A person may act "as if" he has such a motive (but is not conscious of it); however, he does not have it "in fact." It argues that when Freud calls a motive "unconscious" he breaches the rules that give the meaning of "motive." Therefore the phrase "unconscious motive" is literally without sense. Freud frames this part of the objection in parallelist terms, but its essence may be found in other, nonparallelist, philosophies of mind. This "literal nonsense" view is indeed at the heart of more recent critiques of Freud's ideas on unconscious motivation. Philosophers discussing Freud's theory have often been concerned that "unconscious motive" is a puzzling and apparently self-contradictory phrase. However, it is only puzzling because of the tendency of "ordinary language" philosophy to assume that the ordinary sense of a term is definitive (for example, Alexander, 1962; Dilman, 1972; Flew, 1956; McGuinness, 1956–1957; MacIntyre, 1958; Peters, 1958), and that it is a necessary part of the concept of motive that it is consciously accessible.

The second part of the objection is the idea that the so-called unconscious processes, being outside the realm of reasons or motives (which would have to be conscious) can only be physical phenomena. This is an attempt to find a solution to the first part of the objection that has been raised; to say what these "unconscious" processes are if they do not belong to the domain of reasons, purposes, and motives. Now Freud answers the first part of this objection by saying, "Our reply is that it would be unjustifiable and inexpedient to make a breach in the unity of mental life for the sake of propping up a definition" (p. 286). At first sight this appears to be merely a counterassertion, stating that conventional definitions do not have legislative force. But it is more than this. Freud backs up this assertion with an illuminating comment:

> It is clear in any case that consciousness can only offer us an incomplete and broken chain of phenomena. And it can scarcely be a matter of chance that it was not until the change had been made in the definition of the psychical that it became possible to construct a comprehensive and coherent theory of mental life.

With these comments we return to themes that I dealt with in Chapter 7, on the explanatory functions of theoretical concepts. Freud is stressing that theory legitimately and informatively redefines aspects of its subject matter. He is arguing for the same point that I made above: that the power and value of a concept like the unconscious lies in its theoretical function. In fact, Freud points out, the very idea of unconscious (motivational) processes is theoretical, and its justification lies in the explanatory worth of psychoanalysis. He mentions the same theoretical functions as I did in Chapter 7: the concept of the unconscious brings coherence into our accounts of behavior enabling psychoanalysis to "construct a . . . coherent theory"; it also serves heuristic functions: "it has led to a knowledge of the characteristics of the unconscious psychical . . . and it has discovered some of the laws which govern it" (1940b, p. 286).

The second part of the objection is handled by Freud in a similar way; he argues that it is a theoretical decision to approach unconscious processes from a psychological rather than a physical standpoint. As he has said, theories in the natural sciences cannot penetrate to the essence of what it is that they are explaining; they only have knowledge through theoretical inference. Similarly,

> the processes with which it [psychoanalysis] is concerned are in themselves just as unknowable as those dealt with by other sciences, by chemistry or physics for example; but it is possible to

establish the laws which they obey . . . [and] to arrive at an 'understanding' of the field of natural phenomena in question [1940a, p. 158].

This has to be done through "framing fresh hypotheses and creating fresh concepts" (p. 158), through theoretical endeavor.

From these remarks we may draw together Freud's view of the mind-brain relation.

IDENTITY OF MIND AND BRAIN

Freud recognizes that the mind-brain issue is an issue of the relations between theories pitched at different levels of their common human subject matter: it is a theoretical problem, and has to be solved theoretically. The problematic relations are not between two objects existing in the universe completely independently of our conceptions of them, that is, a naive realism. They are between two theories existing "in the mind of the beholder."

For Freud, we do not have direct access to unconscious processes. Yet he insists that mental life is a "function of an apparatus . . . extended in space" (1940a, p. 145) and that its "bodily organ, and scene of action, [is] the brain" (p. 144). He expects that one day we will be able to explain mental life by referring directly to neurological and chemical processes. Since we are unable to gain direct knowledge of unconscious processes, we need to make plausible hypotheses about them to gain an understanding of the area and to explain their behavioral consequences. So psychoanalysis creates its mental model. This, considers Freud, is exactly the practice of other natural sciences, for in doing this, psychoanalysis is modeling wholly natural processes. What makes psychoanalytic inferences psychological, rather than physical, is not any essential difference between the mental and the physical. It is that as yet we do not know enough about the brain and its functioning to be able to say exactly what brain processes give rise to psychological phenomena, nor how they do so. Thus the language and terminology of psychoanalysis is designed to cohere with the "original" psychology, the everyday terminology used to explain the phenomena of consciousness.

FUNCTIONALISM

The structures and processes of Freud's mental model are postulated according to function. Freud argues that there must exist certain structures, and that there must occur certain processes in these structures that would produce the behavioral effects he observes and wishes to explain. Yet whatever it is that gives rise to our psychological functions must be, Freud assumes, located in the brain. The psychoanalytic constructs are postulated to explain precisely the same functions that a complete neurophysiology of brain processes would be designed to explain. Implicit in Freud's treatment of the mind-brain relation, then, is the idea that brain (neurophysiological) concepts and mind (psychoanalytic) concepts are functionally identical. This identity is a theoretical one. The constructs of psychoanalysis, provided psychoanalysis gives a good explanation of the facts (according to usual theoretical standards of coherence, intelligibility, predictive power, and so on), would be functionally isomorphic to the constructs of an equally good neurological theory that accounts for the same facts.

A SCIENTIFIC REALISM

Motives as Causes

Freud treats the concepts of his motivational theory as characterizations of real processes, the causes of behavior. The problems raised by this philosophy are then: Do such constructs satisfy the criteria for being causes, and do they satisfy the criteria for being real? Of course, the issue here is a very broad one. Strictly, it is not confined to psychoanalysis but is a problem in theories of motivation in general, and indeed in all psychology. It is the problem: What are the referents of mental terms? And what is the relation of such referents to behavior?

However, I am specifically concerned here with the application of a general scientific realism to psychoanalytic theory.

CAUSES AND LAWS

It is widely held that any causalist theory of mind has, on Humean grounds, to demonstrate that (1) the regular co-occurrence of mental and behavioral events may be observed (so psychological laws could be formulated) and, to enable this, (2) mental events and the behavioral events they are supposed to cause are "separate existents."

This returns us to the themes in Chapter 6 on meaning. There I made several points about mental constructs, and about the hypotheticals that can be used to unpack their meaning. To summarize:

1. No hypothetical is analytically true. Some are more central to the concept than others. However, sharp distinctions between analytic and synthetic hypotheticals are not possible in the case of complex mental concepts. So no one behavior is either a necessary or a sufficient criterion for the ascription of a wish.

2. Systematic empirical relations are expressed in the hypotheticals. Hypotheticals state (a) the behavioral tendencies consequent on having an unconscious wish; and (b) relationships that exist between the mental state and other properties of the person or his conditions (some of these are not directly observable properties but are also in need of unpacking).

3. In both these respects this contrasts with a purely dispositional analysis. In the dispositional view, regular empirical relations hold only between the different sets of observables (in psychology, behaviors or external conditions) that conjointly define a person as being in some mental state.

4. There is an indefinitely large number of hypotheticals generated in the unpacking of a mental notion such as wish. This makes empty any claim that a mental state

ascription is reducible to, or "merely" equivalent to, a series of statements about observables.

5. When a mental property is ascribed to someone, especially in the context of a full psychological theory like psychoanalysis, this goes beyond predictions about immediate behavioral properties. The ascription is categorical.

The "everyday" and the psychoanalytic theories of motivation do not contain laws in the sense of simple empirical generalizations; neither, of course, do many established theories in the natural sciences. Indeed, wherever there is a theoretical, ordinarily nonobservable concept it is not possible to discover simple empirical generalizations that include it. But there do exist in the wish case what may be described as "systematic empirical relations." These are expressed by the hypotheticals. They say that, for example, having an unconscious wish is usually (in certain conditions) followed by, or associated with, certain other events. These may be behaviors or other properties of the individual—the sorts of behaviors and other properties I have already illustrated in the unpacking of the unconscious wish concept.

CAUSES AND INDEPENDENT EXISTENCE

The complement to this point about the lawlike nature of the hypotheticals is that about the independent existence of the motivational processes Freud posits. These have to be ontologically distinct from the behaviors they are supposed to cause. However, there are two features of motives that, at first sight, make it appear that they are not specifiable independently of the observables upon which they are based, and which they are designed to explain. First, motives, including all those psychoanalysis calls upon, are known by inference. The second and related problem is that motives always imply goals: they are always "motives for something." They are even named according to that for which they are motives. Motive explanations then seem irreducibly teleological. In the Wolf Man example used, the unconscious motive is the wish for sexual relations with the father. Thus, saying what the motive is involves stating what it is the "motive for." This criticism, that the logical relation between mental properties (motives) and actions precludes a causal relationship, is widely used against causal theories of mind. A particularly nice summary of the issues is by Melden (1966).

However, there is a solution to these apparent difficulties: briefly, the independent specification of a motive, which establishes its credentials as a causal candidate, consists of discovering further predictions that flow from its postulation. In this way the motive is more than merely a shorthand for the evidence that leads to its assumption. This sense of independence can be illustrated both for the concepts of general science and for psychology.

In science the starting point of an explanation is generally the inference from some phenomenon to be explained to a mechanism whose initial characterization is little more than "whatever causes the phenomenon." For example, in the case of the germ theory, the germ was initially merely the unseen living thing that causes disease. Today a variety of kinds of germs can be observed under the microscope and identified by criteria other than as disease-causing entities. Similarly, in genetic theory genes were at one stage nothing more than "whatever carries hereditary characteristics." Now the gene is a construct related to virtually every part of biochemical knowledge, and it is more or less chemically identifiable apart from its function in carrying hereditary factors.

We accept that there do exist such things as genes and germs because they did not remain defined merely in terms of the observables upon which they were first postulated. These concepts are something over and above mere shorthand, true by definition, formulations of the data. It is their role in fulfilling explanatory functions (those discussed in Chapter 7) that confirms them as good characterizations of real causal processes. Each further confirmed prediction, each piece of information, each link forged with other theories that a theory gives establishes its concepts (the germ, the gene, the electron) as real processes. The observability of these postulated processes is not critical. We can "see" germs with the aid of a theory of optics that gives us the microscope. We cannot see genes in quite the same way. If we could, we could only do it with the aid of an enormous amount of equally theoretical notions that give us the electron microscope. We surely cannot see electrons in any literal sense.

In psychology the motive case is similar. We can only know motives by inference, and the existence of some postulated motive is only given through the way that postulation performs explaining behavior.

An ordinary motive explanation. Consider an example. A man is seen talking to a woman. An observer is asked why, and a reasonable answer is given: he has a sexual interest in her. This is a motivational explanation. The man's motive is sexual interest. Now, in a causalist analysis, such as I have been putting forward, this interest is the cause of the particular behavior (talking to the woman), and the explanation is achieved by citing that cause. The cause in turn is known by inference.

In this explanation, the citing of the motive gives the questioner more information than he had initially, when only the behavior had been observed. (This is so even though the explanation offered is only a very simple one, unlike the complex Freudian case studies.) That is, the facts do not necessarily imply the motive. Many different motives could have led him to talk to her. Conversely, the statement of the motive (the man has a sexual interest in the woman) does not imply the action that is specified in the datum (he was talking to her). It could be that this or any other man does not act on his sexual motive by talking to the object of his interest.

The statement of the motive is then not merely a reformulation of the behavioral facts, and is not reducible to data statements. The motive ascription is something over and above the behavior it explains. It is this that makes the motive ontologically distinct from the observable events it causes.

What is a motive? If we ask, "What then *is* the motive?" we are back to the themes discussed in Chapter 6: What does it mean to say that someone has a motive? We can spell out a series of hypotheticals for our "man talks to woman" example. These follow the pattern of the B list of hypotheticals given in Chapter 6. The B list spelled out the hypotheticals associated with the general concept of wish, and here we have a specific wish, that of a particular person's sexual interest in another. The spelling out, modeled on the B list, looks like this:

E1. If the man A has a sexual interest in the woman B, then he will behave in ways that usually bring about sexual contact with respect to B.

E2. If . . . , then, if A believes that talking will lead to such sexual contact, he will talk to B.

E3. If . . . , then, if he is prevented from achieving sexual contact, he will show negative emotions (anger, disappointment, and so on).

E4. If . . . , then A will show an interest in matters related to sexual contact with B.

E5. If . . . , then A's talk about sexual contact with B and related matters will become more frequent.

E6. If . . . , then he will contemplate the thought of sexual contact with B with pleasure.

E7. If . . . , then, if this sexual contact is achieved, A will be pleased.

E8. If . . . , then, if he wishes equally for another state of affairs which is incompatible with achieving sexual contact with B, A will show hesitation in acting toward the contact, will vacillate emotionally, and so on.

E9. If . . . , then, when asked, A will say he wants sexual contact with B.

In this list "sexual contact" could be a series of activities ranging from flirting and holding hands to sexual intercourse. It is as diverse as sexual practice itself. Further, just as for the general case of wish, (1) it contains concepts (like belief) that are themselves in need of unpacking; (2) its hypotheticals vary in their centrality to the concept of sexual interest, but no hypothetical is analytically true; (3) it allows for the fact that a person may hold more than one wish at a time, including incompatible wishes; (4) there is an indefinitely large number of hypotheticals associated with the concept of sexual interest, for the possible manifestations of such a motive are innumerable.

Sexual interest, like the concept of wish, operates as a construct in a theory. The meaning of "sexual interest" is given by its position in a network of hypotheticals that relate it both to observables and other mental terms. It changes as we get more information about the nature of sexual motivation (say, its physiology, or roots in childhood), and it changes as sexual activity varies from culture (kissing) to culture (rubbing noses). The use of the concept systematizes a large amount of information, behavioral and theoretical. The use of the concept in explanation is also heuristic; it leads us to expect other things about A which we would not have expected from knowledge of only the initial activity (talking to B).

When we want to say what A's motive—sexual interest—actually is, we say much more than merely that it is whatever causes him to talk to B, or even whatever causes his sexual behavior toward B. It is not merely the "motive for" some specified sexual activity; it is a mental state that involves beliefs about the consequences of certain actions; it is a state with certain physiological concomitants; it is a state associated with pleasurable feelings; it is dependent on cultural norms; and so on. The ascription of a sexual interest to A is something whose meaning cannot be defined in a finite number of observation statements.

A psychoanalytic motive explanation. The explanation in terms of sexual interest may be satisfactory for some contexts. However, explanations differ with different situations. Psychologists, for example, might want to say more about what A's sexual motivation is, both in the specific case where there is a puzzle to be solved about A's behavior, and in the general case where the psychologist is required to provide a theory of motivation.

Let us then take the example further. Suppose that the man concerned is Wolf Man and the woman is the peasant girl bending by the pond side (see Appendix). In the first place Freud explains the Wolf Man's behavior by saying he has an unconscious desire for a woman inferior to himself. Thus far the account, though it is a new and more informative one, still ascribes a motive that is named after its object. But this first part of the account is the tip of the iceberg for Freud. Freud brings to bear his general theory of motivation on this specific matter, just as he does in other parts of the Wolf Man case (see Appendix). The postulated "wish to debase" is lodged in the complex of Freud's case study account. It is linked by Freud to events of childhood, to events of adulthood, to other symptoms, to other experiences, to other motives, and indeed to Freud's theory of mind, just as is his dream explanation.

The important point about this is that within psychoanalytic theory a wish, such as a wish for sexual relations with a peasant girl, only possesses its characteristics by virtue of its ontogenesis, its derivation from a more basic source of motivation. The motives we introspect, or see in others, have the tripartite structure already discussed. In particular, they are goal-directed, they are "motives for." But this characteristic is not irreducible. It is there because an ordinary motive is the psychological outcome of more basic processes with similar characteristics. In psychoanalysis, the goal or object of an ordinary motive is the learned substitute for other ontogenetically prior objects. These latter were objects of instinctual drives and were instrumental in their fulfillment.

If a causal analysis is to stand, of course, then at some point in this regress the notion of an object or goal has to be defined and stripped of its teleological connotations. This is exactly what Freud's mental model attempts to do. Freud (see Chapters 3 and 4) provides a theory that explains the directionality of the motivational process in a nonteleological way. He sets out a mechanistic theory of purpose. At its most basic the object of a wish is merely a set of external conditions associated with the previous release of drive tension. The object of a motive does not define the motive, and the motivational state is independent of the object. It is rooted in the evolutionarily developed requirements of the organism, what the individual needs to do to survive.

Motives exist, and may be defined, independently of any finite set of behaviors they are posited to account for. They are contingently related to these behaviors in a lawlike way. Motive ascriptions are not merely dispositional attributions; they state categorical properties of the individual.

Qualified realism. The discussion here is about approaches to the ontological status of theoretical concepts, so it is worth mentioning how the view being put forward fits into the realist-instrumentalist dichotomy. Instrumentalism as a philosophy of science depends on the idea that it is not possible to draw a distinction between what is true and what is false in scientific theory, precisely because it is theory, known on inference, and is not fact. On the other hand, realism, of the usual kind, assumes that it is possible to draw the distinction. So in a realism there are true theoretical statements and false ones, respectively characterizing and failing to characterize real processes, states, or events. I am putting forward a realism here, but one with qualifications that may at times appear instrumentalist! I argue that theoretical knowledge is inferential, and this includes knowledge about one's own and others' minds. The distinction between those theoretical statements that describe real states of affairs and those that do not is more complicated than ordinary realisms or instrumentalisms allow. We are dependent on inference and theory for knowledge of which postulated processes are real and which are not. It is rarely, if ever, that one can simply and unequivocally observe a postulated process and so confirm its existence. Rather, we are dependent on the overall functioning of the theory (the functions discussed in Chapter 6) to tell us whether its constructs are a "good characterization" of the real processes they are supposed to describe. Even thinking of constructs as "good" or "not so good" characterizations of existent, causal processes can be deceptive. For we have no access to the "real" causes of behavior other than through the theories that we have about them. The information that we get back from the testing of the theory does not, as Popper (1934, 1963a) has pointed out, tell us what is true about our theoretical constructs but rather what is not true about them. In Popper's view the truth of theories is a guiding principle (1963b), something to aim at, not an achievable object. Yet scientific statements do assert something about reality, for they forbid certain states of affairs and become falsifiable because of this. Freud does not discuss falsification in any Popperian way. However, like Popper, he combines a realism with a recognition that final and exact descriptions of unobserved processes are never achieved.

Functionalism and the Mind-Brain Relation

FUNCTIONAL EXPLANATION

Much of psychology is concerned with functional explanation. That is, behavior is treated as the function of some hypothesized mental process, and in this type of explanation the postulated process is individuated, and consequently often named, according to its supposed behavioral consequences. This functionalist approach to explanation in psychology has become an important part of the debate on the mind-brain issue (for example, Fodor, 1968a, 1968b, 1978; and Dennett's collection of essays, 1978a). There has even been some discussion of functionalism and psychoanalysis (Wilson, 1973). This fits the motive case. When motives are identified and named it is according to their function. They are named according to their behavioral consequences. It is this that leads some philosophers wrongly to suppose that they are actually defined by that for which they are motives.

A series of behaviors, perhaps not obviously correlated, are designated as functions because it makes explanatory sense to treat them all as consequences of the same hypothetical process. Freud's notion of the sexual drive has this effect. It makes a large range of behaviors the function of one mental process. The characterization of drive as the "sexual drive" is a functional one in that it is characterized according to its presumed behavioral consequences. Freud, in his complex theory of sexuality, is attempting to describe a mental process that would have as a consequence just those behaviors he wants to explain. He does this by using models, on the assumption that like mechanisms have like consequences. He also hopes that this functional postulate will lead to new hypotheses and to more information about sexuality in human life. In a similar way Freud posits the mental structures of the structural theory. These correspond to behavioral functions. Philosophers sometimes consider this type of psychological explanation to be conceptually muddled. But, as was pointed out above, explanation in other sciences also starts like this. What does seem different about psychology is that its constructs are not obviously material (brain) processes. This raises the worry that we can go no further than functional explanation, that psychology is stuck there.

MIND AND BRAIN

Freud's belief is, of course, that we are not stuck at this point, at least not for conceptual reasons. In time, he expects, a second stage of explanation can take place and the neurochemistry of mind will be discovered. In psychology no attempt is usually made to specify the material processes of which behavior is a function. Yet it is clear that intelligent and motivated behavior is a function of brain processes. A purely psychological explanation could be taken further; we could attempt to find out what neurological mechanisms have the same functional properties as those specified in the psychological theory. This could be done if there was available a sophisticated enough neurophysiology. So in principle we may develop an explanation of some series of behaviors—say, sexual behavior—in purely psychological (functional) terms, then proceed to look for those brain processes that would be capable of exhibiting the same functions (see Fodor, 1968a, pp. 109ff.). The psychological theory may be a good one, and may have led to an integration of information about sexual and related behaviors. If so, then the search for the neurological embodiment of the psychological constructs will be constrained by the psychological theory. Conversely, the psychological mechanisms cannot be other than those allowed by neurophysiology.

Functional identity. In this process we do not have to discover a one-to-one correspondence between psychological and brain structures. It is rather that an adequate neurophysiology must describe brain mechanisms that can carry out the same functions as those of the psychological mechanisms—where the psychology is in turn an adequate one. There is here an identity between mind and brain. It is a "functional identity."

There is another feature of this identity between mind and brain processes: the identity is a theoretical one. Both of these processes are postulates: they are theoretical. What distinguishes them has to do with the theories that contain them. That is, the difference between the inferred brain processes and the inferred mental processes lies in the respective theories of brain and mind, certainly not in the fact of inference. We have access to mind and to brain processes only through theory anyway. There is no means other than the goodness of the theories to tell us if we are characterizing the posited causal mechanisms correctly. Mental mechanisms are described in a language that coheres with other psychological theory —sometimes everyday psychological language. Brain mechanisms are given in the language of neurophysiology. Whereas psychological mechanisms admit of no direct material specification, neurophysiological ones do, though the latter are less theoretical because of it.

Computer Analogy. Functional explanation, and the type of identity involved in the mind-brain relation, can be illustrated through the use of a common analogy. Consider a computer. What a particular computer can do can be explained at a number of different levels. Suppose the considered computer takes as input any number and then lists the next ten whole numbers. We can enumerate several different sets of mathematical operations that are compatible with this behavior. These sets would be functionally equivalent. However, unless it is a very odd computer (such as a human), only one of the sets is used. There are further levels of the system we could explore; the language in which these operations were programmed into the computer; the commands from that language that were used; the supplementary (noncomputational) aspects of the system; the means and size of memory storage; the system for addressing information; and so on. At each level the number of possible computer procedures (theoretical mechanisms) compatible with the result compounds, and still we have said nothing about the actual hardware of the system. Everything so far is at a level abstracted from the actual material of the system. It would not matter if the system were made of blue cheese, so long as it was functionally compatible with the processes required to perform our mathematical operation. In fact, the simple task mentioned could be done by a nonelectronic machine. Further, just as different hardware configurations are compatible with one computational capacity, so the one hardware arrangement can be responsible for many different computational abilities. Even when we get down to the specification of the computer hardware, we find ourselves referring to these in terms that are at least partially characterized by their functions in the computer system: "central processing unit," "micro-processors," "random access memory chips," and so on.

Analogously, the explanation of some human capacity might be given in terms that make no direct reference to the wetware of the brain. Instead, the postulated mechanisms—mental mechanisms—are described in terms abstracted from actual brain processes. They are specified according to the functions for which they are supposedly responsible. But the mental mechanism explains the behavior as does the description of the computational capacities and program of the computer.

SUMMARY

At the conclusion of this chapter it is appropriate to compare Freud's treatment of ontological issues with the one adopted here. The convergence and compatibility of these two treatments in a variety of respects should be clear. The following points express (a) the essential characteristics of Freud's view (as discussed in the earlier part of this chapter), and (b) how these fit in with the "theoretical construct" view presented here.

1. Psychology (psychoanalysis) describes the mechanisms that cause behavior.
2. These descriptions, however, are forever "approximations," as the mechanisms can be known only inferentially. This is normal in science.
3. Knowledge of familiar mechanisms and their functions enables us to model the mechanisms of mind. Freud uses, among other things, neurophysiological processes as models in constructing his theory. The result is a functional type of explanation. Once again, this is normal in science.
4. Behavior is a function of brain processes. In principle, it is possible to give an explanation of behavior in neurophysiological terms. However, we do not yet know enough about these brain processes (which are also known by inference) to do this.

5. As a consequence, psychology (psychoanalysis) does not tie itself to neurophysiology, or attempt localization of psychological functions in the brain. It works at specifying mental structures and processes according to their functional characteristics. One day perhaps, we will have a neurophysiology that will specify the neural processes that underlie the processes that psychology (psychoanalysis) now gives in mental terms.

Freud's philosophy of science is a realism, and his approach to psychology is a materialist one. But it is one qualified by an understanding that the processes of which science, including mental science, speaks can be known only indirectly. This means that even the specification of the neurophysiology of mental processes is a theoretical matter. It is a matter of elaborating in neurophysiological theory a set of brain mechanisms that are able to carry out the functions assigned to the mental ones by psychology—mechanisms, that is, which are functionally equivalent to the psychological mechanisms.

PART III

FURTHER ISSUES

10

PRELIMINARIES

In the essay so far,

1. I have given an exposition of Freud's theory of motivation, illustrating its form and its content.
2. I have also tried to show how this theory developed and changed out of ideas that existed prepsychoanalytically. Certain of these ideas remain as principles that persist through all changes in Freud's theory.
3. Further, I have argued that these principles—embodied in Freud's metapsychology and model of mind—give psychoanalysis its characteristics as a theory of motivation, for they deal with the energizing, the precipitating, and the directing factors in motivated human behavior.
4. I have also argued for a "theoretical construct" approach to psychological explanation. This is a scientific realism, qualified by an appreciation of the tentative nature of all theoretical knowledge.
5. This theoretical construct analysis, I have tried to show, provides a coherent account of the psychoanalytic concept of motivation, and of Freud's causal theory of mind. Moreover, this approach largely concurs with Freud's own philosophy of explanation.

ISSUES RAISED BY THIS ANALYSIS

This approach to psychological explanation raises certain philosophical issues. Some examples are: one might object that

177

the phrase "unconscious motive" is self-contradictory and violates the ordinary meaning of motive; or one might object that motives cannot be theoretical constructs as we can get to know our motives in a way we could never know anything theoretical; or one might object that motives cannot be causes as their relation to action is not appropriately contingent. I have tried to cover these and other issues in giving the theoretical construct point of view.

But the application of this analysis to psychoanalytic theory raises further issues. Many of these are themes in post-Freudian literature on psychoanalysis. These issues are in the first place theoretical, rather than philosophical, because they specifically have to do with supposed inadequacies of Freud's theory. For example, it is argued that the clinical data and principles are not dependent on the metapsychology, and that the latter is theoretically redundant. These theoretical arguments are, however, largely based on tacit philosophical ideas, and once they are examined closely the underlying conceptual doctrines emerge. For instance, in arguing that the clinical principles are independent of the metapsychology, the assumption is that the metapsychology, which embodies a causal method of explanation, is incompatible with clinical descriptions, because these consist of patients' reasons for acting: a causes-reasons distinction is assumed.

The work in the last part of the essay consists of (1) discussing some of the major theoretical issues in the area, and (2) making explicit the philosophical objections they contain to the sort of analysis I have offered. (3) Further, since many of these are on conceptual points I have already discussed, they can be countered by referring them back to the arguments of earlier chapters.

Sources of the Issues

A wide and varied range of thinkers, for the most part working independently of each other, have argued toward a position (or rather a cluster of closely related positions) on the topic of psychoanalytic explanation. This is remarkable because they come from different disciplines and traditions. Some few of the very many that may be included in this range are: the social philosophers and theorists Habermas (1972), Ricoeur (1970, 1981), and Sartre (1943); the British philosophers MacIntyre (1958) and Peters (1958); the American psychoanalysts and psychologists, including thinkers identified with the "ego psychology" tradition, Atwood and Stolorow (1984), Bettelheim (1982), Gill (1976), Holt, (1976), George Klein (1976), Schafer (1976), and Spence (1982, 1983); and the British psychoanalyst Rycroft (1966). Some analysts following Melanie Klein (Meltzer, 1978, and Segal, 1973) have adopted the same position on psychoanalytic explanation (see Mackay, 1981). Further, these views on psychoanalysis appear in very different contexts, in textual critiques of Freud, in reformulations of psychoanalytic theory, in extensions to that theory, in rival psychodynamic theories, and in philosophical analyses. Thus they might have been expected to have had radically different views on psychological phenomena and on how to explain them.

THE SEPARATE DOMAIN THESIS

The position toward which they argue is that psychoanalytic explanation has solely to do with meanings. It has to do with the articulation of the person's understanding and misunderstanding of himself, his relationships, and his experienced world. The arguments also stress—and this is the important part for our purpose—that such an articulation can be achieved only within a language that eschews the causal vocabulary of natural science, a language that keeps away from the concepts of mental forces, structures, and causes. Such an articulation, it is held, can have no truck with accounts of action that treat it as the causal outcome of interactions between hypothesized mental structures, as a causally determined phenomenon on the natural science model.

This position on psychological explanation is what Sherwood (1969) has dubbed the "separate domain" view. In this view explanations of human behavior belong, on philosophical grounds, to a domain of explanation separate from explanations of nonhuman phenomena. This separate domain thesis follows much older views, for example, Dilthey's well-known division between human sciences (sciences of understanding) and natural sciences (sciences of explanation). On several grounds it stands in opposition to the theoretical construct analysis that I have been presenting here.

What I am calling the separate domain view allows for a large variety of positions within it, and of course covers much more than merely psychoanalysis. The separate domain debate on psychoanalytic explanation consists of a number of overlapping subdebates carried on in psychoanalysis and the various disciplines that relate to psychoanalysis, each using different terms and frames of reference. One part of the psychoanalytic debate, for example, derives its terminology from the European philosopher Paul Ricoeur and concentrates on the notion of a hermeneutic science. Hermeneutics has become perhaps the central concept in recent psychoanalytic theoretical debate, particularly since Grünbaum (for example, 1984) has cast his critiques of the separate domain view in terms of the hermeneutic exegesis of psychoanalysis versus Freud's own natural science view of psychoanalysis, and he assimilates the psychoanalysts like Gill, George Klein, and Schafer to the hermeneutic position. Another subdebate is on the thesis of the "narrative" nature of psychoanalytic explanation. Spence (1982, 1983), following themes in Schafer (1980) and Ricoeur (1981), elevates the distinction between what the patient (and analyst) believe to be the facts—and which therefore affect him—and what are the facts into a distinction between "narrative truth" and factual truth, once again separating the domains of knowledge in the social, specifically psychoanalytic world from that of science.

With participants in the separate domain debates coming from such a variety of disciplines, it is not surprising that there is a mix of terms, concepts, and styles of argument. I hold, however, that there are important common themes in these debates. I am not suggesting that theorists as far apart in their interests as, say, the psychoanalyst Roy Schafer and the philosopher Paul Ricoeur have identical views on explanation and on psychoanalysis. Rather, both put forward arguments that embody the separate domain principle, and this is the important point for the discussion here. Even within psychoanalysis there are several versions of the separate domain position, using a variety of arguments. The extent to which a revised notion of causality can be incorporated in psychoanalytic theory, the role of avowal in the confirmation of psychoanalytic hypotheses, the importance of subjective experience to psychoanalysis, the relation of the language of intentions to that describing neurological processes; on these and other issues there is no simple consensus.

I have chosen to concentrate largely on a group of psychoanalytic authors, representatives of what Schafer (1976, p. x) calls a "new critical movement concerned with the logic, language, [and] implications . . . of Freudian psychoanalysis." Their idiom, unlike that of, say, the hermeneuticians and phenomenologists, is closer to mine. Certainly the themes in their works are easier to disentangle than in writers like Ricoeur. Further, I believe that their works contain most of the matters that need to be dealt with here. Some of the important works of modern psychoanalytic theory come from these writers. In the 1970's and into the early 1980's the critique of Freud's philosophy of science that they endorse gained momentum to the point where the anti-natural science position on psychoanalytic explanation was accepted, as Grünbaum says, "as being at the cutting edge of the field, if not [in some quarters] *de rigueur*" (1984, p. 1). Some major works by the authors on whom I concentrate are Schafer (1976), Klein (1976), both collections of previously published works; and the series of essays in memory of George Klein by Holt, Wallerstein, Loevinger, Schafer, Gill, and others (Gill and Holzman, 1976). I also refer to the earlier work (1958) of the British philosopher MacIntyre, because he discusses with exemplary clarity many of the philosophical themes upon which the anti-metapsychologists depend. I shall also draw occasionally on works by other writers, but the literature is now too large and too diverse to sample representatively all its different branches.

On the part of this critical movement there is a clear recognition that it owes much to other sources. Schafer (1976, pp. 7–8) says: "I have used, as best I could, certain ideas culled from modern philosophical writings on existentialism, phenomenology, mind, and action; e.g., by Binswanger (1936, 1946),

Sartre (1943), Wittgenstein (1958), Ryle (1949), and others."
Similarly Klein (1976, p. 26) acknowledges "certain philoso-
phers of science to whom we owe a debt of gratitude—particularly
R. S. Peters (1956) of the English school tracing to Wittgenstein,
Ricoeur in France (1970), and in this country Kohut (1959),
Apfelbaum (1965, 1966), Loevinger (1966), Holt (1965, 1968)
and others."

Even those psychoanalytic authors on whom I shall concentrate are not always consistent on the several related issues that
go into the debate. Klein's work (1976), for example, contains
both an antitheoretical, phenomenological strand of thinking
as well as emphasis on the value of theory to psychoanalysis.
However, the common thrust of the writers I shall consider is
away from the type of approach I have been taking, and in
their discussion they raise issues that need to be addressed here.
Also, there is acknowledgment on their part of a vital common
element in their thinking. This is why Schafer can describe
himself as part of a "new critical movement" in psychoanalysis
(1976, p. x).

The separate domain issue is particularly important for psychoanalysis today. Formerly, the received view of psychoanalytic
theory was that psychoanalysis could and should be regarded
as offering explanations of the natural science type. This view
is expressed particularly clearly in the works of, for example,
Rapaport (1960a, 1960b), and Rapaport and Gill (1959). In this
view, Freud's metapsychology is his general theory and it legitimately attempts to explain the clinical principles and
data—much as I argued earlier. The metapsychology is about
the mental processes, structures, and forces hypothesized by
Freud. The clinical principles are about the relations among
personality characteristics, symptoms, actions, and experience.
In this view the mental structures and their interactions cause
the actions and experience. However, this received view has
changed toward a different consensus. Under the impact of
such leading psychoanalytic theorists as Gill (1976), Holt (1976),
Klein (1976), and Schafer (1976), the move has been to disengage the metapsychology and the clinical principles on the
grounds that they embody different and incompatible modes
of explanation. This move is perhaps a response to the enor-

mous problems met in the attempt to validate psychoanalysis using traditional empirical methods. This has been noted by other authors. Blight asks in the title to his (1981) article "must psychoanalysis retreat to hermeneutics?"

THE TWO THEORIES OF PSYCHOANALYSIS

The separate domain perspective can be imposed neatly upon psychoanalysis because the latter itself naturally fractures into two domains. The metapsychology and the clinical principles have long been regarded as "the two theories in psychoanalysis," even by those not opposed to the metapsychology. Rapaport (1960a) talks of the distinction between clinical theory and the general theory of psychoanalysis. The latter is identified as the metapsychology. The clinical part of psychoanalytic theory is usually seen as the lower-level theory and includes data. The metapsychology is the general theory that is put forward as an explanation (the anti-metapsychologists would say pseudo-explanation) of the clinical. Traditional psychoanalytic theoreticians, such as Rapaport, and before him Hartmann, Kris, and others, have often shown dissatisfaction with Freud's metapsychology, considering it to be wrong or outdated. But their objections have been to specific aspects of the metapsychology, not to its very idea. They may have rejected, say, the drive conception, but not the need for some explanation of the energizing aspects of motivation. They were not philosophically opposed to explaining clinical phenomena in terms of a higher order set of hypotheses that made reference to causal mental processes.

The Metapsychology versus the Clinical Principles. The writers mentioned above, Klein, Holt, Schafer, Gill, and others of this "new critical movement," argue that there can only be one true theory of psychoanalysis, and this is the clinical one; metapsychology is redundant. These writers treat the metapsychology and the clinical principles of psychoanalysis in the terms of the separate domain dichotomy. Klein (1976), for example, says:

Psychoanalysis is unique, I believe, among psychological disciplines in containing within itself two kinds of theory, one clin-

> ical, and one metapsychological; or as Rapaport has expressed
> this distinction, the "clinical principles" and the "general psy-
> chological theory." The distinction is exemplified in Chapter
> Seven of Freud's *The Interpretation of Dreams,* where his expla-
> nations are on a level entirely different from that of the first six
> chapters of the same book. I am referring to Freud's attempt to
> discuss the mental apparatus in terms of a quasi-thermodynamic
> energic system. In moving to that level Freud believed . . . that
> he was on the most fundamental level of explanation [p. 41].

Similarly, Holt talks of "two psychoanalytic theories of motivation" (1976, p. 162) and says "the clinical theory" of psychoanalysis is "opposed to metapsychology, which Rapaport called
the *general theory* of psychoanalysis" (p. 161).

In accordance with the separate domain view they argue that,
first, this division is a philosophical matter: "The . . . profound
point of distinction [between clinical psychoanalysis and meta-
psychology] is that they derive from two different philosophies
of inquiry and explanation" (Klein, 1976, p. 26); they belong
each to a "different universe of discourse" (Gill, 1976, p. 86).
Second, they see the division as between a type of explanation
appropriate to natural phenomena and one appropriate to human activities. Klein expresses this: metapsychology attempts
"to place psychoanalysis in the realm of natural science by providing an impersonal, nonteleological view of the organism as
a natural 'object,' subject ultimately to the laws of physics, chemistry and physiology" (1976, p. 2). On the other hand, clinical
explanation attempts to "read the experiences of a person and
to account for them, that is, understand them" (p. 1), "it [clinical
explanation] has to do with an accounting in terms of reasons
and origins, significance and meaning, of behavior, rather
than . . . causation" (p. 3). Third, they therefore reject the metapsychology arguing in favor of what Holt terms "clearing
away the deadwood of metapsychology" (1976, p. 161).

In fact there is a series of contrasts made between the two
theories of psychoanalysis by those who wish to remove metapsychology from psychoanalysis:

Biology versus Psychology. The metapsychology, it is argued, is
just biology: "the metapsychology deals with the neurology and
biology, with the physical substrate, of psychological function-

ing" (Gill, 1976, p. 85). It is identified with Freud's Project model: "the Project contains the first comprehensive statement of the major principles of what we now call metapsychology" (p. 73). It is also seen as the "residues of nineteenth-century physiology" in which Freud received his training (Holt, 1976, p. 163). The British philosopher MacIntyre, writing in the "ordinary language" tradition (1958, p. 22) argues that Freud took a theory originally intended as neurology and then rewrote it in psychological language. Further, it is regarded as purely speculative (for example, Gill, 1976, pp. 82–83).

In contrast to this, it is asserted, "clinical psychoanalysis is a 'pure' psychology which deals with intentionality and meaning" (Gill, 1976, p. 85), and "clinical theory is quite close to the factual observational core of psychoanalysis" (Holt, 1976, p. 161). Indeed MacIntyre (1958) argues that Freud's true discoveries are all at the level of description, in his insightful "redescriptions" of action.

Mechanism versus Purpose. The metapsychology, it is argued (for example, by Holt, 1976, p. 170), is mechanistic, and its "mechanistic" nature is pejoratively described:

> The metapsychological points of view are the natural-science framework of structure, energy, and force. . . . If the metapsychology is employed to *explain* clinical propositions, the effort to state psychoanalytic propositions in terms of physics and chemistry, or in terms of biological concepts like structure, function and adaptation, becomes inevitably reductionistic [Gill, 1976, p. 85].

Klein comments on causal explanation in the metapsychology:

> Issues of causal explanation, impersonal causal processes and mechanism, the desire to establish interfaces with the natural sciences, and the theory of evolution and biology . . . have all created a momentum for a mode of theoretical explanation quite different from the clinical mode [Klein, 1976, p. 2].

He equates this with an attempt to answer "how" questions in psychology. Freud's "positivistic bent," says Klein, made him ask of phenomena like repression, "*how* do they occur? What is their mechanism?" (p. 43). "To explain something meant to know *how* it worked" (p. 44; italics added).

In contrast to this, the anti-metapsychologists argue, psychoanalysis should be attempting to "usefully answer psychological why-questions" (Schafer, 1976, p. 201). "Psychoanalysts [in the application of clinical notions] are theorists not on the 'how' but on the 'why' of behavior" (Klein, 1976, p. 53). "None of them [the clinical conceptions] has much to do with an account of 'how,' or mechanisms. . . . Psychoanalysis [the clinical enterprise] is a psychology of . . . *meanings*" (p. 54). Schafer says, "meaning (and intention) is . . . at the center of clinical psychoanalytic work" (1976, p. 100); and Gill comments, "Psychological propositions [as opposed to metapsychological ones] deal with intention and meaning" (1976, p. 103). The anti-metapsychologists identify the clinical principles as the true psychoanalysis and they see this as nonmechanistic and distinct from natural science. Explanations in this specifically human science articulate the person's reasons, his purposes, and the (conscious or unconscious) *"personal meanings* of . . . events" which require, says Klein, "mentalistic and teleological terms" (1976, p. 49).

The contrasts can be summarized thus:

Metapsychology	*Clinical Principles*
Biology	Psychology
The Project model	The Project rejected
Early medical Freud	Later psychological Freud
Speculative theory	Data
"Explanation"	Description
Natural science model	Human science
Mechanism	Purpose
Causal explanation	Intentional
"How"	"Why"

In the remaining chapters I shall argue against these distinctions, and against the conclusions drawn from them: that the clinical principles must be disentangled from the metapsychology; that psychoanalysis must "recover and rehabilitate the clinical theory of motivation by clearing away the deadwood of metapsychology" (Holt, 1976, p. 161).

Before I proceed with this, it is important to note that this debate is over the psychoanalytic theory of motivation. A number of those attacking the metapsychology are quite explicit about this. The quotation immediately above, from Holt, is one example. Holt's (1976) paper is entitled "Drive or Wish? A Reconsideration of the Psychoanalytic Theory of Motivation." Klein (1976) says: "The general ingredients of the clinical mode of explanation are as follows: It is first of all a theory of motivations. It is concerned with the specification, the conditions and the origins of motivations, their development and their pathological miscarriages" (p. 3).

11

METAPSYCHOLOGY AS BIOLOGY

The biological argument used against the metapsychology says: "the metapsychology is disguised neurology and is not a genuine explanatory system for psychological data." The first part of this, that metapsychology is neurology, is usually supported by showing how similar are the Project model and the later metapsychology. Klein, Gill, Holt, and the philosopher MacIntyre (1958) all do this. They also point out that concepts like drive, energy, force, and structure are concepts used in the analysis of material systems. To this I have no objection. It is true as far as it goes, and I have argued similarly. The second part of the biological argument asserts that neurology can have no part in psychological explanation. Even psychoanalysts who wish to defend the metapsychology often assume the latter is true. Kanzer (1973), for example, attempts to defend the model of the Project by arguing that it is not neurology. This second part of the argument rests on a number of suppositions, often not made explicit by those who support it.

Against this I shall argue that (1) without any proper justification, this simply assumes that if metapsychology is biology (neurology), then it cannot figure in any sort of psychological account; (2) the sense in which Freud's metapsychology is biology is misunderstood by the anti-metapsychologists; and (3) they mistake the way hypothetical constructs work in explanation.

188

DUALISM ASSUMED

The biological argument is fundamental for the anti-meta-psychologist's position. But its supposed justifications are often not explicit. It is assumed to be self-evident that if the metapsychology contains neurological propositions then it cannot be used in psychological explanation. Gill, for example, spends most of his (1976) paper making the points that "metapsychological propositions are in the natural-science framework of force, energy, and structure," and that "psychological propositions deal with intention and meaning" (p. 103). Little time is spent in arguing from this to his conclusion "that metapsychological and psychological propositions are in different universes of discourse" (p. 91), that is, they are of different explanatory orders. Rather, it is assumed that showing both (1) that the metapsychology uses neurological constructs, and (2) that clinical accounts involve ascriptions of intention means that there is an unbridgeable ontological gulf between them.

MacIntyre (1958) makes similar assumptions. Most of his book is spent showing that Freud uses the term "unconscious" adjectivally to (re)describe actions to further our understanding of the reasons for those actions. Little time is spent telling us what is wrong with using "unconscious" in its substantive, metapsychological sense to stand for a theoretical entity involved in the explanation of behavior.

Both MacIntyre and Gill, like others critical of the metapsychology, assume rather than justify the explanatory dualism of the separate domain thesis. But since intentional action is the end product of the evolution of a wholly natural system, such a dualism needs justifying and should not be assumed. Motivation theorists like Freud attempt to identify which aspects of this natural world are the causes of intentional action. Of course, differences do exist between explaining action in terms of intentions and explaining actions in nonintentional terms. The former is the everyday way of doing things and it provides us with a fairly efficient way of understanding and predicting human behavior in the ordinary context. Explanations of the latter kind are tenuous, and we have little information about the relation between their constructs and the "wetware" of the brain. This, however, does not mean that there is any fundamental ontological break between the two. The supposed break between the two modes of explanation is in need of demonstration.

FREUD'S BAD BIOLOGY

Another reason offered for the rejection of the metapsychology is not just that it is biology but, it is argued, it is bad biology. Holt, for example, comments: "the metapsychology of motivation is an explicit, coherent, but untenably mechanistic theory, which has the virtue of being testable and the misfortune of being mostly wrong" (1976, pp. 162–163). In an earlier paper Holt (1965) characterized Freud's Project model as a "passive reflex model" of nervous functioning. Holt argued there that the Freudian conception of the nervous system was out of date; his biology was wrong, and that "*many—perhaps most—of the obscurities, fallacies, and internal contradictions of psychoanalytic theory are rather direct derivatives of its neurological inheritance*" (p. 109). Similarly the philosopher R. S. Peters (1958) says that Freud's physiological orientation spoils his theory because his physiology was out of date (p. 77).

It is not my present purpose to defend Freud's neurology or his concepts of the functioning units of the brain. Others have done this, or at least have shown Freud's model to compare with modern information-processing concepts (for example, Erdelyi, 1985; Innes, 1971; Pribram, 1965; Pribram and Gill, 1976). It is true that the language Freud uses is old-fashioned, and some of the ideas he uses are out of date. However, the model he builds does not depend on neurological specifics. Freud was concerned in the Project (1895a), as are neuropsychologists today, with setting out the operational principles of a cybernetic model. He is trying to state in general neurological terms the mechanisms that would provide the psychological functions (see Chapter 8) in which he is interested. It is clear that many neuropsychological principles now stressed, though they go by different names, are present in Freud's Project model: "many of the neurological conceptions contained in his model have a current ring to them" (Pribram, 1965, p. 81). In the same article Pribram proposes that "we take seriously the detail—in its *structured* combination of the neurological and psychological—with which the psychoanalytic model is replete" (p. 82).

The contrast between the assessments of the neuropsychology by Holt and Peters on the one hand and by Pribram on the other points to a problem in Freudian scholarship. Freud stressed infantile sexuality, unconscious motivation, and that they were inextricably bound up. He then proceeded to analyze every aspect of personality, normal and abnormal, in these terms. This aspect of his work is the most widely known, the most controversial, and the most striking. But stressing this aspect of Freud's work obscures the complex metapsychology upon which it is built. It takes attention away from the sophistication of the motivational model that Freud uses. Personality textbooks, for example, tend to discuss the broad outline of Freud's theory, simplistically classing it as a "tension reduction" or "drive" theory. Upon this assumption they then treat Freud's theory of motivation as standing or falling with drive theory. But Freud's is not a simple theory of motivation at all. Demonstrating that the model includes reflex principles does not mean that it is merely what Holt (1965, p. 96) terms a "passive reflex model." Nor does the fact that Freud's theory involves drive concepts mean that it excludes postulates about cognitive mechanisms or that it cannot deal with the role of learned incentives—the type of motivational formulations that modern motivation theorists consider a necessary part of any worthy and topical theory of motivation. An examination of Freud's Project model shows "that the formulations of memory-motive mechanisms, attention, consciousness, and thought processes are as sophisticated as any available elsewhere" (Pribram and Gill, 1976, p. 11).

However, the quality of Freud's neurology cannot strictly be relevant to a conceptual attack on the metapsychology, nor to its defense. This point is recognized by Gill (1976, p. 77). What is really at issue is whether the propositions of the metapsychology, with their neurological content, could possibly serve as explanations of psychological phenomena. Arguing that they are not good neurology, as does Holt and in places Klein, would not exclude better neurological propositions from being explanations for psychological phenomena.

REDUCTIONISM

One critical word that is mentioned—though it is hardly developed as a full argument against the metapsychology as neurology—is "reductionism." Klein mentions reductionism in discussing "Freud's two theories of sexuality." These two are the "drive-discharge" theory of the metapsychology and the "clinical theory" which "centers upon . . . the values and meanings associated with sensual experiences" (1976, p. 73). Klein comments: "This psychoanalytic clinical view should not be confused with the reductionist position of the drive-discharge theory. . . . The clinical theory of sexuality does not reduce motivations" (p. 94). And Gill (1976) comments:

> If the metapsychology is employed to *explain* clinical propositions, the effort to state psychoanalytic propositions in terms of physics and chemistry, or in terms of biological concepts like structure, function, and adaptation, becomes inevitably reductionistic [p. 85].

He expands:

> Insofar as these metapsychological concepts are alleged to be explanations of, or higher-order abstractions from, the clinical propositions, they are pseudo explanations and pseudo abstractions which, to the extent that they are related to the clinical propositions at all, are restatements of them in another, albeit systematic, language relating to a different universe of discourse [p. 86].

Schafer (1976, p. 201), too, argues that traditional motivational explanations in psychoanalysis are merely translations of the data statements into an alien language.

In this accusation of reductionism, they assert that the metapsychology *restates* psychological phenomena in biological terms.

They imply, that is, (1) that the metapsychology simply is biology; and (2) that the metapsychology attempts to carry through an elimination of psychological terms in favor of biological ones. They consider then (though there are degrees to this) that terms like "ego," "id," "cathexis," and "drive" are actually biological. Gill (p. 85) talks of "biological concepts like structure, function, and adaptation."

The reductionist accusation contains misunderstandings: (1) it mistakes the sense in which Freud's metapsychology is biological; and (2) the metapsychology does not lead to reductionism—at least not any sort like the "translation" version. A return to the theoretical construct analysis of metapsychological terms illuminates these points.

Functional Explanation and Reduction

In Chapter 9, I argued that Freud's theory attempts to give functional characterizations of those processes that give rise to action and experience. These mental processes are distinguished—for example, into conscious and unconscious motivations—according to their presumed consequences. One source on which Freud models his characterizations of mental processes is the speculative neurological theory of his day. This, we should note, was itself as much determined by psychological considerations as neurological. As a materialist, Freud assumes that the processes he constructs are realized neurally; there are working parts of the brain that carry out just such functions. He also makes some attempt to see that his postulations are neurologically plausible. This does suppose an identity between mind and brain. But this is, as I argued in Chapter 9, a functional identity. It is not an identity that allows simple reduction: it is not a matter of "translating psychological phenomena into biological terms." On this reading, psychoanalytic constructs are putative characterizations at a high abstract level of the neural working parts. They describe the working parts at a functional and organizational level, and not in terms of the brain wetware.

Consider Freud's (1916–1917) theory of sexual motivation. This involves a complex of energic and structural notions. The various postulated mental processes are differentiated according to their supposed psychological consequences; the sexual objects of such a motive, how sexuality develops in the child, and so on. This postulated drive process is made biologically plausible by incorporating notions of adaptation. Of the precise biology of these sexual motive processes Freud remains agnostic:

> . . . the phrase 'sexual metabolism' or 'chemistry of sexuality' is a term without content: we know nothing about it and cannot even decide whether we are to assume two sexual substances . . . or whether we would be satisfied with *one* sexual toxin which we should have to recognize as the vehicle of all the stimulant effects of libido [pp. 388–389].

Yet the next sentence states, "The theoretical structure of psycho-analysis that we have created is in truth a superstructure, which will one day have to be set upon its organic foundation" (p. 389). There then must be working parts of the organic substructure that carry out the sexual functions. How it does it (one substance or two?) does not matter. The identity is a functional one. A single function might be compatible with several organic substructures, and one organic system might carry out several different functions. In such an identity the neurochemistry is as much conditioned by the psychology as the other way around. This weakens further the accusation of reductionism—which implies a one-way process of theory elimination.

We may also recall from the argument in Chapter 9 that what makes a construct itself neurological or psychological is not, as the reduction accusation supposes, something absolute. It depends on the theory in which it inheres, and which gives the theoretical concept its content, and it depends on the data from which the construct is inferred. Much of this is convention. A simple motive construct named "the sexual arousal factor" might be considered psychological if it is inferred from behavioral data such as periodicity of sexual arousal, experienced excitement, selectivity of objects in states of excitation, and so on. On the other hand, if the inference is made from the presence of certain chemicals during times of arousal, we would consider it a neurochemical hypothesis. Kanzer (1973) makes out a strong case for treating the Project hypotheses as psychological, on the grounds that they are established on psychological data and differentiated according to psychological functions.

So the accusation of reductionism made by the anti-metapsychologists errs both in its understanding of the nature of theoretical constructs and in the senses that Freud's metapsychological constructs are biological. Now, this second point needs elaborating since, as I have argued (Chapters 2, 3, 9), both the fact of the Project and the lingering influence of his neurological education show that Freud was not always so philosophical and agnostic on the relation of his theoretical concepts to neurology.

Biology and Metapsychology

Freud uses his understanding of neural processes to model his metapsychological theory. This is the first way that biology enters into psychoanalysis. His metapsychology and mental model bear formal resemblance to the then current ideas about neural processes. This, however, does not make his hypotheses biological. After all, a supply-demand theory of economics may be modeled directly upon a hydraulic pressure system, and that does not make it a physical theory. The anti-metapsychology critics (for example, Gill, 1976, p. 76) do not make the necessary distinctions between the constructed theory and that upon which it is modeled. Gill argues that much of the Project model is a "neurological metaphor" (1976, p. 76)—it has formal similarity to neurological theory—and he notes that the "Project contains the first comprehensive statement of the . . . metapsychology" (p. 73). Yet he also asserts that "by metapsychology, Freud meant a set of biological assumptions" (p. 72). Gill, however, is mistaken. Science uses metaphor (modeling) a great deal. There is good argument that it is a necessary part of theory (for example, Harré, 1970, 1972; Hesse, 1966, 1967).

But the source of the model does not define the nature of the theory constructed, as Gill assumes.

Freud also incorporates evolutionary, adaptive notions into his metapsychology. This reflects his view that man is part of the natural living world and must be understood in those terms. But it hardly makes his constructs directly biological. Rather it is that evolutionary knowledge places constraints upon the picture that we paint of man's psyche.

Freud at one stage, at the time of the Project (1895a), believed that the causes of behavior can be characterized quite directly in biological terms. Even then he was aware of how speculative are the neurology and physiology that he uses, and he realizes how much psychological factors have determined his hypotheses (see Kanzer, 1973). However, Freud does talk as though the neural or material event corresponding to a psychological event or process could be identified. For example, "remembering X," he seems to believe, corresponds to "the recathexis of a group of neurones previously associated with the percept X"—or some such formulation. However, as I have recorded (Chapter 9), he later rejects this simple correspondence picture of the mind-brain relation. He soon abandons the parallelism that supports it. After this he lets the psychoanalytic hypotheses "float," while he still believes that the relation between psychoanalytic hypotheses and neurology will one day be made clear.

Freud does not then reduce psychological data to biology—at least not in the way the anti-metapsychologists argue. Nor does biology enter into his metapsychological explanations in the way that Gill, Klein, and others argue. The latter fail to justify their objections to Freud's "biological" metapsychology. In general, they rest their views on unproven philosophical doctrines.

12

THE METAPSYCHOLOGY, THE CLINICAL PRINCIPLES, AND THEIR INTERDEPENDENCE

The various calls for the disengagement of the metapsychology and the clinical principles assert the independence of the latter from the former. Variously, they view the metapsychology as irrelevant to, as inconsistent with, as incompatible with, or as harmful to, the clinical principles. A quotation from Gill (1976) makes this point nicely: "Metapsychological propositions are not an abstraction from psychological [clinical] propositions, nor are they derivable from, translations of, or explanatory of such propositions. There is therefore no direct connection between metapsychology and psychology" (p. 103).

There are, in the literature, several versions of the view that "metapsychological propositions are not psychological and are not relevant to psychoanalysis" (Gill 1976, p. 92):

1. The metapsychology is not "explanatory of" the clinical principles specifically in that the metapsychology does not in fact aid in clinical explanation.
2. The clinical data and principles are logically independent of the metapsychology.
3. The metapsychology is logically inconsistent with the clinical data and principles.
4. The metapsychology is theoretically inconsistent with the clinical principles and data.

197

In this chapter I shall consider these in turn.

METAPSYCHOLOGY AND CLINICAL EXPLANATION

I need to counter the view that the metapsychology is not "explanatory of" the clinical principles (1) in the general sense that the metapsychology does not inform the clinical aspects of psychoanalysis, and (2) in the specific sense that it does not help particular clinical accounts. In both the general and the specific cases the idea I want to criticize is that metapsychology is an inappropriate superimposition upon clinical material, of no heuristic worth, and is *post hoc*.

Prepsychoanalytic Principles and Clinical Explanation

In Chapter 2, I argued that many of the metapsychological principles existed prepsychoanalytically, and that Freud synthesized these into a model of mind. One such principle is the very general one that man (including mind) is a part of nature. He is subject to natural laws. So mind is lawful and explicable. Now this notion, general as it is, does have consequences for Freud's clinical approach. It is a lawfulness not simply in rationalist terms, picturing man as a creature of reason. Indeed, Freud's discoveries about the importance of the unconscious would not sit comfortably with a purely rationalist version of the lawfulness of mind, for the latter implies a certain logic and self-consistency in action that is quite the opposite of Freud's description of unconscious, primary process activity. This rationalism would make unconscious reasons an anomaly and a puzzle. Rather, for Freud, mind is lawful in natural biological terms. It is causally explicable. From this perspective, the individual is primarily unconscious, and if there is a puzzle then it is this: What is the function of consciousness? So, while Freud's general physicalism does not lead directly and specifically to clinical hypotheses, it sets the stage for the clinical approach and for the emphasis on unconscious motivation.

There are other general principles that predate but condition Freud's clinical theory. For example, Freud sees endogenous stimulation (drive) as the outcome of evolutionary processes. Now, because the individual cannot fly from internal stimulation as he can from external, he must master it to survive. In turn, this is the basis of conflict: on the one hand there are the demands of the real world (and this comes to include the social), and on the other are the individual's drives that have to be satisfied. Mastery of the environment and the delay of gratification (the opposition of primary and secondary processes) are necessitated. The idea of intrapsychic conflict is of course fundamental to Freud's clinical explanation.

The relation of these very general principles to the clinical explanations Freud offers is not simple. Freud's physicalism, his theory of drives, his Darwinian perspective, and the various other principles that predate his clinical work do not lead directly to his clinical hypotheses. Nor are such general principles logically necessary for such hypotheses. Yet they do condition and inform the particular clinical principles that Freud uses, and his metapsychological principles themselves are affected by his clinical work, and the clinical work of others. While the idea of intrapsychic conflict is present in Freud from the outset, it also receives reinforcement from clinical practice. In Breuer's patient "Anna O" (Breuer and Freud, 1895) there was a clear distinction between two mental states, the hypnoid and the normal. These states conflicted with one another, and this fact helped form Freud's notions of an unconscious over and against the conscious mind (the structural counterparts to the primary and secondary processes).

Sexuality, too, is a notion that is informed both by the prepsychoanalytic concepts and by clinical experiences. The clinical data may have forced the importance of sexuality on a reluctant Freud. Yet to a great extent he was already prepared for its importance by his emphasis on evolution: psychological processes were bound to be oriented toward activities necessary for the continuation of the species.

The Wish Concept

Freud's use of the wish concept is a more specific example of the way in which the metapsychology and the clinical principles interact. In Chapter 6, I argued that wish serves as an explanatory construct for Freud in his case studies (1918; see also my Appendix). In the Wolf Man case Freud postulates an unconscious wish as the cause of symptoms and dreams. This wish postulate implies a tripartite model of motivation, one in which precipitating, directing, and energizing elements make up a full motivational account. These three types of factors are in fact metapsychological. They are detailed in the theory of mind with its energic and structural concepts, its hypotheses about learning and development, the primary and secondary processes, and so on.

The wish concept is the interface between the metapsychology and the clinical data, the means by which the metapsychology is brought to bear upon the data. The wish concept provides, as I argued, an explanation of the data in that it helps systematize them, is heuristically valuable, and performs various other conceptual functions that are essential to explaining (see Chapter 7). I pointed out, too, that the very meaning of "unconscious wish" as Freud uses it is given by the theory within which it resides: a metapsychological theory.

The Metapsychology and the Freudian Case Study

On examination of the Wolf Man case, we find that Freud's (1918) clinical explanation is dependent on the metapsychology. The essence of Freud's hypotheses about the phobia is: *The wolf is a substitute for the father, whom he feared because castration was an implied condition for the satisfaction of the passive-feminine and sexual wish he had for his father.* Freud uses three sources to construct this and other hypotheses (see Appendix). The first is the data themselves. Freud draws upon the wolf dream, other dreams, associations to these, the Wolf Man's reminiscences, reactions to interpretations, and so on. These are gathered over the years. The second source is his working clinical principles—many of them "clinical rules of thumb" (see Appendix). These are gathered from Freud's earlier experience and used to extract data, interpret dreams, and move the analysis along. Third, and most important for present purposes, there is the mental model, the metapsychology itself.

THE MENTAL MODEL AND THE PHOBIA EXPLANATION

On the Wolf Man case Freud (1918) comments:

> There are in any case narrow limits to what a psycho-analysis is called upon to explain. For, while it is its business to explain the striking symptoms by revealing their genesis, it is not its business to explain but merely to describe the psychical mechanisms and instinctual processes to which one is led by that means [p. 105].

By "a psycho-analysis," in contrast to simply "psycho-analysis," Freud means the "overall clinical explanation." Within this he is identifying two elements. One is what I have termed the "clinical account" (see Appendix). It simply states the phobia data and unconscious wishes that lie behind it. The second I have termed the "theoretical account." This consists of more general psychoanalytic propositions. It is not derived from the clinical data of this particular case, and there is no attempt to justify it within the case study. Rather it is brought from without the case study and its descriptions of mental workings serve as explanations of the clinical account.

For Freud a descriptive statement on one level of the explanatory hierarchy is explanatory for a lower level. In fact Freud (see Appendix) divides the case study into two main parts. The first derives and justifies the clinical account (roughly, pp. 7–103). The second is the theoretical account. It *explains* the first, clinical, account by *describing* the "psychical mechanisms and instinctual processes" that underlie the unconscious wishes mentioned in the clinical account (pp. 104–122). That is, it attempts to explain the clinical account in terms of the mental model.

Now the principal features of the mental model (outlined in Chapters 2–4) are its general physicalism (its use of the force and structure concepts and its evolutionism); and its specific physicalism (its detailing of the mental mechanics of instincts, of primary and secondary processes, of the structural division of mind, and of the "wish-impulse" structure). These can be seen exemplified in the case study, particularly in the theoretical section.

GENERAL AND SPECIFIC PHYSICALISM IN THE CASE STUDY

Structure. The explanation that Freud gives of the wolf phobia is clearly based on the structural division of the mind. The id is not yet part of his theory at the time of Wolf Man. However, he does discuss the different distinctions that may be made between consciousness and unconsciousness, as qualities of mental events and as systems of the mind. He says, for example: "We are constantly guilty of making a confusion between the phenomenon of emergence as a perception in consciousness and the fact of belonging to a hypothetical psychical system to which we ought to assign some conventional name, but which we in fact also call 'consciousness' (the system *Cs.*)" (p. 105). The unconscious is distinguished from the ego and from the "moral ego" (a forerunner of the superego; p. 110), and is used throughout the study in its systematic, structural sense to explain clinical phenomena.

Force and Energy. The concepts of energy and force are mutually implicative. Force is energy with direction, and energy always exists in conserved quantities. At the beginning of the case study Freud (p. 106) refers to mental energy derived from an instinct. He talks of "a failure on the part of the organism to master its sexual excitation." The assumption of the quantitative, conserved nature of mental energy is clear when he comments that the repression of a homosexual wish is a "withdrawal of libido" and that the "libido . . . [is] converted into free anxiety and subsequently bound in phobias" (p. 113). And again, Freud refers to Wolf Man's "power of maintaining simultaneously the most various and contradictory libidinal cathexes" (pp. 118–119). These quantities of energy derive from instinctual sources and appear as impulses (wishes) directed onto objects. Mental activity consists of the interplay of forces as, for example, when the "homosexual wishful impulse" (p.

113) conflicts with that of the ego whose "motive force" (p. 110) is narcissistic masculinity.

Evolution. There are also some references to the evolutionary nature of psychic structures where Freud comments that "pre-genital organizations in man should be regarded as vestiges of conditions . . . of animals" (p. 108). He is using this hypothesis to explain the transference of the "receptive passive function . . . from the oral zone . . . to the anal zone." He also argues that the Oedipus complex is one of many "phylogenetically inherited schema . . . concerned with the business of 'placing' the impressions derived from actual experience" (p. 119). He argues that this is a source of the wish that conflicts with the homosexual one. He also, of course, treats instincts, such as the "nutritional instinct" (p. 106), as somatically based. Yet these determine mental events; mental activities, such as Wolf Man's oral and anal predilections, are ultimately in the service of somatic needs.

Conflict. Freud explains clinical material in terms of the conflict between the two mental systems. The unconscious is characterized by the primary process and its mode of operation is neither logical nor reality oriented. Thus Wolf Man is able to act simultaneously as though castration is the condition of homosexuality and as though sexual intercourse takes place at the anus. Freud explains the contradiction: "our bewilderment arises only because we are always inclined to treat unconscious mental processes like conscious ones" (pp. 78–79). It is in the unconscious that wishes represent instinctual tendencies. The unconscious contains the homosexual wishful impulse which simply presses for discharge, regardless of reality. It is the ego that modifies.

Associationism. In Wolf Man's mind associations are registered; for example, there are associations between the wolf and the father. These associations are in the form of traces (p. 112)—left presumably by passages of excitation. When prevented from expression, the homosexual wish cathexis passes over into the wolf phobia.

Primary Process. The primary process itself is not explicitly mentioned, nonetheless it remains an essential ingredient in the Wolf Man case study. Quantities of energy arise from instinctual sources (nutritional, sexual) and add a load of excitation to the system. This excitation must be "mastered" (p. 106); that is, its pressure to discharge must be controlled by secondary-process structures or dysfunctional (neurotic) activity will result. This is what happens in the case of Wolf Man.

Secondary Process and Ego. The ego contrasts with the unconscious. Its secondary-process nature is indicated in that, for example, "the ego, by developing anxiety, was protecting itself against what it regarded as an overwhelming danger" (p. 112). This danger was the intense homosexual wish. This is used to explain Wolf Man's motive for repression. Freud also points out that the energy the ego uses is ultimately libidinal. This concurs with his theory of instincts at the time. However, the ego's instincts are not strictly sexual. It has an "interest [Freud often uses this synonymously with 'instinct'] in its own self-protection and in the preservation of its narcissism" (p. 112). Indeed, it is clear that these derivative instincts draw energy from the libido but have modified, secondary-process aims. So the conflict between the homosexual impulse and the narcissistic one in the Wolf Man's case is founded upon the division of the instincts into object-libido and ego-libido; between that which operates toward immediate satisfaction and that which is bound and modified toward ego-syntonic ends.

Mental Mechanics. In a number of places Freud becomes quite specific about the mental mechanisms behind the phobia formation. In the passage already quoted he outlines the "micro" mechanisms of repression: the ego withdraws libido from the homosexual impulse and the withdrawn quantity is converted to anxiety and bound in the wolf phobia (p. 113). Wolf Man's psychological experiences—fearing, forgetting, desiring, becoming phobic—are the concomitants of changes in the energy conditions of the elements of the mental apparatus. Once again Freud explains clinical phenomena by referring back to the model of mind.

Wishes, like instincts, are complex phenomena in psychoanalytic theory. As the mental representatives of instincts they share the latter's general characteristics: pressure, source, object, and aim. The pressure is set up by the cathexis of energy from some somatic, instinctual source. Thus the "homosexual wishful impulse" (p. 113) gets energy from the sexual instinct of an intensity that is threatening to the maintenance of ordinary ego-directed activity: its pressure is too great. The object is in this example the father, and the aim is the satisfaction that Freud talks about (p. 112)—that is, the release of tension.

THE UNITY OF THE OVERALL CLINICAL ACCOUNT

Freud considers it natural that the clinical should be subsumed by the theoretical account, and indeed that the two comprise a single explanation. He wants to explain the case, and explanation at one level is description at another in the explanatory hierarchy; the description of mental mechanisms is an explanation of the behavioral phenomena. The essential unity of the overall explanation is then indicated by the way Freud interweaves his different levels of explanation.

Another point to note is that the role of the metapsychology in clinical accounts is an explanatory one in just that sense of "explanatory" discussed in Chapter 7. In particular I have been pointing out the heuristic role that the metapsychology performs in clinical accounts.

The view that the clinical principles are in fact independent of the metapsychology is then wrong on at least two counts. One is that many of the clinical principles are conditioned by metapsychological principles that predate them and the stage is set for individual case explanations by these metapsychological assumptions. The second is that as a matter of fact Freud depends on his metapsychological model of mind when he forms his clinical accounts in the case studies.

LOGICAL INDEPENDENCE

One may object that it is not Freud's use of the metapsychology that is in question but rather the logical independence of the clinical data and the metapsychology. This, however, is quite simply dealt with. It is not a requirement of a theory offered in explanation of a set of data that the former be logically derivable from the latter. To hold that it should be is to return to a brand of logical positivism. A theory that is nothing more than a logical restatement of a set of data will not function as a theory should, for it will have no heuristic function and no "surplus meaning" over and above the data upon which it is founded. It may work to systematize data, but that is all. Just this is not a full explanatory role, and so this is not a telling argument against the metapsychology.

THEORETICAL INCOMPATIBILITY

The metapsychology, it may be argued, is independent of the clinical principles not for the reasons discussed above, but because it is theoretically inconsistent with the clinical data. This is an argument that Holt (1976) adopts, and in fact one with which I have already dealt (Chapter 11). Holt argues that Freud's metapsychology is empirically inadequate, in particular it is bad biology. This argument fails as a support for the separate domain thesis. First, there is a good case made out by Pribram and others that Freud's neurology in his psychoneurological model of mind is surprisingly good. Second, the quality of Freud's neurological speculations is not relevant to his philosophy of explanation. It is the latter with which we are concerned.

LOGICAL INCONSISTENCY

The final of the senses of "independence" is a more complex matter to deal with. However, it is more appropriately handled in the next chapter—on meaning. It asserts that the mode of explanation (causal) implied by the metapsychology is not appropriate for clinical, psychological data, and that the latter, being about meaning, needs an explanation of an intentional kind.

13

PSYCHOANALYSIS AND THE PSYCHOLOGY OF MEANING

Central to the argument against the metapsychology, and against Freud's causal theory of mind, is the view that true psychoanalysis is a "psychology of meaning." Another way of saying this—in the terms of the last chapter—is that the metapsychology is logically inconsistent with the clinical principles. It is argued that the causal, explanatory concepts of the metapsychology are of a different logical order to those of the purposive, clinical data. This is what Gill (1976) means when he says of the clinical propositions that they are in a "different universe of discourse" (p. 86) from the metapsychology and that the latter cannot articulate meaning.

Gill asserts that "clinical psychoanalysis is a 'pure psychology' which deals with intentionality and meaning" (p. 85). Psychoanalysis, Klein (1976) comments, is "a psychology . . . of . . . *meanings*" (p. 54), and Schafer (1976), "meaning (and intention) is . . . at the center of clinical psychoanalytic work" (p. 100). Holt (1976) condemns the metapsychology because it is at variance with the true value of Freud's work, in reality Freud "dealt always and almost exclusively with patterns of meanings" (p. 168).

In this chapter I want to (1) tease out the concept of meaning as it is used in this context; (2) show that the anti-metapsychologists' views on meaning are dependent on certain mistaken philosophical doctrines (ones with which I have already dealt); and (3) show by referring back to my arguments in Part II that

207

Freud's causal theory of mind is compatible with a psychology of meaning.

MEANING IN THE WORKS CRITICAL OF THE METAPSYCHOLOGY

One feature about the above and other comments on psychoanalysis as a psychology of meanings is how vague they are about why a causal theory of mind cannot deal with meaning. Generally the critics show on the one hand that clinical psychology is concerned with meaning, and on the other that the metapsychology is a causal model of mind. This is taken by them to be adequate enough to establish their position. The detailed justification for this position—that a causal model of mind and the articulation of psychological meanings are incompatible—is omitted.

George Klein on Psychoanalytic Ascriptions of Meaning

Klein (1976) gives the clearest and most comprehensive account of clinical psychoanalysis as a theory of meaning. It is worth looking at his account in more detail. He says:

> Psychoanalysis, first of all, attempts to specify coherences in behavior in terms of purpose, not only conscious intention but also that arising out of the dynamics of aborted wish, conflict, defense, anxiety, guilt, and unconscious fantasy. When an analyst sees a pattern of behavior functioning as a "defense," for example, he is stating the *significance* of a pattern of behavior; he is making a statement about its purpose or intention. The coherences to which an analyst becomes sensitized are unique in their distinctive concern with purpose—aims frustrated, conflicted, aborted, regressed, defended against. This discovery of intention is the primary objective of the analyst in the psychoanalytic situation [pp. 51–52].

This is an exclusive concern with purpose. It comes in response to "why" questions about behavior (p. 53).

Klein takes an essentially phenomenological view of these meanings, criticizing the metapsychology because it cannot deal with the "personal meaning" of events for individuals (p. 49). Statements of the *"personal meanings* of . . . events—their psychological significance—require so-called mentalistic and teleological terms." Yet he is less radical in his conceptual surgery than others—for example, Schafer. Klein at least allows that there is theory in clinical psychoanalysis (p. 49) and that in it are two categories of "concepts of meaningfulness" (p. 52). One group he terms "phenomenological" or "experiential." The other he terms "functional" or "extraphenomenological." The experiences that an analyst attributes to the patient are in the phenomenological category (p. 50). But,

> concepts like projection, introjection, and repression, which point to something in the mind of the patient which the patient does not experience but is part of his reality, are functional or extraphenomenological concepts. These are of the class of concepts which are meant to account for, or in some way to illuminate or elucidate, those experiences of the patient which are not accessible directly. Thus an analyst plunges into phenomenology, but goes beyond it to generalizations that connect accessible and inaccessible levels of experience. . . . The analyst's extraphenomenological concepts are meant to illuminate, in these terms of purpose, function and accomplishments, the *significance* of the experiences he infers and the actions he observes—not simply the existential meanings which are based on conscious experience, but also the meanings or significance of inferred unconscious fantasies [pp. 50–51].

From the above, and from elsewhere in Klein's book, we can identify a number of concepts that recur in the anti-metapsychologist's discussions of the psychology of meaning. These seem to hang together. These concepts include motive, intention, goal (aim), purpose, reason, action, teleology, phenomenology, meaning, significance. They fit together in an account that runs like this: clinical psychoanalysis is attempting to articulate the motives (in the sense of intentions, goals, aims, purposes) of the person. These are the reasons for his action. Such a method is phenomenological in the loose sense that the person's subjective, though often unconscious, apprehension of the world is being described in psychoanalytic accounts. Stating a person's goals in explanation of what he does is teleological. Finally, the whole procedure consists of elucidating the meaning, the significance, of the person's action and of expressing the meaning that events have for him.

In this view, then, psychoanalytic accounts state the meanings of actions and of objects for the agent or perceiver. Let me illustrate this by going back to the Wolf Man case that I have been using as an example. Wolf Man makes sexual advances to a particular peasant girl. Freud says what this action means (besides the conscious wish) by stating some of its unconscious aims: to debase a woman unconsciously perceived as like his sister; to assume his father's sexual position in dominance of his mother, and so on. In the same case Freud states what Wolf Man's phobia means by stating its personal, unconscious meaning to him: the wolf is the father (in certain respects).

About Klein's Views

Klein elaborates upon his statement of the basic aims of clinical theory (pp. 56–60). He discusses, following Polanyi (1965a, 1965b, 1966), the notion of "coherence" and sketches a picture of inference in psychoanalytic explanation. He argues that an analyst identifies an intention in an array of behaviors, thereby specifying a "coherence" which links the data. This reading of intention is an inferential process, and remarkably, Klein seems to be suggesting at this point that the structure of clinical inference is the same as in natural science, or as in the perception of ordinary events. For example, he says a chair is a coherence identifiable in an array of data. Klein even makes ontological comparisons, suggesting that an intention is just as real as a physical property since they are both "coherences" (p. 58).

Now, Klein is clearly correct in pointing out that psychoanalysis is concerned with identifying the hidden meanings of actions and of events for the experiencer. His account of inference, as far as it goes, is also not incompatible with the one I have given. He even talks of functions and distinguishes the functional specification of a process from a description of its machinery: a watch is a watch by virtue of its function, not its machinery; we now have watches without springs and balances (p. 59). However, he is unable to take the step to a causal theory of mind, based on a theoretical construct approach, even though he is much less tied to a descriptive phenomenology of meaning than, say, Schafer or MacIntyre. Instead, he asserts the metapsychology is unable to account for meaning at all: "metapsychology throws overboard the fundamental intent of the psychoanalytic enterprise—that of *unlocking meanings*" (p. 48).

Klein offers a variety of reasons for this view, though there are still others that remain implicit. First, he makes such disparaging comments as "what neurophysiologist studies his datum by talking to it?" (p. 48), and he describes the language of the metapsychology as "wholly impersonal" (p. 48), and as a "historical aberration" (p. 43). Most important, he argues that "physiological [read: 'metapsychological'] terms cannot substitute for psychoanalytic terms descriptive of the meanings of object relations. . . . The *personal meanings* of such events—their psychological significance—require so-called mentalistic and teleological terms" (p. 49). And, "A statement of the meaning of behavior is of a different level of coherence from a statement of physiological laws. . . . But, knowing only the physiological rules of operation of a machine or system, and without an observer who recognized its purpose, we shall look in vain for a 'purpose' structure in the machine or system" (p. 61). Also, "to confine theoretical effort to the enterprise of deciphering meanings" is, he says, "to remain on the level on which the discoveries themselves were formulated" (p. 60).

In these quotations we can see some of the reasons why Klein does not allow that metapsychology could deal with meaning. To begin with, he is expressing a general opposition to any picture of the person that smacks of mechanism. This is a motive for most versions of the separate domain view. Against it stands a simple fact: that man is a naturally evolved animal, a biological system. The assertion that Freud was "really" concerned only with purpose, and that the causal model of mind is merely a historical aberration, misses the point. Freud started off with the idea that man is a physical, specifically biological, system explicable wholly in causal terms. *His concern is not simply with meaning, but with how meaning relates to man's biological nature.* This is the motive for constructing the metapsychology. It is an attempt to show how meanings are analyzable, and that they do not require a language all of their own, in a domain separate from other explanation.

Klein is also saying, of course, that the metapsychological language simply is neurological. This crude equivalence I have already argued against. It misrepresents the ways in which biology and metapsychology are related (Chapter 11, above).

However, the view that Klein is most obviously expressing here is the "logical order" one: Klein is saying (like Gill, 1976, p. 91) that there is a language, a set of concepts, that is logically appropriate for the articulation of meaning, and so for explaining human action; this set, however, is of a different logical order to the metapsychological one of cause and structure. I have already named some members of this set, or family, of concepts: motive, intention, goal (aim), purpose, reason, action, teleology, phenomenology, meaning, significance. These are those concepts that recur in anti-metapsychologists' discussions of meaning. Now, many of these are familiar concepts in philosophical psychology. There is a philosophical literature, that of the ordinary language philosophers, which argues that in this family the concepts are logically interrelated in such a way that it means that motives cannot sensibly be cited as causes of actions. Klein and other critics of the metapsychology have adopted the doctrines of the ordinary language philosophers, even acknowledging their philosophical debt. However, they apply them without offering any analysis of the logic of mental terms in justification of these doctrines.

The philosophical literature referred to (for example, Melden, 1961; Peters, 1958) uses a "logical connection" argument to show that reasons explanations are not causal explanations. It is this distinction that is at the philosophical heart of the critique of Freudian metapsychology. Schafer (1976, pp. 204–205, 229) makes clear that his "new language for psychoanalysis" (the title of his book) depends on a distinction between reasons and causes. Similarly, Klein says that psychoanalysis must give accounts in terms of reasons, not causes (1976, p. 3). The logical connection argument says that the statement of the motive or reason for an action is not logically independent of the statement of that action, and that such an independence would be necessary for the reason to count as the cause of the action. Thus, the argument goes, if citing a reason is an explanation for an action, this "reasons" sort of explanation is not causal and is of a logically different order from causal explanations.

The paradigm of the psychological account inherent in this is that where an action is explained by stating the motive (also describable as the reason, purpose, aim, or goal) *for* which it was done. Motives, the argument proceeds, always imply actions because they are defined as "motives for," and so they do not possess the required logical independence of actions that would allow them to be causes of those actions. It is in this sense that the purpose family of concepts are related, and form a group of concepts appropriate to the articulation of psychological meanings (goals) but not for specifying causes. In ontological terms, the argument goes, reasons are not ontologically distinct from actions and so cannot be counted as their causes.

The paradigm of explanation on which authors such as Klein depend is essentially the same. Klein is clear, in conveying his views, that psychoanalytic explanation (even when he allows that it includes "functional" concepts) has to do with the articulation of purposes, the statement of the goals of action, and cannot be causal. Holt draws upon the idea that causes and effects must be "independent existents," for example, when he says that "tension" is a redundant concept in psychology. Tension cannot, he argues, be measured and "for a concept like tension to have scientific value, it must be measurable (at least crudely) in some way that is *independent* of the behavior it is invoked to explain" (1965, p. 110).

What Is Wrong with This View of Explanation?

The first point to make against this view of explanation is the general one that I argued in Chapters 7 and 8. This is that the best way to understand psychoanalytic motive ascriptions is to compare them with the ascriptions of theoretical properties in standard scientific explanation. The structure of inference in everyday psychological, psychoanalytic, and scientific explanation is the same in essential respects. The broad explanatory functions that psychological constructs serve are also the same as for other sciences. It is these functions that give theoretical constructs their meaning, their epistemological characteristics, their ontological status, and mark them as the (hypothesized) causes of observed phenomena. If it is reasonable to adopt a realism toward the concepts of the natural sciences, then it is reasonable to do the same toward mental concepts such as those belonging to psychoanalytic theory.

More specifically, I argued in Part II that the meaning of a psychoanalytic motive ascription, typically the ascription of a wish, may be unpacked into a series of hypotheticals. These hypotheticals state the conditions under which a person can be said to have the particular wish. I made two points that are against the "logical connection" argument in that analysis. First, systematic empirical relations are expressed by the hypotheticals. Such hypotheticals state the behavioral tendencies consequent upon "having such and such a motive." They also state relationships that exist between the ascribed motive and other properties of the person or his conditions. Second, no one hypothetical is analytically true. While some behaviors are more central to the wish concept than others, no one behavior is either a necessary or a sufficient criterion for the ascription of a wish.

Further, I argued that while there is a sense in which motives are always "motives for" something, this is not unusual in scientific explanation (Chapter 9). Theoretical constructs are commonly known by inference, and often named in the first place by reference to those data upon which they were based. This does not mean (as positivist arguments would have it) that these constructs have no existence independently of those data upon which they are based. Similarly, motive ascriptions are independent of the actions upon which they are based, and of the aims they are supposed to imply. The independent specification of a motive, which establishes its credentials as a causal candidate, consists of discovering further predictions that flow from its postulation, and of the demonstration that it performs its explanatory functions well.

To distinguish sharply between reasons-explanations and causes-explanations is to miss the basic similarities between mental constructs, such as motivational ones, and those of science. They are similar in both their inference and their justification. The psychoanalysts who follow this separate domain philosophy of psychology make the same mistake and suppose that the ascription of meaning—that is, of motives and purposes—is irreducibly noncausal.

THE PHENOMENOLOGICAL PICTURE OF EXPLANATION

Klein's picture of psychological explanation is restricted by a perception of human motivation and action that psychoanalysis should have altered dramatically, for it is essentially phenomenological and experiential. (This is so despite Klein's discussion of the importance of "extraphenomenological" concepts.) Indeed, there is a strand of phenomenological thinking, only sometimes acknowledged, in the works of most anti-metapsychologists. This is so in two senses. First, they hold that the key to understanding action lies in grasping the meaning of events to the individual concerned. Klein states as two of his three guidelines for constructing a revised psychoanalysis: "First, an effort to point to the concepts that are constructed from the patient's standpoint; second, an emphasis on phenomenological experience" (1976, p. 5). Such a phenomenological approach places emphasis on the subject's perception of himself, of events, and of his relationships. Yet there is no satisfactory means of combining such an emphasis on the subjective perspective and the facts of unconscious motivation —where the meaning of an action is opaque to the subject.

The second sense in which their perception of motivation is phenomenological is the way in which they emphasize that psychology is concerned with the description and redescription of (largely subjective) data rather than with theory. Klein is the most theoretical of those against the metapsychology. (He is not at all consistent on these matters of theory and has even been criticized by Frank [1979] for straying into theorizing that is of

a metapsychological kind.) However, his programmatic statements convey a different attitude in which he seems to identify
theory in clinical psychoanalysis with a type of description. He
wishes to "confine theoretical effort to the enterprise of deciphering meanings, i.e., to remain on the level on which the
discoveries themselves were formulated" (p. 60). Holt comments similarly: "It is virtually a hallmark of the clinical theory
that it is quite close to the factual, observational core of psychoanalysis, as opposed to metapsychology" (1976, p. 161).

One source for this rejection of theory in favor of description
is the Wittgensteinians' idea that ordinary language, with a few
extensions, is able to express the Freudian insights. MacIntyre,
for example, argues that Freud extends ordinary mental language in an informative way when he talks of unconscious
wishes, and that this is an essentially descriptive, or redescriptive
exercise (1958, p. 48), putting the facts in a clear light and so
showing what the facts really are (p. 61). MacIntyre, like the
later "new critical movement," rejects the explanatory constructs of the metapsychology. One of his reasons is that sticking
to this descriptive mode prevents the conceptual confusion that,
he asserts, Freud creates when he treats unconscious motives
as both causal and purposive in character (p. 60).

Schafer, in his influential (1976) book, rejects the idea of
theory for psychology in an even more radical and direct way.
He takes the philosophical themes that concern MacIntyre and
systematically applies them to psychoanalysis. His argument is
that a number of conceptual problems in psychoanalysis can be
solved through one linguistic move. This is to create an "action
language." In this language all psychological processes, events,
experiences, and behaviors are regarded as actions, and each
action is designated by an active verb, or adverbial locution
stating the mode of the action. Insofar as it is sensible to do so,
nouns and substantives are not used. This new language for
psychoanalysis also involves changes in the use of verb forms.
The active rather than the passive voice is used, so individuals
are seen as agents and not sufferers in their behaviors. The
verb "to have" is not used, as it implies entities are the referents
of psychological propositions. For Schafer, one "feels" and does
not "have a feeling." The latter locution might suggest that

there is an entity called a "feeling." Similarly, individuals are never said to "have" impulses, habits, dispositions, unconscious wishes, symptoms, or sublimations.

These changes do away altogether with the need to make mental state ascriptions and thereby preclude their treatment as states in the causal processes underlying behavior—an echo of behaviorism. There are, for Schafer, no egos, no unconscious impulses, no drives, and no cathexes. In fact, there is no model of mind as Freud conceives of it. One important consequence of this is that it removes the possibility of reifying mental concepts (a point to be discussed further below). But most important for present purposes, it renders psychological theory redundant: it establishes a purely (re)descriptive language for psychoanalysis. The similarity to MacIntyre is clear: "using action language . . . one answers why-questions in terms of reasons. Essentially, in giving reasons for particular actions . . . one restates these actions in a way that makes them more comprehensible" (Schafer 1976, p. 210).

The phenomenological picture of motivated action is one where entertained goals are the sources of action, and citing these goals gives an adequate explanation of the action. The anti-metapsychologists want to stick to the level of the (re)description of action, and of the elucidation of purposes. This is the level of phenomenal givens, and in this their perception of motivation is phenomenological.

Much of the force of the arguments of the psychologists of meaning, like those of the phenomenologists, derives from the subjective, experiential fact of purpose. It seems to the subject that his entertained purposes, or at least those upon which he can call in justification of his actions, are basic for the understanding of his actions. To deny the importance of entertained purpose for the understanding of action seems, from the subjective point of view, to be nonsensical. However, our actions may be motivated unconsciously. This surely is essential to the psychoanalytic view, and requires us to recognize that the subjectively experienced reason for an action is not of paramount importance nor even necessary in the explanation of that action. The person is, in the senses that I sketched in Chapter 8, "object" to himself when he identifies his own motives, just as he is when others ascribe motives to him. His own state of mind is inferentially known to him, and his knowledge of it is subject to error. The theoretical construct approach fits the psychoanalytic fact naturally. Those accounts of motivation that retain phenomenological elements—such as the view that the person has strong privileged access to his own state of mind—do not.

The account of the psychologists of meaning is deficient in another sense. It restricts motivational explanation to the specification of the goals of behavior, that is, of its directions. Klein, for example, makes this explicit when he describes the psychoanalytic enterprise as about the *"meaning, purpose, direction, aim* of behavior" (1976, p. 70). The energizing and precipitating aspects of motivation are omitted. It is sometimes legitimate, as I discussed in Chapter 9, to mention only the directional component of the motivational factors in answer to a question about motivated action. However, such an explanation of action is elliptical and depends on the context. Further, of course, it also allows that only the energizing or only the precipitating factors may also serve as explanatory ellipses. This latter the anti-metapsychologists would reject. Answering motivational questions solely by pointing to goals—events that have not yet occurred—is avowedly teleological (Klein, 1976, p. 49).

Theoretical Construct Approach to Motivation and Meaning

Klein (1976, p. 49) asserts that the metapsychology cannot deal with meaning. The same point is argued by Gill (1976, p. 85). Schafer (1976, p. 103) says of the metapsychology with its natural science language that "it is inconsistent with this type of scientific language to speak of intentions, meanings, reasons or subjective experience." In particular the criticism is that metapsychology "reduces" meaning. Now, since the articulation of meaning is clearly equated with the statement of goals or directions of action, the question is: Can the metapsychology deal with the directional aspects of motivation? The short answer is yes, and the theoretical construct approach illuminates how.

We must return to the starting point of the approach I took

in Part II: motives are inferred states of the individual. This means that the goals of action are inferred, and as I have already discussed, the motives, though they may be named in relation to their goals, are neither defined in terms of their goals nor defined in terms of the data upon which they were first postulated. A "wish to have X" is named after X, which may be mentioned in the data to be explained. However, the wish is specifiable independently of X. Nor is the motive defined in terms of, nor restricted to, the entertained goals of the individual, for it may be that the individual has no awareness of the motives for his actions.

The directional aspects of a particular motive derive from precursors in the individual's history, though of course it is also affected by aspects of the current environment. A particular reason for doing something is the causal outcome of complex processes located in the survival requirements of the organism. In principle, the current motive is traceable to the evolved mechanisms for maintaining and enhancing human life and their operation in the individual from the start of his life. Now, Freud attempts to outline these evolved mechanisms and how they interact with the social and physical environment. The directionality of specific wishes derives from that of the instinctual drives, which are linked to specific somatic needs. This latter directionality is hardly intentional. Instincts do not seek ends, and initially (at birth or more probably before) the individual has no knowledge of the objects that will effect drive reduction. Nor does a homeostatic drive system "intend to satisfy itself." Klein is wrong in saying "that a drive seeks its own gratification is a banality; it is part of the definition of drive" (1976, p. 47). Such a teleological definition of drive has no place in a physicalist account of human motivation, such as Freud's.

THE PSYCHOANALYTIC CONCEPTS AND REIFICATION

The last of the issues to be discussed here is that of reification. It is about the referents of psychoanalytic terms. The anti-metapsychologists insist that clinical psychoanalysis, at least, is about reality. Schafer, for example, states that " 'psychic reality' refers to subjective meaning" (1976, p. 89). Later he links this notion with the concepts I have just been discussing: ". . . in order to take into account psychic reality or the world as experienced, which is the world of meaning and private activity, one must shift to explanations in terms of reasons rather than causes or conditions" (p. 229). Gill states "I believe a self-contained 'pure' psychological theory [that is, psychoanalysis purged of metapsychology] . . . enables us to arrive at valid truths about reality" (1976, pp. 94–95). At the same time these authors reject the model of the mind as "reifying." Holt says the reader "must be struck by another feature of Freud's discussion of motives or instincts—his treating them constantly as if they were real, concrete entities. In short he reifies" (1976, p. 168). Klein, in discussing the ego concept, argues that "within the process-mechanism theory . . . ego is reified as a *system of regulation*" (1976, p. 29). And of course Schafer's whole new language is constructed without any mental substantives, to avoid the reification that he sees as an essential mistake of Freud's metapsychological language.

The phenomenological perception of motivated action means that purposes are real by virtue of their place in subjective experience. This perception, as we have seen, affects the critique made by the anti-metapsychologists. Once again this is at odds with psychoanalytic discovery: that the reasons we give for our actions are often not the real ones. However, the most important point is that the accusation of reification assumes it is wrong to hypothesize psychological entities and then to treat them as existent. In other words, the criticism will not allow that theoretical constructs in psychology refer to real entities and processes. The objection is of two parts. One part is that which we encountered in the critique of metapsychology as biology (Chapter 11): Freud's metapsychology is poor neuro-physiology and cannot seriously be taken to refer to real neural processes, and is not consistent. Holt in particular (1965, 1976) argues in this way. The other part of the objection is a philosophical one. This is not merely that Freud's constructs are empirically and theoretically inadequate. Rather, it is asserted, there is something conceptually wrong in the theoretical concepts of Freud's mental model. These, if they refer to material processes, are irrelevant to the concerns of true psychoanalysis—namely, meanings.

One reason for this notion of "psychic reality" is that the anti-metapsychologists have no means for dealing with the referents of mental terms comparable to that of the physical sciences. The latter are shown to be real by the fact that they are quite apparently materially indentifiable. It is not so easy to see what mental terms could refer to since the brain cannot be inspected to verify the presence of a thought or the operation of an ego-executive. The notion of psychic reality is a way out for the critics of Freud's materialism. Psychic reality makes no attempt to be material reality.

However, the reification criticism may be answered briefly. It requires an analysis that makes sense of the ontology both of psychological and of nonpsychological concepts. The theoretical construct approach, I have already argued (Chapter 8) does this. It is possible to apply the same general criteria of reality to the psychological concepts as to others in the physical sciences. Doing this asserts one order of reality, not two. The principle for which I argued offers a pragmatic conception of what is real: roughly, concepts are as real as the theories which contain them are good at explaining. In turn, explaining (Chapter 6) consists of effecting a systematization of the data, cohering with other theories, performing various conceptual functions, being heuristically valuable, and so on. The ontological status of the Freudian concepts cannot be decided *a priori,* and one cannot assess individual theoretical concepts without taking into account the performance of the general theory. There are parts of Freudian theory that are clumsy, parts that are inconsistent with others, and parts that are simply wrong. This, however, does not prevent the application of a scientific realism to its constructs. Theoretical constructs are putative descriptions of real processes: they are approximations. Freud's theory has given us some real information about mental processes, and we hope that other psychologies will give us more.

14

CONCLUSION

I have offered in this essay a realist account of Freud's concept of motivation. This has involved two main tasks:

First, I attempted to dissect Freud's theoretical writings to show which of his principles and ideas make up the motivational core of psychoanalytic theory. I argued that certain principles persist through changes in Freud's theoretical formulations. Despite inconsistency and some lack of clarity in Freud's writings, there is an identifiable model of mind with which Freud works, and which remains intact—even across the change from the explicit neuropsychology of the Project to the later psychological formulations.

I argued that the central and enduring themes in Freud's theory grew out of, and were shaped by, ideas that Freud took from the science of his time. In particular, there is a philosophy of explanation that lies at the basis of his theory of motivation. The way he sets up his motivational constructs and uses them to explain action depends on his materialism. Freud not only wanted to make sense of symptoms, character, and experience, but he wanted to make sense of them in the terms of natural, specifically biological, science. This idea always remained with him—though he soon realized that what is currently known of neurological processes is not enough to explain the complex phenomena of psychology. His concept of motivation remains a causal one, and motives, he always believes, are material processes.

I also tried to point out the interrelations of the various theoretical concepts in Freud's motivational theory, and to show how Freud uses his mental model to give causal explanations of behavior.

Second, I argued that Freud's motivation concepts perform the same functions as do the theoretical constructs of natural science. If, as I also argued, we take a realist view of the constructs of natural science, then we must do the same for psychoanalytic concepts. There is no *a priori* reason to exclude these concepts from science. The worth of such concepts can be decided only on other grounds—how *well* they carry out the usual explanatory duties required of a theory. Treating the psychoanalytic motivation concepts as theoretical constructs, I argued, illuminates the way they explain psychological data, the kind of knowledge we have of motives (especially unconscious ones), the relation of these motives to behavior, and their ontological status.

It is apparent, too, that Freud's own philosophy of explanation accords with this. The "theoretical construct" analysis is not an alien imposition upon psychoanalytic theory.

Now, much recent criticism of Freud's theories is not empirical, but philosophical. Many critics argue that Freud is conceptually muddled and that he operates with a mistaken philosophy of explanation, rather than that he is actually wrong about the determinants of neurosis or personality. (Some philosophers, following Popper, assert that psychoanalysis is unscientific because it is untestable, and also say little on the content of the theory.) I have, similarly, not discussed the empirical standing of Freud's theory. What has concerned me is how Freud explains symptoms and behavior, and what sense can be made of the theoretical constructs he uses to do this. Of course, my study does assume that psychoanalysis expresses important truths about behavior—the study would be pointless without that assumption. However, an adequate assessment of the empirical value of psychoanalysis is a separate topic and demands a separate treatment, too long to be included in this essay.

Against critics who say that Freud is conceptually muddled, I have argued that his is a respectable philosophy of science. Freud's comments on matters such as causation, the role of theoretical constructs in explanation, materialism, the mind-brain relation, inferential knowledge, and others are often insightful and sophisticated. Many philosophers appear to be unaware of the range and detail of Freud's writings on these topics. They are misled by their narrow focus into thinking that Freud was philosophically naive and muddled—for example, in his belief that motives can be both causes and reasons.

On the other hand, much conceptual work done by psychoanalysts themselves is equally problematic. It has become common among psychoanalysts to accept the philosophers' thesis that Freud is conceptually weak. Some, such as the anti-metapsychologists, attempt to defend Freud's clinical insights by reformulating them in a noncausal language—a language free of Freud's "conceptual muddles." In particular, Freud's theory has been restyled as a psychology of meaning, or hermeneutic science, and located in a branch of knowledge separate from natural science. This is an unnecessary defense. Psychoanalytic theory is philosophically viable without the reformulation. Such a reformulation would raise other important problems for psychoanalysis. For example, we should still want to know what are the rules of evidence in this separate, special, human science; and what would be the relation of this science to other psychologies?

Most of the issues I have discussed—the relation of mental processes to behavior, the ontology of postulated mental processes, the problem of explaining intentional action, the place of meaning in psychological accounts, and others—are just as important for the wider discipline of psychology. In particular, the separate domain issue is perennial in psychology. Theorists are divided on what role the individual's perception of himself and the world plays in determining his actions, and they are divided on how one might construct a psychology to take meaning into account. The argument that psychology is a special sort of science and occupies a separate domain of explanation is common in all those branches of the discipline that treat motivation—for example, social psychology, personality theory, psychopathology. Psychoanalysis is, of course, controversial and intriguing in its content in a way that perhaps no other psychology is. However, what makes psychoanalysis a good subject for a conceptual study is not that its conceptual problems are radically different from the rest of psychology, but rather that so many of psychology's problems are represented in the one theory.

APPENDIX

ASPECTS OF THE WOLF MAN CASE

Freud wrote up the "Wolf Man" case in *From the History of an Infantile Neurosis* (1918). It is the most complex and detailed of his published studies.

Wolf Man was a Russian aristocrat born in the late nineteenth century. From early years he showed a tendency toward psychopathology. At three he underwent a character change, becoming an irritable and violent child (pp. 24–28). At four, after a terrifying dream, he developed the wolf phobia from which the clinical pseudonym derives. Later the phobia itself gave way to an obsessional neurosis, characterized by compulsive religiosity (pp. 61–71). He displayed a host of other symptoms: he hallucinated injuries to himself (p. 85), reacted irrationally in money matters (p. 83), and displayed bizarre anal-erotic symptoms (pp. 74–75). At eighteen, a breakdown following a gonorrheal infection left him psychologically incapacitated. He began his four-year analysis with Freud in 1910.

A section (pp. 7–103) of the case study is devoted largely to a discussion of what I wish to call "the clinical account." This comprises the clinical data, what they mean, and how they are derived from the analysis with the aid of interpretive rules and techniques. Another section (pp. 104–122) gives the "theoretical account." In this Freud attempts to explain the clinical account by describing the "psychical mechanisms and instinctual processes" (p. 105) that underlie the unconscious wishes of the clinical account.

226

CLINICAL ACCOUNT

Although Freud was originally called in to understand and help Wolf Man in an adult breakdown, his approach takes him back to the patient's childhood. He gathers from Wolf Man memories of his childhood, rich in pathological material. These memories provide the first data to be explained. They cover the mother's ill health (1918, p. 13), the change in Wolf Man's character, his wolf phobia (p. 15), his sadism toward animals (p. 16), and other details. After recounting these memories Freud says:

> Here, then, in the briefest outline, are the riddles for which the analysis had to find a solution. What was the origin of the sudden change in the boy's character? What was the significance of his phobia and of his perversities? How did he arrive at his obsessive piety? And how are all these phenomena interrelated? [p. 17].

Freud's hypothesis is that Wolf Man is motivated by a passive unconscious wish for sexual satisfaction from his father. This hypothesis runs through all of Freud's accounts of Wolf Man's many pathological characteristics and his symptoms. The hypothesis is erected on the basis of the data mentioned above. However, as we shall see, Freud also uses supplementary hypotheses, clinical rules-of-thumb, and much analytic probing as well to reach this explanation. Freud answers the three "riddles" that the case sets him:

1. The change of character is a regression. Wolf Man is first seduced by his sister (p. 20) and this helps establish the passive aspect of his sexuality. But, when he attempts to reproduce this situation with his nurse "Nanya," he fails and is threatened with castration (p. 24). His passive sexuality becomes unconscious and his sexual organization regresses to an earlier anal stage. Its form is consequently sadistic/masochistic (p. 26). He also returns to an earlier object choice, his father. He has in any case a marked bisexual predisposition. This is then the change in his character: he becomes irritable and aggressive. He also uses the naughtiness to provoke punishment from his father (p. 28).

2. I discuss the phobia and its relation to the unconscious wish in more detail below.

3. The obsessional symptoms are a compromise of several unconscious elements. A major element is the homosexual wish. Wolf Man identifies with the suffering Christ—they share the same birthday (p. 64). This satisfies his masochistic wish for the father, since Christ suffers at the hands of God-the-Father. But this wish threatens to break into consciousness: he wonders if Christ has a behind (p. 63) and if Christ defecated. Underneath this is the fear whether he himself could be used by his father like a woman, receiving the penis in the anus. Against these blasphemous ruminations, and the wish behind them, is an ego-syntonic masculine protest. The piousness and ritual formulas protect him against the acknowledgment of the wish and counteract the blasphemies.

The Phobia

The phobia was not of wolves themselves, but rather of pictures and thoughts of wolves. Its first expression came in a dream near Wolf Man's fourth birthday. He woke up in a panic after dreaming of still, white, staring wolves with bushy tails and sitting in a tree. He was afraid of being eaten by them (p. 29). After this he was "most tremendously afraid" of a certain picture of a wolf (from a storybook of Little Red Riding Hood). In this the wolf was upright and striding forward. His sister would torment him with it (pp. 29–30).

There were a number of other behaviors and fears directly associated with the phobia. When he was seven or eight he dreamed of an expected tutor "in the shape of a lion that came towards his bed roaring loudly and in the posture of the wolf in the picture; and once again he awoke in a state of anxiety" (p. 39). Later he was to have a Latin master called Wolf of whom he was greatly afraid, and whom he tried to appease with money (p. 39).

Yet other behaviors were less directly associated with the wolf phobia but could easily be seen to have a bearing on it. For example, Wolf Man showed a distinct preference for *coitus a tergo, more ferarum* (p. 41), felt a compulsive attraction to women bending over, as the female animal is copulated (he was not afraid of pictures of wolves on all fours), and he felt a fear and loathing of certain other animals that seemed to him to be like men rather than women (pp. 16, 89). And these were a small part of his myriad symptoms.

Freud's hypotheses about the unconscious reasons for the phobia are scattered throughout the text. But in essence they are as follows: *The wolf is a substitute for the father* (p. 112). *The Wolf Man feared his father because castration was an implied condition* (p. 42) *for the satisfaction of the passive* (p. 64), *feminine, and sexual wish he had for his father* (p. 42).

Sources of the Clinical Hypothesis

There are three types of source for a clinical hypothesis, like this one about the phobia: first, there are the clinical data; second, there are clinical rules—therapeutic, exploratory, and interpretive techniques that Freud uses; and third, there is the mental model or metapsychology that sets the stage for his clinical work.

CLINICAL DATA

Freud uses the first anxiety dream as a major source for clues about the phobia and its unconscious basis. A rule-of-thumb for dream analysis makes it likely that some elements in the manifest dream symbolize the opposite in the latent content. For example, Freud suspects that the bushy-tailed wolves signify the opposite, tailless wolves—in turn a symbol of castration. Indeed, one branch of associations to the dream wolves leads to a children's story. In this story a wolf, who also during the story lets other wolves "climb upon him" (p. 42), is deprived of its tail. The story ends in further humiliation for the tailless animal. A second branch of associations leads to stories of a wolf that devours little goats and to the striding wolf that threatened Little Red Riding Hood. The aggressive action of this latter type of wolf is represented by another opposite—the stillness of the dream wolves. Thus at the very minimum the dream provides Freud with the idea that the fear is of castration, of the aggressive male wolf who castrates, and that being climbed on while on all fours was associated with castration.

Information about Wolf Man's passive sexuality was gathered from further material. He showed an identification with women (pp. 76–77) and a wish to provoke beatings from his father (p. 28). In addition, he had fantasies of being beaten (pp. 46–47). His clearly erotic relations with his sister started with his seduction by her, and when as a teenager he was sexually rejected by his sister he turned to a peasant girl who shared the sister's name. Subsequently he showed a strong preference for women who were inferior to him: "inferior" both in that they were servant girls, and thus his social inferiors; and in that overwhelming erotic feelings were aroused in him on seeing women bending over and engaged in menial tasks, thus physically inferior (pp. 93–94): "This was clear, for instance, in the episode of Matrona. He was walking through the village which formed part of their . . . estate, when he saw a peasant girl kneeling by the pond and employed in washing clothes in it. He fell in love with the girl instantly and with irresistible violence" (p. 93). His active sexuality toward these women then seemed to be a reaction to the frustration of his underlying passive sexual wish. Freud argues he had a wish to "debase his love-object" (p. 93).

Material on his castration fear was given in Wolf Man's recollections: of castration threats (p. 24); of his keen interest in the (absent) genitals of girls; and even of hallucinations—for example, that he had cut his finger "so that it was only hanging on by its skin" (p. 85). It was an "attack" on his genitals, gonorrhea, that precipitated his breakdown (p. 7). Finally, for Wolf Man "fear of his father became the dominating factor" (p. 17) in his late childhood.

The ascribed unconscious homosexual wish is also supported by material from Wolf Man's other symptoms. For example, his feminine, masochistic, and ambivalent attitudes toward his father were indicated in his obsessions (pp. 63–65). In addition, his castration fears could be seen in aspects of his obsessions (p. 66), and in his anal eroticism Freud saw his identification with women and the lingering fear "whether he himself could be used by his father like a woman—like his mother in the primal scene" (p. 64).

CLINICAL RULES

Freud does not just depend on clinical data (Wolf Man's dreams, associations, recollections, and symptoms) to formulate his clinical hypothesis. He also uses clinical rules-of-thumb gathered from previous experience. That is, he uses practical information on what symptoms usually go together, what common dream symbols usually mean, typical symbolic equivalences, and so on. One example of this is his use of the symbolic equation feces = baby = penis to unravel the anal-erotic symptoms. Another is the equivalence of opposites (thick-tailed wolves = tailless wolves) in dream interpretations.

Yet another example, an important one for the Wolf Man case, is the hypothesis of the primal scene. This forms an explanatory nucleus to which various pieces of the case material are attached. Freud hypothesizes that the infant Wolf Man was witness to a parental sexual intercourse, and that this "primal scene" became a paradigm for many of his symptoms. The wolf dream conveyed a powerful sense of reality to the dreamer. Freud says "we know from our experience in interpreting dreams that this sense of reality . . . assures us . . . that the dream relates to an occurrence which really took place" (p. 33). Wolf Man's associations, plus some of the striking qualities of his dreams, lead Freud to a series of significant fragments to be reconstructed: *"A real occurrence—dating from a very early period—looking—immobility—sexual problems—castration—his father—something terrible"* (p. 34). Freud's theory of the time suggests a copulation scene as the witnessed event. The features of Wolf Man's sexual fears and preferences suggest to Freud that sexual intercourse was *a tergo, more ferarum* (from behind, in the manner of the wolf): with the male upright and the female bending over. The two concerned are father and mother.

To this postulated primal scene Freud ties almost every aspect of the case history: the fear of the upright-wolf picture (p. 39); the compulsive attraction for bending-over women (p. 41); his anality (p. 41); his fear of castration (p. 36), and so on. Freud is well aware of the heuristic value this postulation has: "It is indispensable to a comprehensive solution of all the conundrums that are set us by the symptoms of the infantile disorder, that all the consequences radiate out from it, just as all the threads of the analysis have led up to it" (p. 55).

The third source for the clinical hypothesis takes us to the theoretical account.

THEORETICAL ACCOUNT

Freud weaves his theoretical account about the vicissitudes of Wolf Man's instinctual life. In doing this he sticks to the features of the instinctual processes that he had given elsewhere (1915a, pp. 122–123)—namely, that an instinct has source, aim, object, and pressure. The development of character is the story of instinctual vicissitudes, the objects that lead to their satisfaction, the forms they take, and so on.

Freud recounts the genesis of Wolf Man's mature sexual organization. In this he refers to the psychosexual phases and interruptions to "normal" instinctual development in Wolf Man. Then he discusses the principal conflict in Wolf Man's pathology. The instinctual force underlying the main, homosexual wish is the libido, so its source is sexual (p. 112). This force is complicated by aggression (which Freud at the time does not allow the status of an independent instinct). Consequently, the wish is expressed in sadistic and masochistic forms. The object of the libido is the father. Freud fills out the wish hypothesis with references to instinctual processes. There is a second wish behind the phobia. This is described as "ego-syntonic" (p. 110). This wish is "normal" masculine sexuality, directed toward women, and compatible with the ego interests. One major ego interest is not to become emasculated. Clearly the two wishes are in conflict.

The contradictory and conflicting aspects of Wolf Man's characteristics are an expression of the primary-process nature of their unconscious determinants. Freud also gives the mental process involved in anxiety hysteria, which underlies the phobia itself. According to Freud's anxiety theory of the time, the withdrawn libido of repressed wishes turns into anxiety: "The ego, by developing anxiety, was protecting itself against what it regarded as an overwhelming danger, namely, homosexual satisfaction" (p. 112).

Freud gives a much fuller theoretical account than I can give here. It is fragmentary, and doubtfully coherent. However, at each stage it employs the metapsychology and general theory of mental processes. It covers Wolf Man's psychopathology and offers explanations for much of the clinical narrative Freud gives in the earlier part of the case study. Its detail and flavor may be illustrated by this passage on the mental mechanics of repression:

> It may truly be said that the anxiety that was concerned in the formation of these phobias was a fear of castration. This statement involves no contradiction of the view that the anxiety originated from the repression of homosexual libido. Both modes of expression refer to the same process: namely, the withdrawal of libido by the ego from the homosexual wishful impulse, the libido having then become converted into free anxiety and subsequently bound in phobias. The first method of statement merely mentions in addition the motive by which the ego was actuated [p. 113].

REFERENCES

ALEXANDER, P. (1962). Rational behaviour and psychoanalytic explanation. *Mind,* 71:326-341.

——— (1974). Wishes, symptoms and actions. *Proc. Aristotelian Soc.,* 68:119-134.

ALSTON, W. P. (1967a). Motives and motivation. In *Encycl. Philos.,* ed. P. Edwards. New York: Collier-Macmillan, Vol. 5, pp. 399-409.

——— (1967b). The logical status of psychoanalytic theory. In *Encycl. Philos.,* ed. P. Edwards. New York: Collier-Macmillan, Vol. 5, pp. 512-516.

——— (1971). Dispositions and occurrences. *Canad. J. Philos.,* 1:125-154.

AMACHER, P. (1965). Freud's Neurological Education and Its Influence on Psychoanalytic Theory. *Psychol. Issues,* Monogr. 16. New York: Int. Univ. Press.

——— (1974). The concepts of the pleasure principle and infantile erogenous zones shaped by Freud's neurological education. *Psychoanal. Q.,* 43:218-223.

ANSCOMBE, R. (1981). Referring to the unconscious: a philosophical critique of Schafer's 'action language.' *Int. J. Psychoanal.,* 62:225-241.

APFELBAUM, B. (1965). Ego psychology, psychic energy, and the hazards of quantitative explanation in psycho-analytic theory. *Int. J. Psychoanal.,* 46:168-181.

——— (1966). On ego psychology: a critique of the structural approach to psycho-analytic theory. *Int. J. Psychoanal.,* 47:451-475.

ARKES, H. & GARSKE, J. (1982). *Psychological Theories of Motivation* (2nd ed.). Monterey, Calif.: Brooks/Cole.

ARMSTRONG, D. (1968). *A Materialist Theory of Mind.* London: Routledge & Kegan Paul.

——— (1973a). *Belief, Truth and Knowledge.* Cambridge, Eng.: Cambridge Univ. Press.

——— (1973b). Beliefs as states. In *Dispositions,* ed. R. Tuomela. Dordrecht, Holland: Reidel, 1978, pp. 411-425.

——— & Malcolm N. (1984). *Consciousness and Causality: A Debate on the Nature of Mind.* Oxford, Eng.: Blackwell.

ATKINSON, J. W. (1964). *An Introduction to Motivation.* Princeton, N.J.: Van Nostrand.

ATWOOD, G. E. & STOLOROW, R. D. (1984). *Structures of Subjectivity: Explorations in Psychoanalytic Phenomenology.* Hillsdale, N.J.: Analytic Press.

BARCLAY, J. R. (1964). Franz Brentano and Sigmund Freud. *J. Existentialism,* 5:1-36.

234

BARRATT, B. (1978). Critical notes on Schafer's action language. *Annual Psychoanal.*, 6:287-303.

BERNFELD, S. (1944). Freud's earliest theories and the school of Helmholtz. *Psychoanal. Q.*, 13:341-362.

——— (1951). Sigmund Freud, M.D., 1882-1885. *Int. J. Psychoanal.*, 32:204-217.

BETTELHEIM, B. (1982). *Freud and Man's Soul.* New York: Knopf.

BINSWANGER, L. (1936). Freud's conception of man in the light of anthropology. In *Being-In-The-World.* New York: Harper.

——— (1946). The existential analytic school of thought. In *Existence: A New Dimension in Psychiatry and Psychology,* ed. R. May, E. Angel & H. F. Ellenberger. New York: Basic Books, 1958, pp. 191-213.

BLIGHT, J. (1981). Must psychoanalysis retreat to hermeneutics? Psychoanalytic theory in the light of evolutionary epistemology. *Psychoanal. Contemp. Thought,* 4:147-205.

BORST, C. V., Ed. (1970). *The Mind-Brain Identity Theory.* London: Macmillan.

BRAITHWAITE, R. B. (1953). *Scientific Explanation.* Cambridge, Eng.: Cambridge Univ. Press.

BRANDT, R. & KIM, J. (1963). Wants as explanations of actions. *J. Philos.,* 60:425-435.

BREUER, J. & FREUD, S. (1895). Studies on hysteria. *S. E.,* 2.

BRÜCKE, E. (1874). *Vorlesungen über Physiologie.* Vienna: Braumuller.

BURNHAM, J. (1974). The medical origins and cultural use of Freud's instinctual drive theory. *Psychoanal. Q.,* 43:193-217.

CIOFFI, F. (1970). Freud and the idea of a pseudo-science. In *Explanation in the Behavioural Sciences,* ed. R. Borger & F. Cioffi. Cambridge, Eng.: Cambridge Univ. Press, pp. 471-499.

——— Ed. (1973). *Freud: Modern Judgements.* London: Macmillan.

——— (1974). Wishes, symptoms and actions. *Proc. Aristotelian Soc.,* 68:97-118.

COFER, C. & APPLEY, M. (1964). *Motivation: Theory and Research.* New York: Wiley.

CRAIG, W. (1956). Replacement of auxiliary expressions. *Philos. Rev.,* 65:38-55.

DAVIS, S. (1983). *Causal Theories of Mind: Action, Knowledge, Memory, Perception and Reference.* New York: W. de Gruyter.

DENNETT, D. C. (1969). *Content and Consciousness.* London: Routledge & Kegan Paul.

——— (1978a). *Brainstorms: Philosophical Essays on Mind and Psychology.* Hassocks, Sussex: Harvester Press.

——— (1978b). Artificial intelligence as philosophy and psychology. In *Brainstorms: Philosophical Essays on Mind and Psychology.* Hassocks, Sussex: Harvester Press, pp. 109-126.

DILMAN, I. (1972). Is the unconscious a theoretical construct? *Monist,* 56:313-342.

——— (1984), *Freud and the Mind.* Oxford, Eng.: Blackwell.

EDELSON, M. (1984). *Hypothesis and Evidence in Psychoanalysis.* Chicago: Univ. Chicago Press.

ELLENBERGER, H. (1970). *The Discovery of the Unconscious.* New York: Basic Books.

ERDELYI, M. (1985). *Psychoanalysis: Freud's Cognitive Psychology.* New York: Freeman.

ERIKSON, E. H. (1955). Freud's 'The origins of psycho-analysis.' *Int. J. Psychoanal.,* 36:1-15.

EXNER, S. (1894). *Entwurf zu einer physiologischen Erklärung der psychischen Erscheinungen.* Vienna: Deuticke.

FANCHER, R. (1973). *Psychoanalytic Psychology: The Development of Freud's Thought.* New York: Norton.

FARRELL, B. A. (1972). Clothing the Freudian model in a fashionable dress. *The Monist,* 56:343-360.

———— (1981). *The Standing of Psychoanalysis.* Oxford, Eng.: Oxford Univ. Press.

FECHNER, G. (1873). *Einige Ideen zur Schopfungs—und Entwicklungsgeschichte der Organismen.* Leipzig: Breitkopf und Hartel.

FEYERABEND, P. (1975). *Against Method: Outline of an Anarchistic Theory of Knowledge.* London: New Left Books.

FLAX, J. (1981). Psychoanalysis and the philosophy of science. *J. Philos.,* 78:561-569.

FLEW, A. (1956). Motives and the unconscious. In *Minnesota Studies in the Philosophy of Science,* Vol. 1, ed. H. Feigl & M. Scriven. Minneapolis: Univ. Minnesota Press, pp. 155-173.

FODOR, J. (1968a). *Psychological Explanation.* New York: Random House.

———— (1968b). The appeal to tacit knowledge in psychological explanation. *J. Philos.,* 65:627-640.

———— (1978). Computation and reduction. In *Minnesota Studies in the Philosophy of Science,* Vol. 9, ed. C. Savage. Minneapolis: Univ. Minnesota Press, pp. 229-260.

FRANK, A. (1979). Two theories, or one? Or none? *J. Amer. Psychoanal. Assn.,* 27:169-207.

FREUD, S. (1887-1902). *The Origins of Psychoanalysis 1887-1902.* New York: Basic Books, 1954.

———— (1894). The neuro-psychoses of defence. *S. E.,* 3.

———— (1895a). Project for a scientific psychology. *S. E.,* 1.

———— (1895b). A reply to criticisms of my paper on anxiety neurosis. *S. E.,* 3.

———— (1900). The interpretation of dreams. *S. E.,* 4 & 5.

———— (1910). The psycho-analytic view of psychogenic disturbance of vision. *S. E.,* 11.

———— (1912). A note on the unconscious in psycho-analysis. *S. E.,* 12.

———— (1913a). The disposition to obsessional neurosis. *S. E.,* 12.

———— (1913b). The claims of psycho-analysis to scientific interest. *S. E.,* 13.

———— (1914). On narcissism: an introduction. *S. E.,* 14.

———— (1915a). Instincts and their vicissitudes. *S. E.,* 14.

———— (1915b). Repression. *S. E.,* 14.

———— (1915c). The unconscious. *S. E.,* 14.

———— (1916-1917). Introductory lectures on psycho-analysis. *S. E.,* 15 & 16.

———— (1918). From the history of an infantile neurosis. *S. E.,* 17.

———— (1920). Beyond the pleasure principle. *S. E.,* 18.

———— (1923). The ego and the id. *S. E.,* 19.

———— (1924). The economic problem of masochism. *S. E.,* 19.

———— (1926). The question of lay analysis. *S. E.,* 20.

—— (1927). Postscript to the question of lay analysis. *S. E.,* 20.

—— (1933). New introductory lectures on psycho-analysis. *S. E.,* 22.

—— (1940a). An outline of psycho-analysis. *S. E.,* 23.

—— (1940b). Some elementary lessons in psycho-analysis. *S. E.,* 23.

FRIEDMAN, L. (1976). Problems of an action theory of the mind. *Int. Rev. Psychoanal.,* 3:129-138.

GEEN, R., BEATTY, W. & ARKIN, R. (1984). *Human Motivation: Physiological, Behavioral, and Social Approaches.* Boston: Allyn & Bacon.

GILL, M. M. (1963). *Topography and Systems in Psychoanalytic Theory. Psychol. Issues,* Monogr. 10. New York: Int. Univ. Press.

—— (1976). Metapsychology is not psychology. In *Psychology versus Metapsychology: Psychoanalytic Essays in Memory of George S. Klein,* ed. M. M. Gill, & P. Holzman. *Psychol. Issues,* Monogr. 36. New York: Int. Univ. Press, pp. 71-105.

—— & Holzman, P., Eds. (1976). *Psychology versus Metapsychology: Psychoanalytic Essays in Memory of George S. Klein. Psychol. Issues,* Monogr. 36. New York: Int. Univ. Press.

—— (1983). The point of view of psychoanalysis: energy discharge or person. *Psychoanal. Contemp. Thought,* 6:523-551.

GOLDMAN, I. A. (1970). *A Theory of Human Action.* Englewood Cliffs, N.J.: Prentice-Hall.

GRÜNBAUM, A. (1984). *The Foundations of Psychoanalysis: A Philosophical Critique.* Berkeley: Univ. Calif. Press.

HABERMAS, J. (1972). *Knowledge and Human Interest.* London: Heinemann.

HANLY, C. & LAZEROWITZ, M., Eds. (1970), *Psychoanalysis and Philosophy.* New York: Int. Univ. Press.

HANSON, N. R. (1958). *Patterns of Discovery.* Cambridge, Eng.: Cambridge Univ. Press.

HARRÉ, R. (1970). *The Principles of Scientific Thinking.* London: Macmillan.

—— (1972). *The Philosophies of Science: An Introductory Survey.* Oxford, Eng.: Oxford Univ. Press.

HARTMANN, H. (1959). Psychoanalysis as scientific theory. In *Psychoanalysis, Scientific Method, and Philosophy,* ed. S. Hook. New York: N.Y. Univ. Press, pp. 3-37.

—— KRIS, E. & LOEWENSTEIN, R. M. (1949). Notes on the theory of aggression. *Psychoanal. Study Child,* 3/4:9-36.

—— —— —— (1964). *Papers on Psychoanalytic Psychology. Psychol. Issues,* Monogr. 14. New York: Int. Univ. Press.

HEBB, D. O. (1955). Drives and the CNS. *Psychol. Rev.,* 62:243-254.

HEMPEL, C. (1965). The theoretician's dilemma. In *Aspects of Scientific Explanation and Other Essays.* New York: Free Press, pp. 173-226.

HERBART, J. F. (1816). *A Textbook in Psychology.* New York: Appleton, 1901.

HESSE, M. (1966). *Models and Analogies in Science.* Notre Dame: Univ. Notre Dame Press.

—— (1967). Models and analogy in science. In *Encycl. Philos.,* ed. P. Edwards. New York: Collier-Macmillan, Vol. 5, pp. 354-359.

—— (1970). Is there an independent observation language? In *The Nature and Function of Scientific Theories,* ed. R. Colodny. Pittsburgh: Univ. Pittsburg Press, pp. 35-37.

HOLT, R. R. (1965). A review of some of Freud's biological assumptions and their influence on his theories. In *Psychoanalysis and Current Biological Thought*, ed. N. Greenfield & W. Lewis. Madison: Univ. Wisconsin Press, pp. 93-124.

———— (1968). Sigmund Freud. *Int. Encycl. Soc. Sci.*, 6:1-12.

———— (1972). Freud's mechanistic and humanistic images of man. In *Psychoanal. Contemp. Sci.*, 1:3-24.

———— (1976). Drive or wish? A reconsideration of the psychoanalytic theory of motivation. In *Psychology versus Metapsychology: Psychoanalytic Essays in Memory of George S. Klein*, ed. M. M. Gill & P. S. Holzman. *Psychol. Issues*, Monogr. 36. New York: Int. Univ. Press, pp. 158-197.

HOLZMAN, P. S. (1986). Psychoanalysis: Is the therapy destroying the science? *J. Amer. Psychoanal. Assn.*, 34:725-770.

HOOK, S., Ed. (1959). *Psychoanalysis, Scientific Method, and Philosophy*. New York: N.Y. Univ. Press.

INNES, J. M. (1971). Freud's 'Project for a scientific psychology.' *Brit. J. Med. Psychol.*, 44:249-257.

JONES, B. (1975). Cioffi on Freud. *Mind*, 84:106-110.

JONES, E. (1953). *Sigmund Freud: Life and Work. Vol. 1: The Young Freud, 1856-1901*. New York: Basic Books.

———— (1955). *Sigmund Freud: Life and Work. Vol. 2: Years of Maturity, 1901-1919*. New York: Basic Books.

———— (1957). *Sigmund Freud: Life and Work. Vol. 3: The Last Phase, 1919-1939*. New York: Basic Books.

KANZER, M. (1973). Two prevalent misconceptions about Freud's "Project." *Annual Psychoanal.*, 1:88-103.

KLEIN, G. S. (1976). *Psychoanalytic Theory: An Exploration of Essentials*. New York: Int. Univ. Press.

KLINE, P. (1981). *Fact and Fantasy in Freudian Theory* (2nd ed.). London: Methuen.

KOHUT, H. (1959). Introspection, empathy, and psychoanalysis. *J. Amer. Psychoanal. Assn.*, 7:459-483.

KUBIE, L. (1959). Psychoanalysis and scientific method. In *Psychoanalysis, Scientific Method, and Philosophy*, ed. S. Hook. New York: N.Y. Univ. Press, pp. 57-77.

LOEVINGER, J. (1966). Three principles for a psychoanalytic psychology. *J. Abnorm. Psychol.*, 71:432-443.

McGUINNESS, B. F. (1956-1957). I know what I want. *Proc. Aristotelian Soc.*, 57:305-320.

MacINTYRE, A. C. (1958). *The Unconscious: A Conceptual Analysis*. London: Routledge & Kegan Paul.

MACKAY, N. (1979). Knowing one's motives. *J. Theory Soc. Behav.*, 9:125-138.

———— (1981). Melanie Klein's metapsychology: phenomenological and mechanistic perspectives. *Int. J. Psychoanal.*, 62:187-198.

———— (1986). Freud, explanation and the mind-brain problem. *Psychoanal. Contemp. Thought*, 9:373-404.

MASSON, J. (1984). *The Assault on Truth: Freud's Suppression of the Seduction Theory*. New York: Farrar, Straus & Giroux.

MAXWELL, G. (1962). The ontological status of theoretical entities. In *Minnesota Stud. Philos. Sci.*, 3:3-27.

MAZE, J. R. (1983). *The Meaning of Behaviour*. London: Allen & Unwin.

MEISSNER, W. (1979). Methodological critique of the action language in psychoanalysis. *J. Amer. Psychoanal. Assn.*, 27:79-105.

MELDEN, A. (1961). *Free Action*. London: Routledge & Kegan Paul.

—— (1966). Desires as causes of actions. In *Current Philosophical Issues*, ed. F. Dommeyer. Springfield, Ill.: C. C. Thomas, pp. 127-150.

MELTZER, D. (1978). *The Kleinian Development*. Strath Tay, Perthshire: Clunie Press.

MERLAN, P. (1945). Brentano and Freud. *J. Hist. Ideas*, 6:375-377.

MEYNERT, T. (1884). *Psychiatry*. New York: Hafner, 1968.

NAGEL, E. (1959). Methodological issues in psychoanalytic theory. In *Psychoanalysis, Scientific Method, and Philosophy*, ed. S. Hook. New York: N.Y. Univ. Press, pp. 38-56.

NELSON, B., Ed. (1957). *Freud and the 20th Century*. New York: Meridian.

PETERFREUND, E. (1980). On information and systems models for psychoanalysis. *Int. Rev. Psychoanal.*, 7:327-344.

—— & SCHWARTZ, J. (1971). *Information, Systems and Psychoanalysis. Psychol. Issues*, Monogr. 25/26. New York: Int. Univ. Press.

PETERS, R. S. (1956). Freud's theory. *British J. Philos. Sci.*, 7:4-12.

—— (1958). *The Concept of Motivation*. London: Routledge & Kegan Paul.

POLANYI, M. (1965a). On the modern mind. *Encounter*, 15:12-20.

—— (1965b). The structure of consciousness. *Brain*, 88:799-810.

—— (1966). *The Tacit Dimension*. New York: Doubleday.

POLLOCK, G. (1980). Freud as scientist and psychoanalysis as science. *Annual Psychoanal.*, 8:3-18.

POPPER, K. (1934). *The Logic of Scientific Discovery*. London: Hutchinson, 1959.

—— (1963a). Science: conjectures and refutations. In: *Conjectures and Refutations: The Growth of Scientific Knowledge*. London: Routledge & Kegan Paul, pp. 33-65.

—— (1963b). Truth, rationality, and the growth of knowledge. In *Conjectures and Refutations: The Growth of Scientific Knowledge*. London: Routledge & Kegan Paul, pp. 215-250.

—— (1983). *Realism and the Aim of Science*. Totowa, N.J.: Rowman & Littlefield.

PRIBRAM, K. (1965). Freud's "Project": an open biologically based model for psychoanalysis. In *Psychoanalysis and Current Biological Thought*, ed. N. Greenfield & W. Lewis. Madison: Univ. Wisconsin Press, pp. 81-92.

—— & GILL, M. M. (1976), *Freud's 'Project' Reassessed*. London: Hutchinson.

PUTNAM, H. (1962). What theories are not. In *Logic, Methodology and Philosophy of Science: Proceedings of the 1960 International Congress*, ed. E. Nagel, P. Suppes, & A. Tarski. Stanford: Stanford Univ. Press, pp. 240-251.

RAPAPORT, D. (1960a). *The Structure of Psychoanalytic Theory: A Systematizing Attempt. Psychol. Issues*, Monogr. 6. New York: Int. Univ. Press.

—— (1960b). On the psychoanalytic theory of motivation. *Nebraska Symposium on Motivation*, 8:173-247.

—— & GILL, M. M. (1959). The points of view and assumptions of metapsychology. *Int. J. Psychoanal.*, 40:153-162.

REISER, M. (1984). *Mind, Brain, Body: Toward a Convergence of Psychoanalysis and Neurobiology*. New York: Basic Books.

RICOEUR, P. (1970). *Freud and Philosophy: An Essay in Interpretation*. New Haven, Conn.: Yale Univ. Press.

——— (1981). *Hermeneutics and Human Sciences: Essays on Language, Action, and Interpretation,* ed. & trans. J. B. Thompson. Cambridge, Eng.: Cambridge Univ. Press.

RITVO, L. (1972). Carl Claus as Freud's professor of the new Darwinian biology. *Int. J. Psychoanal.,* 53:277-283.

——— (1974). The impact of Darwin on Freud. *Psychoanal. Q.,* 43:177-192.

ROSEN, G. (1972). Freud and medicine in Vienna: some scientific and medical sources of his thought. *Psychol. Med.,* 2:332-344.

RUBINSTEIN, B. (1967). Explanation and mere description. In *Motives and Thought: Psychoanalytic Essays in Honor of David Rapaport,* ed. R. R. Holt. *Psychol. Issues,* Monogr. 18/19. New York: Int. Univ. Press, pp. 18-77.

——— (1976). On the possibility of a strictly clinical psychoanalytic theory: an essay in the philosophy of psychoanalysis. In *Psychology versus Metapsychology: Psychoanalytic Essays in Memory of George S. Klein. Psychol. Issues,* Monogr. 36, ed. M. M. Gill & P. S. Holzman. New York: Int. Univ. Press, pp. 229-264.

RYCROFT, C. (1966). Introduction: causes and meaning. In *Psychoanalysis Observed,* ed. C. Rycroft. New York: Coward-McCann, pp. 7-22.

RYLE, G. (1949). *The Concept of Mind.* London: Hutchinson.

SARTRE, J-P. (1943). *Being and Nothingness.* London: Methuen, 1958.

SCHACHTER, S. & SINGER, J. E. (1962). Cognitive, social and physiological determinants of emotional state. *Psychol. Rev.,* 69:379-399.

SCHAFER, R. (1976). *A New Language for Psychoanalysis.* New Haven, Conn.: Yale Univ. Press.

——— (1980). Narration in the psychoanalytic dialogue. *Critical Inquiry,* 12:29-53.

SEGAL, H. (1973). *Introduction to the Work of Melanie Klein.* London: Hogarth Press.

SEROTA, H. (1974). The ego and the unconscious: 1784-1884. *Psychoanal. Q.,* 43:224-242.

SHALOM, A. (1985). *The Body/Mind Conceptual Framework and the Problem of Personal Identity: Some Theories in Philosophy, Psychoanalysis and Neurology.* Atlantic Highlands, N.J.: Humanities Press.

SHERWOOD, M. (1969). *The Logic of Explanation in Psychoanalysis.* New York: Academic Press.

SKINNER, B. F. (1950). Are theories of learning necessary? *Psychol. Rev.,* 57:193-216.

SMYTHE, T. W. (1972). Unconscious desires and the meaning of "desire." *Monist,* 56:413-425.

SOLOMON, R. C. (1973-1974). Reasons as causal explanations. *Philosophy and Phenomenological Research,* 34:415-428.

——— (1974a). Freud's neurological theory of mind. In *Freud: A Collection of Critical Essays,* ed. R. Wollheim. New York: Anchor, pp. 24-52.

——— (1974b). Freud and "unconscious motivation." *J. Theory Soc. Behav.,* 4:191-216.

SPENCE, D. (1982). *Narrative Truth and Historical Truth.* New York: Norton.

——— (1983). Narrative persuasion. *Psychoanal. Contemp. Thought,* 6:457-481.

STERBA, R. (1974). The humanistic wellspring of psychoanalysis. *Psychoanal. Q.,* 43:167-176.

STEWART, W. (1969), *Psychoanalysis: The First Ten Years, 1888-1898*. New York: Macmillan.

SULLOWAY, F. (1979). *Freud, Biologist of the Mind*. New York: Basic Books.

TICHO, E. & TICHO, G. (1972). Freud and the Viennese. *Int. J. Psychoanal.*, 53:301-306.

TUOMELA, R. (1977). Dispositions, realism and explanation. *Synthese*, 34:457-478.

———— Ed. (1978). *Dispositions*. Dordrecht, Holland: Reidel.

VON ECKARDT, (1982). Why Freud's research methodology was unscientific. *Psychoanal. Contemp. Thought*, 5:549-574.

WHYTE, L. L. (1960). *The Unconscious Before Freud*. New York: Basic Books.

WILSON, E., Jr. (1973). The structural hypothesis and psychoanalytic metatheory. *Psychoanal. Contemp. Sci.*, 2:304-328.

WITTGENSTEIN, L. (1942-1946). Conversations on Freud (1942-1946). In *L. Wittgenstein: Lectures and Conversations on Aesthetics, Psychology and Religious Belief*, ed. C. Barrett. Oxford, Eng.: Blackwell, 1966, pp. 41-52.

———— (1958). *Philosophical Investigations* (2nd ed.). Oxford, Eng.: Blackwell.

WOLLHEIM, R. (1971). *Freud*. London: Fontana.

———— Ed. (1974). *Freud: A Collection of Critical Essays*. New York: Anchor.

———— & HOPKINS, J., Eds. (1982). *Philosophical Essays on Freud*. Cambridge, Eng.: Cambridge Univ. Press.

YOUNG, P. T. (1961). *Motivation and Emotion*. New York: Wiley.

NAME INDEX

243

SUBJECT INDEX

245

PSYCHOLOGICAL ISSUES